On Ruins of Empire

Recent Titles in
Contributions in Political Science

Cautious Revolution: The European Union Arrives, Second Edition
Clifford Hackett

The Kingfish and the Constitution: Huey Long, the First Amendment, and the
Emergence of Modern Press Freedom in America
Richard C. Cortner

Unions and Public Policy: The New Economy, Law, and Democratic Politics
Lawrence G. Flood

U.S. Foreign and Strategic Policy in the Post–Cold War Era: A Geopolitical
Perspective
Howard J. Wiarda, editor

Comparing State Polities: A Framework for Analyzing 100 Governments
Michael J. Sullivan III

Federalism and the Environment: Environmental Policymaking in Australia, Canada,
and the United States
Kenneth M. Holland, F. L. Morton, and Brian Galligan, editors

Public Enterprise Management: International Case Studies
Ali Farazmand, editor

Mainstream(s) and Margins: Cultural Politics in the 90s
Michael Morgan and Susan Leggett, editors

The European Union, the United Nations, and the Revival of Confederal Governance
Frederick K. Lister

The Leviathan in the State Theory of Thomas Hobbes: Meaning and Failure of a
Symbol
Carl Schmitt
Translated by George Schwab and Erna Hilfstein

On Ruins of Empire

Ethnicity and Nationalism in the Former Soviet Union

Georgiy I. Mirsky

Contributions in Political Science, Number 375
Bernard Reich, Series Adviser

Greenwood Press
Westport, Connecticut • London

Library of Congress Cataloging-in-Publication Data

Mirskiĭ, G. I. (Georgiĭ Il'ich)
    On ruins of empire : ethnicity and nationalism in the former
Soviet Union / Georgiy I. Mirsky.
        p.   cm.—(Contributions in political science, ISSN 0147–1066 ;
no. 375)
    Includes bibliographical references and index.
    ISBN 0–313–30044–5 (alk. paper)
    1. Nationalism and communities—Soviet Union—History.
2. Nationalism—Soviet Union—History.   3. Minorities—Government
policy—Soviet Union—History.   4. Soviet Union—Ethnic relations.
I. Title.   II. Series.
HX550.N3M58   1997
305.8'00947—dc20   96–5789

British Library Cataloguing in Publication Data is available.

Library of Congress Catalog Card Number: 96–5789
ISBN: 0–313–30044–5
ISSN: 0147–1066

First published in 1997

Greenwood Press, 88 Post Road West, Westport, CT 06881
An imprint of Greenwood Publishing Group, Inc.

Printed in the United States of America

The paper used in this book complies with the
Permanent Paper Standard issued by the National
Information Standards Organization (Z39.48–1984).

10 9 8 7 6 5 4 3 2

The research described in this book was sponsored and financed by the
John D. and Catherine T. MacArthur Foundation and the London School of
Economics and Political Science.

Contents

1

What Kind of Empire Was the Soviet Union?

The Soviet Union was a unique kind of empire, not only, nor even primarily, because people of the dominant nation—Russia—were by and large worse off economically than those of some of the southern republics. The main peculiarity of the USSR was the unusual character of the system of power in the multiethnic society. In the British and French empires, for instance, local chiefs and rulers in the colonies were given their share of governing, but they remained natives— local bosses—never belonging to the imperial elite of London or Paris. In the Soviet Union, however, republican leaders were an integral part of the overall ruling class; some of them even made it to the Politbureau. This can be explained both by the internationalist ideology of Communism, hypocritical as it was, and by pragmatic experience. All the major decisions, of course, were made in the Kremlin but local elites were given a substantial degree of autonomy. In this way, a strong and quite reliable network of local power centers was created that proved to be totally loyal to the paramount Party leadership. The system achieved a broad and solid foundation.

The native *nomenclatura* played a dual role: First, party and state officials were Communist *apparatchiks* just like their colleagues in Moscow; and second, they were traditional local bosses and patrons. Thus, their system of rule was vertical, and leaders always had a valuable feedback from the grass roots, allowing them to gauge the mood of the population. In Central Asia, for example, the republican or provincial party secretary, all-powerful in the Soviet system, also symbolized and took the place of the traditional clan and ethnic leader. He was a local chieftain and patron, a godfather figure lording it over an entrenched network that often resembled the Mafia. Loyalty to him was paramount, and hardly related to the Communist ideology. This is why those bosses, unlike many of their counterparts in Russia, retained their positions after the collapse of the Soviet system. Former Republican Party secretaries, now presidents of independent states, were elected not because they represented Communist ideology, which is all but forgotten by most people; they are regarded as experienced, elder statesmen with deep, local roots and vast connections.

Parallel to this process of elite-building, which succeeded in creating a stable and viable party-state structure, (thus greatly facilitating the task of governing the enormous country), another important pattern was developing. It can be called "promoting national identities" or—in some cases—even nation-building.

Here we see one of the biggest paradoxes of the Soviet system: A powerful and wholly centralized totalitarian regime organically unable to tolerate any autonomous, unco-opted authority, to say nothing of opposition, was genuinely promoting and encouraging national consciousness of diverse ethnic groups. Great efforts were made to foster native culture, art, language, to rewrite history so as to educate people in the spirit of national identity and pride. Every republic had to have its own academy of sciences, opera, ballet, and so on. Native poets and artists were given an all-Union prominence; native artistic groups were constantly performing in Moscow; third-rate local soccer or basketball teams were sure to be included in the all-Union first-league championships. In Central Asia, in particular, modern nations were almost artificially created where none had existed before the October Revolution.

This phenomenon can partly be explained by the internationalist ideology of Marxism which could not be simply discarded by the Bolsheviks. An even more important reason, however, is a pragmatic one. No matter what the Bolshevik leaders were thinking about the nationalities issues at the outset, they were quick to grasp the advantages they could get by encouraging ethnic identity of the numerous nations and groups under their rule. The key factors were, first, selection: Only completely loyal and trusted individuals were chosen to lead the republics, only those who would never forget that they owed all their power and privileges to the center, to Moscow; and second, education and propaganda value. It is much easier to educate young generations in the spirit of loyalty to the regime if children are being told again and again, from kindergarten on, that their nation, formerly deprived of all rights, has now achieved an unheard-of degree of prosperity thanks to that regime. In this respect, not only the "blossoming of culture" but also industrialization played a major part. Steel mills and machine-building factories built in formerly backward agricultural areas were used by propagandists as visible proofs of modernization and incredible progress. The decentralization of Soviet industry with the negative effects so obvious at this point, after the disintegration of the Union, was initiated to a large degree under the influence of political considerations.

There is no denying that substantial progress was achieved, for instance, in the sphere of education. Some smaller ethnic groups, which before the revolution had been totally illiterate, had an opportunity to study; half-forgotten languages of those groups were restored and adapted to the Cyrillic script. Thus, writers and poets could now write in their own languages.

Ian Bremmer calls the whole arrangement of nationality relations within the USSR an unofficial "nationalities contract," and suggests that

it consisted of the central authorities providing a package of economic benefits to the republics, to be used largely at the discretion of the local elites, in exchange for the compliance of republic citizens with Soviet rule. This deal effectively "bought off" the loyalties of target leadership cadres, such as economic managers, trade union officials, administrative and party heads, and intellectuals. Those not fortunate enough to be so targeted were effectively excluded from the nationalities contract.[1]

Another expert, Victor Zaslavsky, believes that "federal structure, nationality registration in the internal passport, preferential treatment of territorially-based nationalities, and protection of the educational and occupational interests of ethnic middle classes and political elites all contributed to the maintenance of stable nationality relations in the USSR."[2]

The rule of the Kremlin in the republics was indirect. The Soviet pattern of governing was personified by the second secretary of the Central Committee of the republican Communist Party, an extremely important and somewhat mysterious figure. Every central committee had a governing body; on the all-Union scale, in Moscow, it was called Politbureau, in the republics just bureau. The top figures in the bureau were: first secretary, second secretary, and secretary (the word "third" was never used, as it was probably not dignified enough, so the third man in the hierarchy introduced himself as secretary of the Central, or *oblast*, or town committee). The man in charge was invariably the first secretary; officially, the chairman of the presidium of the local supreme Soviet was superior to him but it was purely nominal. Everybody in every republic, or *oblast*, or town and district, knew that it was the first secretary who was the real boss. I remember that, on more than one occasion, I, as a lecturer sent from Moscow, was a guest of honor at the after-talk dinner; each time, without exception, it was absolutely clear from the beginning that I had only one interlocutor. The table conversation was just a dialogue between the first secretary and me; the other dignitaries present, including the two lesser secretaries, the chairman of the Soviet, the head of local government, and so on, would just pronounce toasts, pour more vodka (or cognac) in my glass, and laugh at the boss's jokes. Otherwise, they would not utter a single word.

The first secretary in the republic was an all-powerful lord; in Stalin's era, he was also a sinister and awesome figure. For example, in Azerbaijan the first secretary, Baghirov, used to enjoy the same kind of prestige and inspire the same degree of horror and fear, on the local scale, as Stalin in Moscow. A lifelong friend of the Secret Police Chief Lavrenti Beria, and thus enjoying total impunity (after Stalin's death he was to be executed along with Beria), Baghirov used to copy the Kremlin dictator's ways, sometimes even managing to outdo the Big Boss. It is known that Stalin, after he learned that a sizeable number of the delegates to the 17th Party Congress in 1934 had voted against him in a secret ballot, decided to teach them a lesson; in the next three years, 90% of the delegates were either in their graves or in Gulag camps. Now, Baghirov went further: On learning that the result of the elections to the Central Committee's bureau in Azerbaijan, a year later, was similar to that in Moscow (the difference being that on this occasion his delegates secretly voted against him), he had all of them executed or sent to a Gulag in the course of a couple of years, just to be on the safe side.

In the 1930s, the second most dreaded man in Azerbaijan after Baghirov was the Minister of the Interior. This minister's deputy, many years later, told a story typical of the Stalin era. It appeared that this deputy minister was suddenly summoned to Baghirov; he arrived in the latter's office, trembling with fear like everyone else who had to experience an encounter with the Boss. In the corner of Baghirov's office the man noticed, to his amazement and consternation, his own boss, the powerful minister, who was sitting at the edge of the chair and shaking all over, "like a dog just out of the water." As the Deputy Minister approached Baghirov's table, the Big Man, without even saying hello, just pointed with his finger at the unfortunate minister in the corner and said: "You take this piece of s ____ and escort him to Moscow; now go!" That was it. The same day, the Deputy Minister escorted his arrested boss to Moscow by plane and returned to Baku for a new appointment. The minister, of course, was duly executed by the firing squad in Moscow as "the enemy of the people"; his deputy was sent to a Gulag a few years later. After serving his time, he came back to the Caucasus and, before dying, told this story to his former driver, who by that time was working at the lecturing society. I was to meet that driver many years later as I was lecturing in the Caucasus and he told me all of this while driving.

So much for the figure of the first secretary. The second secretary in the Union republics was almost invariably an ethnic Russian; it was as late as the 1970s, under Brezhnev, that this arrangement was abolished. Contrary to some beliefs, the second secretary was by no means a real boss in the republic; he was just Moscow's "eyes and ears," watching over the first man and reporting to the Kremlin. Without his consent, however, no major personnel changes could be made. It was, of course, the First Man, a native, who made the decisions but the Second Man, an ethnic Russian sent by Moscow, had to okay them. Both men tried to avoid conflicts; if those occurred, however, Moscow was to play the role of arbiter. As a rule, the Kremlin tended to favor the local man so as not to worsen the relations with the republic.

The first secretary was in charge of everything, the second secretary was responsible for industry (in agrarian areas, for agriculture) and often for ideology as well. The third secretary was charged with lesser things such as education and culture, health care, and so on but sometimes also with the organization of political propaganda. In many instances, women were entrusted with this job. In the ruling Republican Party bodies, women were represented, if at all, only at the third level.

Sometimes, representatives of local non-Russian minorities could be given the third position. Once I met with local chiefs in Kirovabad, the second largest city of Azerbaijan. I happened to be sitting next to the third secretary, a woman. She was ethnic Armenian; there was a strong Armenian minority in Kirovabad *oblast*. During a general conversation, I asked her in what language she was thinking—Azerbaijani, Armenian, or Russian. She dodged my question and just gave me a rather embarrassed look; I immediately realized my mistake. In front of her boss, the first secretary, an Azerbaijani, she would not admit that she was thinking in Armenian, and she obviously did not feel like lying.

In matters of culture and tradition, the locals were given a free hand. Once I was a guest at the home of an *oblast* secretary in Uzbekistan. His wife, a member of the local Party committee, behaved like a typical Muslim woman, just bringing food and drinks but never participating in the repast. When the host switched on some music and I told him that I would not mind having a dance, he told me: "You want to dance, you dance with me."

In general, the relations between various ethnic groups appeared quite normal. At an oil refinery in Baku workers told me that there was no tension at all among the Azerbaijanis, Russians, Armenians, Jews, and other people employed at the huge plant. At the end of each year, however, like everywhere in the Soviet Union, bonuses had to be given to the best workers, and they invariably went to ethnic Azerbaijanis. As people of the "core" or titular nation, they had to be the winners of this "socialist competition," as it was called. Likewise, I remember being told in Kirgizia that "red banners" for the victory in the "socialist competition" in agricultural areas used to be entrusted exclusively to ethnic Kirgiz, although everybody knew that the best results were always being achieved by ethnic Germans, descendants of the deportees who had been exiled by Stalin from the European areas of Russia during the war.

Of course, the typically Soviet hierarchical mode of thinking required strict ranking of the republics according to their political weight and importance. The "basic" nations were accorded the status of Union republics; others, that of autonomous republics or national *okrugs* or autonomous *oblasts*. All ethnic groups were divided into four categories, namely fifteen Union-republics, twenty autonomous republics, eight autonomous *oblasts* (regions), and ten autonomous *okrugs* (areas). There were really no meaningful objective criteria—territorial, economic, demographic, or historical—for such a division, which does not mean that there was no political sense in it, no underlying reason. The division of ethnoses made sense for the Kremlin, and the reason was as old as it was simple: divide and rule. The hierarchical setup was a recipe for permanent national-ethnic tension. At the bottom of the ladder, more than fifty ethnic groups had no official statehood at all. Those were the smallest groups that could safely be ignored; their very existence was, although in a minor way, a source of satisfaction to the others, those standing just a notch higher and having the lowest degree of statehood—a constant reminder that there was somebody even lower than you. At the top, there was a "super-ethnos"—the Russians, the big brother, the leading nation.[3]

While not very important within the old structure, this setup became a recipe for disaster, a source of embarrassment, mutual grievances, claims, and counterclaims as soon as the Union collapsed. The status inequality, bitterly resented by many ethnic groups, has been exacerbated by another factor: the existence of sizeable minorities within virtually every one of the newly independent states (except for Armenia and Turkmenistan) as well as the Russian Federation. To what extent this situation originally arose as a result of a deliberate "divide and rule" policy of the Kremlin is a matter of dispute. The fact remains that at present, according to experts, about 180 actual or potential conflicts on ethnic grounds exist in the former Soviet Union. Anyway, the ensuing mess can only be called truly monumental, and the ethnic labyrinth resulting from both the construction of the Soviet Union in its bizarre and unorthodox form and its rapid disintegration is certain to remain an essential factor in the post-Soviet states for decades to come.

As time went by, the dominant position of ethnic Russians began to diminish. In the 1980s, in the least developed republics, the number of native university-educated specialists was increasingly approaching that of the Russian population.[4] As to the leading positions in administration and management, most of them since the mid-1950s belonged to members of local nationalities.[5] The proportion of the indigenous population in the administrative-managerial personnel in Ukraine, for instance, by 1989 reached 79.0%, in Uzbekistan 67.6%, in Georgia 89.3%, in Azerbaijan 93.8%, and so on; only in Kazakhstan was it practically equal to, and in Moldavia less than, that of ethnic Russians.[6]

To sum up, by the time Gorbachev started his *perestroika*, the Soviet Union, as regards its ethnonational situation, could be called a fairly stable state, although with a substantial hidden potential of turmoil. The leading position of ethnic Russians was unchallenged: They constituted more than half of the population while another 20% were also Slavs (Ukrainian and Belorussian). Another 20% were Muslims, 3% were Christian Caucasians (Armenians and Georgians), and 3% were Balts.[7] Local Communist elites were firmly entrenched and, along with the numerous members of the Party, administrative and managerial personnel were on the whole satisfied with their situations. Open manifestations of nationalist discontent were rare and quite efficiently dealt with by the powerful KGB. Thus, the dire predictions of some Western experts (notably the eminent French Sovietologist Hélène Carrère D' Encausse) regarding the nationalities issue as a major potential cause of the collapse of the Soviet Union have proved wrong. The catastrophe, as always in Russian history, came from the Center.

When Gorbachev took over in 1985, his intention, contrary to some later Western opinion, was not to bring democracy to his country and to change the system, but quite the opposite: By carrying out radical, far-reaching reforms he aimed at improving the system, at invigorating and rejuvenating the Communist Party. Gorbachev was determined to get rid of the rot, corruption, and inefficiency which were inexorably leading to the growth of the gap between the Soviet Union and the industrial capitalist nations. As David Remnick emphasized, "there is absolutely no evidence to suggest that Gorbachev was out to undermine, much less destroy, the basic tenets of ideology or statehood of the Soviet Union."[8] The failure of his reforms confirmed the truth of Tocqueville's thesis: "The most perilous moment for the bad government comes when it tries to mend its ways," as well as of Milovan Djilas's warning that Socialism is not reformable, it just disintegrates.

It was not so much the economic *perestroika*, ill-conceived and counterproductive as it was, that doomed the system, as its social and ideological implications. *Glasnost* dealt a mortal blow to the Soviet regime. De-Stalinization that Gorbachev initiated after much hesitation as a means of discrediting his adversaries, the Party hardliners, promptly turned into de-Leninization and the rejection of the whole concept of Marxism-Leninism, thus depriving the Party of its legitimacy and its right to continue in power. Once the horrible crimes committed by the Party during its seventy years of rule became known, the Pandora's box was opened. As criticism of the Party became almost officially sanctioned, people felt free to openly challenge the whole system based on Socialist teachings, while the ruling elite grew confused and disoriented. There was an overwhelming and widespread feeling of a lack of direction, of a definite weakening of the Party's grip. Infallibility of the Party leadership was openly ridiculed, the raison d'être of continued mobilization, ideological committment, and Party discipline was gone as the Cold War ended and even the word "imperialism" disappeared overnight from the official lexicon.

Of course, popular discontent was caused first and foremost by the rapidly deteriorating economic situation. By 1989, the government lost control over the economy; production was falling due to the disruption of the traditional economic ties, sharp decline of labor discipline, and the total confusion of the whole Party and managerial personnel; shortages of foodstuffs and all other kinds of goods became truly menacing. In this situation, however, it would have been strange if latent ethnonationalist grievances and secessionist tendencies had not surfaced. If one felt free to protest and complain about everything else, why should the sphere of national relations be an exemption? And indeed, by 1990, parliaments in each of the fifteen Soviet republics passed resolutions demanding control of their own sovereignty. It was largely symbolic at first; every local elite, far from attempting to challenge the Communist system as such, tried to posture as a champion of the national rights so as not to be outflanked by emboldened and increasingly vociferous nationalist groups of native intelligentsia. At the same time, those ruling elites saw their chance of weakening the Center's control and of increasing their own grip on local affairs. Genuine secessionist feelings were voiced only in the three Baltic republics, notably in

Lithuania, a pioneer of the independence movement, and in Georgia, profoundly shaken by the bloodbath in Tbilisi in early 1989. As to Ukraine, it was just a small group of traditional nationalists that claimed real independence as opposed to symbolic sovereignty. In Central Asia and Kazakhstan all was fairly quiet.

Things changed dramatically, however, after the failure of the abortive Moscow coup in August 1991. An end to the Communist rule was officially proclaimed by Yeltsin. Under these circumstances, local Communist elites were mortally frightened by the prospect of their own imminent demise should they continue to cling to the agonizing regime with its collapsing and openly despised ideology. The best thing for them to do was promptly to turn coats and transform themselves into nationalist leaders. Yet, with the exception of the Baltic republics and Georgia, followed a little later by Armenia and Azerbaijan, the idea of sovereignty was not, in the minds of local leaders and the majority of the population, tantamount to complete independence. It was only when Yeltsin, along with the Ukrainian and Belorussian leaders proclaimed the dissolution of the Soviet Union in December 1991, that independence became an established fact. As regards the Central Asian republics, it can be said that independence was literally shoved upon them or just fell from the sky.

After a brief period of confusion and bewilderment the local leaders realized that the sudden advent of independence could prove beneficial to them. Marshall Goldman explains this in the following terms: ''From a strict economic point of view, political and economic independence may not make sense for the various republics, especially the smaller ones, but many of them concluded that they had less to lose than by being tied to an ineffective union. The Soviet economic situation was deteriorating at an accelerating rate. Would they be any worse off on their own?''[9] This logic is quite correct but it must be remembered that considerations of this kind could emerge only after the event; that is, after the official breakup of the Soviet Union, and not prior to this; the secession was not the result of a freely taken decision of most of the republican leaders but was rather forced upon them. They simply had to go along with the ''big three'' in order to survive as leaders.

As regards Russians, they were at first dumbfounded by the suddenness of the events, but rather quickly reconciled themselves to the new situation. As Michael McGwire put it, ''there were certainly those who were strongly in favor of preserving the imperial borders of the USSR. . . . But other Russians saw 'Russia' as a nation rather than an empire, and while its essential character and boundaries differed between groups of protagonists, such a nation would even gain from relinquishing the non-Russian areas.''[10]

Contrary to some forecasts, the demise of Soviet Communism did not begin with nationalist upheavals and liberation movements bent on tearing apart the vast multinational empire. In fact, the outbreak of nationalist protest proved to be not the beginning but the culmination of a surprisingly short and not too violent process of decline and fall of the Soviet regime. Of course, it had not been completely bloodless. Suffice it to recall Nagorno-Karabakh, Tbilisi, and

Vilnius. Generally speaking, however, most of the really bitter conflicts started in the aftermath of the regime's collapse. Seeds of those conflicts had undoubtedly been sown in the Soviet period; indeed, as mentioned earlier, the whole administrative setup of the Soviet Union made an eventual explosion inevitable. The fact remains that violence erupted in Tajikistan, Georgia, Ossetia, Abkhazia, Moldova precisely when new national entities emerged on the ruins of the empire. It is against these new entities, not against the Communist system and the imperial structure, that people rose in revolt.

At the same time, cracks started to appear in the structure of the newly formed sovereign Russian Federation, thus putting in question the very existence of the state which used to be a kernel and a backbone of the whole empire. Tatarstan and Chechnya were the first ominous signs of potential turmoil in Russia proper. Tension began to grow between Russia and Ukraine; Crimea and Dniester loomed large in the media. Against this background, Russian nationalism emerged for the first time as a potent force. Attention began to focus on the ethnopolitical situation in the post-Soviet space; more violence looked inevitable. Nationalist sentiment, largely ignored during the Soviet era, suddenly appeared as the genie let out of the bottle.

The role of ethnonationalism in the breakup of the Soviet Union cannot be regarded as a major one. This phenomenon, however, became vital in the post-Soviet political life after the collapse of the empire. Yet it must be said that practically all serious conflicts have so far occurred in the periphery, not in the center, of the defunct empire. It is only there that the rise of *ethnonationalism* was followed by *ethnic conflicts*. Thus, it appears that the two phenomena are not inseparable. What is needed now is an analysis of the background of ethnonationalism.

NOTES

1. Ian Bremmer, "Reassessing Soviet Nationalities Theory," in *Nations and Politics in the Soviet Successor States*, ed. Ian Bremmer and Ray Taras (New York: Cambridge University Press, 1993), 10–11.

2. Victor Zaslavsky, "Success and Collapse: Traditional Soviet in Nationality Policy," in *Nations and Politics in the Soviet Successor States*, ed. Ian Bremmer and Ray Taras (Cambridge, Mass.: Cambridge University Press, 1993), 37.

3. In the Tsarist Empire, only 45% of the whole population were ethnic Russians.

4. Ellen Jones and Fred Grupp, "Modernization and Ethnic Equalization in the USSR," *Soviet Studies* 36, no. 2 (1984).

5. Severyn Bialer, *Stalin's Successors, Leadership, Stability and Change in the Soviet Union* (New York: Cambridge University Press, 1980), 214–216.

6. L. L. Rybakovskii and N. V. Tarasova, "Migratsionnyie protsessy v SSSR: Novye yavleniya," *Sotsiologicheskie issledovaniya* no. 7 (1990), 40.

7. Paul A. Goble, "Gorbachev: Facing the Nationality Nightmare," *Washington Post*, March 25, 1990, C1–2.

8. David Remnick, *Lenin's Tomb* (New York: Random House, 1993), 47.

9. Marshall L. Goldman, *What Went Wrong with Perestroika* (New York, London: W. W. Norton & Company, 1991), 227–228.

10. Michael McGwire, *Perestroika and Soviet National Security* (Washington, D.C.: The Brookings Institution, 1991), 355.

2

Ethnos, Nation, and the State

ORIGINS OF NATIONS: PRIMORDIAL GROUPS AND SOLIDARITY

In the words of Karmela Liebkind,

in traditional societies with few group memberships conscious awareness of ethnic allegiance tended to be undeveloped and diffuse. Group consciousness was unnecessary to the extent that social bonds of a primordial nature provided strict rules for conduct and for the prediction of social events. Successive eroding of traditional bonds necessitated increasing self-awareness and explicit group identities.[1]

This assertion can be misleading in the sense that "ethnic allegiance" is seen as tantamount to "group consciousness." The former was obviously lacking in the mentality of the primordial tribes while the latter has been present ever since groups emerged out of isolated families. A group cannot exist without its members' belief in the necessity of the group arrangement for their survival. At this point, homogeneity and collectivism make their appearance; common interest creates a "we-group." "This group consciousness," as Hans Kohn pointed out, "will strive towards creating homogeneity within the group, a conformity and like-mindedness which will lead to and facilitate common action."[2] The sense of cohesion is necessary for the existence and survival of a group. Thus far, there is no trace yet of ethnic element in this group consciousness; what is already evident, however, is solidarity, cohesion, and homogeneity—the prerequisites and ingredients of an eventual ethnic consciousness.

Now, if there is a "we-group," it is logical to be aware of the existence of a "they-group." To what extent is the "boundary mechanism" needed to create the sense of group community and solidarity which is eventually destined to grow into ethnic consciousness? Vamik Volkan writes about "need to belong to a group and have enemies."[3] Certainly, it always comes to just that, sooner or later, but what is primary and what is secondary? Anthony Smith suggests the existence of "a feeling of community, of 'us-ness' and group belonging."[4] In other words, group solidarity consciousness is determined first by positive, rather than by negative, factors. The final result, however, is inevitably the same: The sense of belonging—which means that an individual is not alone but part of a group, a community—creates a certain primary identity that invariably appears to be based on boundaries from other communities. "We" is meaningful only inasmuch as there are "they," the others. The presence of a negative reference group becomes essential for keeping alive the sense of belonging, the newly found communal identity. It can even be called useful if not indispensable for the very existence of group, community, tribe; without the boundaries opposing "us" to "the others"—who become enemies almost by definition—it would have been difficult to maintain the internal cohesion necessary for group survival. Born of shared experiences and values, fed by a feeling of community, group consciousness is being sustained and strengthened by the fact of a hostile environment, of constant presence of "them," the enemies. Each primordial group thus possesses a kind of miniature "besieged fortress" mentality.

"Who am I" is thus defined by the existence of "the others," generally regarded as unfriendly, as potential adversaries. This spontaneous, automatic hostility toward strangers is rooted in the group mentality of prehistoric tribes. How otherwise can we explain the phenomenon noted by Anthony Smith: "Psychological evidence drawn from European children's natural imagery showed that distinctions about 'foreigners' are imbibed at the age of six to eight."[5] A survey made by psychologists from the British Association for the Advancement of Science showed that the first thing most children learned about the people of other nations was to dislike them.[6] Obviously, in the primordial society an individual had to instinctively display a hostile, defensive reaction to everybody who was not of the same tribe. Some authors believe that

just as the body is better prepared to avoid destruction by foreign substances as a result of a generalised tendency to resist the impingement of foreign substances, so an individual or a society may be better prepared to avoid destruction by aliens as a result of a generalised tendency to distrust, avoid or reject foreign-seeming individuals. . . . When it occurs in natural settings, xenophobia is a functional and adaptive trait in that it maintains the integrity of the social group.[7]

Paul Brass describes this basic unit of primordial society as a group the members of which "are similar to each other and collectively different from others," and which uses its sense of ethnic identity "to create internal cohesion and differentiate themselves from other groups."[8] The question is: At what stage is it possible to denote this group identity as "ethnic?" Exactly when does group solidarity, group consciousness acquire traits of ethnicity? Does language play a major role in this process?

Anthony Smith outlined six components of what he calls *ethnie*: a collective name, a common myth of descent, a shared history, a distinctive shared culture, an association with a specific territory, a sense of solidarity.[9] Most of these, though not all, can apply to primordial groups and tribes. It is interesting to note that Smith does not even mention language as a component of an *ethnie*. This appears to be a major omission. The point is that, in the same book, Smith writes: "It is *ethnie* rather than nations, ethnicity rather than nationality, and ethnicism rather than nationalism, that pervades the social and cultural life of antiquity."[10] This postulate, however, implicitly stresses the role of language as the very essence of ethnicity, as a crucial element of the transformation of a mere group or tribe into an *ethnie*. "Primitive man," writes John Armstrong, "was disturbed by the uncanny experience of confronting others who, perforce, remained mute in response to his attempts at communication."[11] At first, the distinction between groups was based on a primitive, personal differentiation. The members of a group just knew each other, and every unfamiliar face was that of "the other," an enemy, even if this "other" spoke the same language. Then, differences of language emerged. It is only at that point that *ethnic* consciousness—which is not the same as *group solidarity*—begins to shape. The "experience" noted by Armstrong continued into the initial stages of state-building, and the first known states that were indeed based on ethnicity had language as a major factor, which made differentiation possible and separate statehood legitimate, as the *ethnies* did not yet possess either shared history or myths of descent, at least not to a sufficient degree.

But even if we add language to the list of ethnic components, some questions remain, for instance: What was it that allowed for the separate existence of ancient Greek states? Almost all of Smith's components making up an *ethnie* were present, including common territory, *Ellada;* nor were those states separated by language or religion. And yet, Spartans obviously felt they belonged to a different *ethnie* than Athenians. What was strikingly absent was the sense of solidarity. Therefore, another factor has to be introduced here, namely, local or parochial interests of both political and economic character, coupled, at least in some cases such as Athens and Sparta, with differences in mentality and value systems.

Things changed as empires emerged. Having at their core solid and well organized, dominant *ethnies* with the criteria listed by Anthony Smith, such empires as the Macedonian and Roman comprised various ethnoses and tribes whose solidarity was rather enforced than natural. Ethnic criteria obviously could not apply in this case; language, however, not only remained as a unifying factor but its role became immeasurably greater. It would have been impossible, for instance, to hold together the Roman empire without the universal spread of

Latin as a powerful instrument, not only of maintaining order and ensuring governance but also of propagating the imperial idea, that legal and spiritual basis of a supraethnic identity in the giant, multiethnic state.

In the end, of course, all multiethnic empires inevitably fall apart, which may rightly be seen as a triumph of "genuine," that is, ethnic, identity over an artificial, supraethnic one. What is important, however, is that, even at that point, ethnic identity did not emerge as overtly paramount. The concept of nation, that logical succesor to *ethnie*, did not make its appearance until much later. The word itself comes from the Latin *nasci*, to be born, and thus is of an ancient origin, but the concept deriving from this term was not a guiding principle of statehood for centuries to come. Cornelia Navari noted that the pre-nineteenth-century state did not serve nations or even communities. "It served God, the Heavenly Mandate, the Law of Allah; it served hereditary rulers . . . since institutions, customs and dynastic habits all cut across ethnic groupings, the expression of nationalism would have been rather perverse. Religion and dynastic loyalty were the main generators of greater group loyalty."[12] Particularly important was the role of religion. It was Arnold Toynbee who pointed out that until the modern epoch, religious identification was usually far more intense than ethnic identity.[13] Carlton Hayes, while noting that "nationalism truly became a religion with the French revolutionaries," wrote that "not until very modern times have whole peoples been systematically indoctrinated with the tenets that every human being owes his first and last duty to his nationality."[14]

All the historical evidence suggests that the communities we currently call nations for many centuries were not wholly conscious of their ethnicity or just did not care about it. "In religious and dynastic wars, Germans fought against Germans, and Italians against Italians, without any realization of the 'fratricidal' nature of the act. Soldiers and civilians entered the service of foreign rulers and served them often with a loyalty and faithfulness which proved the absence of any national sentiment."[15]

It was only with the growth of mass conscription and mass education that most Frenchmen came to feel their "Frenchness" and began to place loyalty to the state—or rather the nation-state—above their various local and regional alliances. Only in the last years of the Hamidian reaction was the concept of "Turk," a term used derogatorily of Anatolian peasants, re-invested with positive ethnic potential and harmonized with a very Western concept of the territorial nation.[16]

In Egypt, prior to the twentieth century, the word "Arab" had not so much ethnic as social connotation, largely meaning *badawi*, a backward nomad. Still another vital issue deserves to be mentioned: in premodern times, it was clan and patronage, rather than ethnic consciousness, that determined an individual's identity, and in many Third World countries this is still the case.

Yet, ethnicity, this seemingly immortal phenomenon, has managed to survive and ultimately to prevail. Anthony Smith presents a comprehensive analysis of this process. In his view, four conditions are necessary for ethnic consolidation: territory, struggle with enemies, religion, sense of ''chosenness.'' He particularly stresses the central role of religious traditions and distinctive priesthoods and rites in maintaining ethnic identity.[17] Among other factors, Smith mentions the role of sacred languages and scripts.[18]

Religion certainly was a crucial factor in keeping alive ethnic solidarity, which always has a tendency to overgrow into a feeling of a common and unique destiny. This is probably best illustrated by the history of Jews who succeeded in surviving as a distinct community in spite of having been deprived of their homeland for two thousand years. This capacity to survive even without a native territory does not invalidate Smith's inclusion of the territorial factor in his list of the prerequisites for ethnic survival. The Jews longed and hoped for centuries to return to their lost land, to their territory; they always prayed ''Next year in Jerusalem.'' Their religion as well as their collective memories were rooted in Palestine. It was religion that helped the Greeks to preserve their identity under the Turkish rule. The same can be said about Armenians and many other nations. Quoting Anthony Smith again,

it was the dream of a restored Byzantine Orthodox empire that most sustained the Greek identity among the poor peasants and shepherds. For it was backed by the dense network of priests in the villages, by the perennial daily ritual of the Church, by its sacred liturgy and texts to which the priests alone had access. . . . What saved a precarious Armenia was Tiridates III's timely conversion to Christianity, and its evolution along local lines during a period of political partition between Rome and Persia after A.D. 387 . . . both organizationally and emotionally, the ethnic Church provided exiled and migrant Armenians with a tangible expression of their identity, a framework for Community and a latent political goal, the restoration of an Armenian kingdom or state.[19]

The sacred books have always remained symbolic reminders of a unique and eternal destiny. The language in which these books had been written was inseparable both from the religious heritage and ancient ethnic roots. There are cases, however, when it was precisely the language, as distinct from religion, that proved to be paramount in ensuring the preservation of identity. For instance, Czechs professed the same religion as their German-Austrian masters; there were also no major cultural or behavioral differences between the two. In these circumstances, language became the main shield protecting the Czech identity, the principal means of resisting Germanization. It is interesting to note that the Czech language is to this day the most ''pure'' of all the Slavic languages; the proportion of the words of Germanic and Latin origin in Czech is substantially less than in Polish, Russian, Bulgarian, or Serbo-Croat. The point is that all those Slavic nations, unlike the Czechs, throughout their history were dominated or challenged by ethnoses which professed hostile religions (Muslims in the case of the Balkan Slavs, Russian Orthodox and German Lutherans in the Polish case) and thus had, in their churches, an even more powerful instrument of preserving their ethnic identity. The Czechs had only language.

Yet another case in point is the history of the Arabs. It has been the Holy Book, the Qur'an, that has preserved the Arab language and, to a very large extent, the Arab identity. However, the Ottoman Turks, who for centuries ruled over the Arab lands, were Muslims, too. This probably accounts for the weakness of the Arab resistance, for the passivity and docility of the Arab population under the Ottoman yoke. Ethnic Arab consciousness was not yet developed, or probably it would be more correct to say that it was inseparable from, and limited by, the Arabs' Muslim identity. The Turks, after all, were people of the same faith; as to the rest, the Arabs were free to speak their own idiom. Besides, linguistic differences did not matter much, and the Arab elite spoke Turkish as well as Arabic. The only genuine revolts against the Turkish rule occurred when heretics, or fringe sects, were taking up arms to foster their new "true faith" (Wahhabis in the Arabian peninsula). These, however, were rather manifestations of protest against the mainstream official Islam, deemed corrupt and decadent, than rebellions of an ethnic nature. When, for the first time, a genuine nationalist, ethnic, and potentially anti-Turkish movement began to shape up by the end of the nineteenth century, it was, quite understandably, language- and culture-oriented. The first champions of Arabism, almost all of them Syrian Christians, focused on the revival of Arabic as a means of restoring Arab identity; they obviously could not use religion for this purpose.

Anthony Smith notes that, in India, "what helped the radical nationalists was the survival of sacred texts like the Gita, the widespread belief in deities like Kali and Shiva, and the existence of well-known symbols and rites of an ancient Hindu culture like the cow, the Ganges and ablutions."[20]

Thus, ethnicity, inseparable from religion and—usually, but not always—from language, has proved its amazing capacity for survival. Just where lies the "magic" of ethnicity, its almost irresistible spell? How does an ethnic group become predominant in the consciousness of people, overshadowing other loyalties and growing into the main vehicle of identity? One of the experts in the field suggests that "ethnic groups throughout the world offer their members two crucial elements usually identified with traditional 19th century nationalism: an effective group identity; and the psychosocial sustenance of affective ties, a sense of peoplehood, self-esteem, and interdependence of fate. This sense of belonging and/or peoplehood forms the basis of ethnicity."[21] In essence, this is nothing but what was already described as the primordial, deep-rooted common consciousness defined by the existence of a "we-group," but in an enlarged context. Purely tribal perception of the world as divided into "us" and "they" becomes more complicated as civilization shapes and develops. Territory and struggle with enemies continue to be basic, determining factors; language remains a barrier and a dividing line; religion and feeling of "chosenness" are introduced by the developing civilization. Out of all this, the primitive group identity providing individuals with a sense of belonging grows into a community of fate; the sheer necessity of ensuring group survival by means of a collective self-defense against "the others" is complemented and "ennobled" by higher, spiritual values such as religion, historical memories and symbols, common destiny, or even a unique mission. It is probably at this point that the group consciousness definitely acquires traits of ethnicity and a genuine ethnic identity is being formed, an identity based not on such transient foundations as loyalty to empires and dynasties, not on religious intolerance inspiring medieval crusades, but on authentic, fundamental cultural, spiritual, and social values.

Jaroslav Krejci and Vitezslav Velimsky believe that "with the weakening of religious and dynastic loyalties, it was the socio-cultural bond of ethnicity which became the main integrative force, a force based on what for men is the most important link of communication—language."[22]

FROM ETHNOS TO NATION

At what point does an ethnos become a nation and ethnic consciousness grow into a national feeling?

Anthony Smith suggests seven features of the nation: (1) cultural differentiae; (2) territorial contiguity with free mobility throughout; (3) a relatively large scale (and population); (4) external political relations of conflict and alliance with similar groups; (5) considerable group sentiment and loyalty; (6) direct membership with equal citizenship rights; (7) vertical economic integration around a common system of labor.[23] Let us look at the cultural dimension first, in the broad context.

Anthony Smith has been one of the first and certainly the most insightful of scholars to focus on such aspects of the cultural heritage as myths and memories. In his view, the "core" of ethnicity resides in this quartet of "myths, memories, values and symbols." Smith stresses, "nations need myths and past if they are to have a future."[24]

John Armstrong is convinced that "a most significant effect of the myth recital is to arouse an intense awareness among the group members of their 'common fate.' " People, looking for origins of their community, feel a certain nostalgia, "a persistent image of a superior way of life in the distant past. It is, therefore, a kind of "collective memory."[25] Glorifying the past, lionizing heroes is indispensable for preserving the historic memory. But the latter also includes negative, sad, and lamentable episodes of the community's history. Vamik Volkan introduces a new cultural-psychological factor, one that he calls "the chosen trauma." A given group feels victimized by another group, and the trauma is being transmitted from generation to generation. Was this trauma real? "Historical truth does not really matter."[26] Paul Brass notes that "every national movement has always justified itself in terms of existing oppression or anticipated oppression by a rival group."[27]

This heritage of shared values, traditions, memories, and myths is the single most powerful factor of nation-creating. Compared to it, such issues, important as they may be, as language or "blood" do not generally appear vital. Hans Kohn noted that "before nationalism, language was very rarely stressed as a fact on which the prestige and power of a group depended."[28] Krejci and Velimsky believe that "ethnic kinship in itself does not necessarily constitute a common ethnic consciousness, that is, a general acknowledgment of being one ethnic nation. Members of an ethnolinguistic community may consider themselves as either one or several nations.[29]

The Bosnian Muslims provide probably the best example of creating a nationality on the basis of religion, shared memories, and consciousness of a distinct and unique destiny. Their community, not distinct by either language or ethnic descent from their neighbors, certainly identifies itself as a nation in its own right. This goes for the Lebanese Maronites, too, who are undistinguishable by language from the other Arabs in Lebanon, as well as for the Ajarians in Georgia, whose only distinction from all the other ethnic Georgians is their Muslim religion. The Irish in the Irish Republic certainly feel that they are a nation although just a small percentage of them use Gaelic in everyday life, while in Northern Ireland people have no doubt that two distinct nations exist in their land, both of them English-speaking. And yet, other cases can be found to prove that in some historic situations it is precisely language—or, to be more exact, language as a major component of a distinct ethnocultural identity—that has been instrumental in forming a nation. Catalans in Spain, Bengalis in former united Pakistan, Kurds in Turkey, Iraq, and Iran, Abkhazians in Georgia, Gagauz in Moldova posess all the characteristics of a distinct nation asserting its identity in a confrontation with a larger, dominant nation *of the same religion*. The point is that in both sets of cases it is not religion as such, or language per se that has been a decisive factor of nation-building. They can become such factors only when something else has already taken root, namely, that "awareness among the group members of their common fate" of which John Armstrong wrote. "A nation exists," to quote Hugh Seton-Watson, "when a significant number of people in a community consider themselves to form a nation, or behave as if they formed one."[30] Krejci and Velimsky suggest the ethnic consciousness is "one of the constituents of ethnic specificity. While some of the other characteristics may be lacking, this subjective consciousness may even serve as a touchstone to decide whether a group is or is not a separate ethnic entity."[31]

E. K. Francis, departing from F. Meinecke's concept of cultural and political nations, offers a theory of "ethnic nation" and "demotic nation," the former being "based on belief in real or mythological common descent, sense of identity and sentiments of solidarity," and the latter "based on common military and administrative institutions, mobility of labour and merchandise within the nation's frontiers combined with protective measures against the outside world."[32] Krejci and Velimsky suggest that in English and French-speaking countries, nation became understood in institutional and geographical terms rather than in ethnic terms. It related to a country which developed as a politico-territorial formation—the state—which by definition was supposed to be a sovereign body. In Central and Eastern Europe, however, state or statehood on the one hand and nation or nationality on the other, were understood as two quite different concepts: statehood implying citizenship, nationality implying ethnic affiliation irrespective of citizenship. Here the basic characteristics of nationality were seen primarily in language and its associated culture.[33]

The authors list five objective factors which make a nation: territory, state (or similar political status), language, culture, and history, and one subjective criterion. "The subjective factor of consciousness is the ultimate factor which eventually decides the issue of national identity."[34] Finally, Krejci and Velimsky offer their own classification of nations according to which three principal groups exist: (1) full-scale nations (English, French, Poles, Russians, etc.), (2) political nations—those which have a state but not a language (Belgians, Austrians, Swiss etc.), and (3) ethnic nations having their own language but no state (Welsh, Bretons, Catalans, etc.).[35]

Louis Snyder defines the nation as "a group or body of people living within a compact or a noncontiguous territory, using a single language or related dialects as a vehicle for common thoughts and feelings, holding a common religious belief, possessing common institutions, traditions, and customs acquired and transmitted during the course of a common history, venerating national heroes, and cherishing a common will for social homogeneity."[36] This definition, like all countless attempts to define the essence of nation, can be said to be vulnerable, lacking some important components and indispensable prerequisites for the formation of a nation. Probably no definition of nation and nationalism that could claim to be satisfying and acceptable to everybody will ever be found. What is beyond doubt, however, is that nations are being forged on the basis of preexisting *ethnies*. What some authors describe as "ethnic nation" can, by definition, be born only out of ethnoses; otherwise we would deal with some artificial formation. It can officially be proclaimed a nation but in fact it is nothing but a conglomerate of various ethnoses created by political will.

Now, let us turn again to Anthony Smith's definitions of *ethnie* and nation. Some of the features that he enumerates are clearly congruous, such as a common myth of descent, a shared history and culture, a sense of solidarity (in his definition of the nation the terms are slightly different—cultural differentiae, group sentiment, and loyalty,—but the essence is the same). What he adds in defining the nation, compared with his characteristics of the *ethnie*, is territorial contiguity, large scale and population, external relations of conflict and alliance, economic integration. As to the territorial contiguity, this is a moot point. The Jews did not have it for two thousand years; on this basis, should they be denied the right to be called a nation? Were they just an *ethnie* throughout their history?

As mentioned earlier, they certainly had an *association* with a specific territory (Palestine). If this term, used by Smith in his definition of the *ethnie*, would be applied to the nation as well, instead of the "territorial contiguity," it would be easier to describe diaspora peoples as nations, too. However, Smith probably used the two different terms with a purpose, to make a point that only those *ethnies* that have achieved statehood, or are on the way to achieving one, can be described as nations. If this is in fact his concept, then certainly diaspora peoples are not nations, and the borderline between *ethnie* and nation is to be found in the former's readiness and capacity to build an ethnic state.

Yet, there is no denying that diaspora communities have long ago constituted separate *ethnies;* they have all the appropriate characteristics. At this point, a question arises: What are modern diaspora communities? Who is an Armenian living in France, or a Jew living in Argentina? They probably feel that they belong to two nations simultaneously. Generally speaking, such a situation is not uncommon. Smith points out that "many individuals today belong simultaneously to two 'nations'—Catalan and Spanish, Breton and French, Scots and British."[37] But here he speaks of those ethnic communities that have a territory of their own and, in some cases, an autonomous status. Diaspora communities are a different case. Their members may feel, just like Catalans or Scots, that they belong to two nations, but from a theoretical point of view it would be more correct to say that they are parts of *two different communities, one ethnic and the other national.* Thus, a French Armenian belongs simultaneously to the Armenian *ethnie* and to the French nation, although in his consciousness, of course, he makes no such distinction. The difference here is that while Catalans or Scots possess—in what degree, it does not matter—rudiments of a national state or an autonomous entity, that is, beginnings and potential of statehood, this is not and can never be the case with American Jews or French Armenians.

Thus, capacity and willingness to create a national entity can be considered major characteristics of nation as different from *ethnie*.

NATION AND NATIONALISM

Peter Sugar writes:

There can be no doubt that nationalism was, and is, probably the most successful belief ever presented to mankind. Even the loftiest religion or philosophy failed in gaining universal acceptance, but there is no corner on our globe today where the leaders of the most significant or the most insignificant state do not constantly use all the means of communications at their disposal to foster nationalism, the state-supporting loyalty.[38]

How old is nationalism? Did it exist before the modern era? Dawa Norbu suggests a new term: "protonationalism," the manifestations of which are tribalism, ethnocentrism, and patriotism.[39] While the first two are rather simple, natural, and easy to understand, patriotism is a much more complex, sophisticated, and controversial phenomenon. Since the term comes from *patria*, it is necessary to know just what people at different epochs meant by the concept of *patria*. Most historians believe that, until recently, this word by and large hardly had any ethnic meaning. Carlton Hayes, a professor at Columbia University, wrote as early as 1926:

Patriotism, which nowadays we connect with nationality, has been historically more closely related to other loyalties of man . . . among ancient peoples, and mediaeval also, the sway of political and military chieftains infrequently coincided with any particular nationality, and consequently patriotism often changed from local sentiment into imperial pride without passing through an intermediate national stage . . . on top of natural local patriotism was superimposed a more artificial imperial patriotism.[40]

Hans Kohn states categorically:

Nationalism is not a modern phenomenon, not a product of "eternal" or "natural" laws; it is a product of the growth of social and intellectual factors at a certain stage of history . . . love of the homeland which is regarded as the heart of patriotism, is not a "natural" phenomenon, but an artificial product of historical and intellectual development. . . . It is frequently assumed that man loves in widening circles—his family, his village, his tribe or clan, the nation. But love of home and family is a concrete feeling accessible to everyone in daily experience, while nationalism is a highly complex and originally an abstract feeling.

Kohn maintains that "it is only in recent history that man has begun to regard nationality as the center of his political and cultural activity and life."[41] Elie Kedourie is of the same opinion: "Nationalism is a doctrine invented in Europe at the beginning of the 19th century."[42] Hedva Ben-Israel notes that nationalism "is one of the modern ideologies springing directly from the Enlightenment principle of the sovereignty of the people. At its core, nationalism refers to the rights of the nation as a collective entity. . . . There is one core idea of nationalism, which is based on an oscillating emphasis on the idea of sovereignty and on the ideal of ethnic continuity."[43] "The most innovative and dominant of the ideas of the Enlightenment was that of the sovereignty of the people, which necessarily implied the recognition of a collective will, that is, the existence of a collective entity differentiated from an accidental collection of individuals. This is the cornerstone of the theory of nationalism. Once collective sovereignty was accepted, the collectivity exercising sovereignty had to be named. The only place it could be found was in the already existing historic nation."[44]

We see that some authors, like Kohn and Kedourie, tend to use the terms "patriotism" and "nationalism" interchangeably, but it is clear that both of them essentially mean patriotism. Of course, the two terms are not synonymous; Hadva Ben-Israel believes that "patriotism is 'natural' in the sense of being common and understandable in ordinary human terms. Nationalism, on the other hand, is not a feeling at all, though it is partly based on feelings. It is an ideol-

ogy: a body of beliefs to which individuals or groups can adhere through con-
viction . . . nationalism is an ideology adopted to justify revolutionary action to
change borders, topple rulers, create or destroy states.''[45] According to Charles
de Gaulle, patriotism is when love of your own people comes first; nationalism
is when hate for people other than your own comes first.

What is that "love of your own people" or "love of nation" that Kohn
considers to be artificial as opposed to the "natural" love of home and family?
It can be argued that the primordial feeling of tribal solidarity came hardly less
naturally to individuals engaged in the daily struggle for existence than love for
the immediate circle, family. In that struggle, group solidarity also can be called
"a concrete feeling accessible to everyone in daily experience." Along with the
solidarity came the fear and hatred of "the others" perceived as a menacing
force. It is from this dual feeling that tribal loyalty was to grow, providing a
basis for ethnic identity. This was happening before the emergence of the state.
Then, primordial ethnic solidarity was mostly, but not always, overshadowed or
superceded by those "other loyalties of man" that Carlton Hayes noted, particularly imperial, dynastic, and religious. But it is exactly this temporary preva-
lence of "other loyalties" that can be called artificial. Some of the old imperial
states which served not ethnic communities or nations but hereditary rulers
proved to be transient; they did not have lasting foundations. Only those remained that succeeded in transforming themselves into nation-states posessing
that lasting, that is, ethnic foundation. *Ethnicity, for long neglected and overshadowed by "other loyalties," returned triumphantly and reasserted itself in
the mentality of peoples.*

Germans fought each other for centuries without qualm or remorse but, in
spite of this, a German *ethnie* was slowly but inexorably taking shape. It is
probably not so much the common language as a vague but unerring feeling of
a shared destiny bred initially on the Teutonic sagas that was vital in providing
the beginnings of an ethnic identity. The German ethnicity was not obvious to
the people; it was, so to speak, dormant, yet it always lurked somewhere in the
background of mentality, only to burst out in the nineteenth century, when the
ideology of nationalism began vigorously to assert itself.

Likewise, the French might not feel their Frenchness until the Revolution, yet
it would be wrong to say that there was no such thing as a French *ethnie* before
the end of the eighteenth century. If anything, the memories of the Hundred
Years' War and Jeanne d'Arc helped to keep alive the sentiment of a common
fate. The surprising ease and swiftness with which the French masses embraced
the ideas of nation and nationalism during the Revolution proves that, just as
in the case of the Germans, *latent ethnicity provided a fertile ground for the
growth of nationalism.*

Yes, for centuries French and Italians did not feel themselves to be an ethnic
whole, and Germans were not Germans, but Prussians or Bavarians; and yet it
was the national idea that eventually prevailed, an idea deeply rooted in ethnicity, temporarily suppressed but never dead. The narrow medieval concept of

patriotism, or rather binding loyalty to locality, prince, and king, gave way to a modern concept, that of loyalty to nation and country. *Patrie* finally came to mean exactly what it is: fatherland, land of forefathers, of people united by a common destiny and history, not a village or province or a cross-ethnic empire. For all practical purposes, patriotism has become undistinguishable from nationalism. Ethnic communities returned to their roots, but on a new basis—that of the state.

This "modern ethnicity," expressed by nationalism as a certain state of mind, is not about "blood" and race, not even about language or religion taken separately, apart from other factors. It is about common destiny, shared history, cultural values. In order to take root in the population, to create a nation out of an *ethnie*, a conscientious effort is needed, a whole set of ideas has to be disseminated among the people. Seen from this angle, nationalism is a "learned sentiment." It has been called "the active solidarity of a group claiming to be a nation and aspiring to be a state."[46] To create this active solidarity, a nationalist vanguard has to emerge.

The mission of this vanguard is none other than *to build a nation out of an ethnos*. The point is that ethnos (*ethnie*), just like family or tribe, is something that exists as such, in a natural way. It is a given, *an objective reality that cannot be changed. Nation, on the other hand, does not emerge naturally and spontaneously*. All the features of ethnicity noted earlier, such as the feeling of a common destiny, a shared culture, historic memories, myths, and symbols, have to be integrated and raised to the level of an *idée-fixe*, ideology of ethnic revival and self-assertion. In this way, nations are being born—and built—out of *ethnies*. It would seem that the latter provide something like a crude foundation on which such a complex, multidimensional and relatively modern phenomenon as nation can be erected. The word "erected" does not seem to be out of place here since, as already noted, nations, unlike ethnoses, are not totally spontaneous creations. Quoting Paul Brass, "cohesive ethnic groups arise not out of the inevitable march toward their historical destiny, but out of unpredetermined struggles, which take three forms: within the group; between ethnic groups; and between the state and its dominant groups, on the one hand, and local elite groups and populations in its outlying territories, on the other hand."[47] This is not to mean that nations are something artificial; they are products of natural evolution of human society, but in order to shape they need an effort made at least by a part of the society—a nationalist vanguard, the standard-bearer of the ideology of nationalism. *This is where a major difference between* ethnie *and nation lies: the former, being, so to speak, a natural and spontaneous phenomenon, does not need ideology while the latter is unthinkable without one*. The ideology of the nation is, of course, nationalism. Nationalist vanguard is a standard-bearer of this ideology.

Probably the first, and highly typical, representatives of this vanguard were the French revolutionaries who stipulated in the declaration of rights of man and citizen: "Le principe de toute souverainete reside essentiellement dans la nation." For the French revolutionaries, the only entity superior to the individual, the citizen, was not the king but a politically organized human collectivity; for them, this collectivity was the nation. It must be noted, however, that their concept of "nation" had virtually nothing to do with ethnicity; for them, the territorial unification of France, inherited from Louis XIX, had to be complemented by civil egalitarianism. Liberty and equality as well as love of the country were the cornerstones of the French revolutionaries' ideology, and the term "patriotism," rather than "nationalism," can be applied in this case. The issue of patriotism, in Istvan Hont's apt observation,

went to the heart of their political system. Nationalism, as the ruling political passion of the subjects or citizens of the "nation-state" is often understood as the opposite to patriotism, and even when the two are seen as connected, it is assumed that nationalism is the pathology of patriotism which develops under specifically modern conditions and chiefly after the French revolution. . . . The historiographical common-place, that the French revolution is the origin of nationalism does not tally with the evidence concerning the use of the word "nationalism," rare as it was, in this period.[48]

True, but there is no denying that the term "nation," no matter how differently from the later sense of the word it sounded at the time, became the key concept of the French revolutionaries' ideology and captured the society.

The idea of nation swept the revolutionary France. "National" became the most popular term. Les Tuileries was renamed Le Jardin National, Le Louvre–le Palais National, the great painter David was charged with designing a "national costume," and so on. The revolutionary war against external enemies quickly transformed the national idea into nationalism. The general conscription under the slogan "The nation in arms" was a major factor in helping the French people to become conscious of their national unity. "Prolonged fighting, intense propaganda, a nationalist mission of solidarity, cohesiveness, sacrifice, common elation—this is the stuff on which nationalism proliferates."[49]

Thus, it can be said that a social revolution followed by a revolutionary war gave rise to French nationalism, although of a nonethnical variety and thus better called patriotism, and helped to forge a nation, although the beginnings of nation-building had been noticeable under the royal-national state. It was different in Germany and Italy. In the former, a nationalist upsurge occurred during the Napoleonic wars as a response to the French invasion, in the latter as a protest against the Habsburg imperial hegemony. In both cases, it was the "intelligentsia of nationalism" that was instrumental in spreading the nationalist ideology. The philosopher Fichte claimed that the German people, alone among the modern peoples, were possessive in the highest degree of a germ of human perfection and of a powerful force in the development of mankind, while Gioberti and Mazzini exalted a historic mission of the Italian nation blessed with a divine predilection. This kind of exaltation is quite common in the nationalist propaganda. One can find innumerable writings on the unique and unparalleled qualities of the Arabs or Chinese, for example.

What about the formation of the Russian nation? Like most great ethnoses, the Russian populace is complex and heterogeneous, by no means "pure" as regards race and blood. The Russians are a blend of diverse ethnic components, including a powerful Tatar element. What matters, however, is the fact that for centuries Russians have felt that they belonged to a community. It was defined sometimes as Russian Christian Orthodox people, emphasizing language and religion first and foremost but also that rather mystical and intangible feeling of belonging together that is indispensable for forming ethnos and nation.

From the Middle Ages, the Russians had three basic elements of ethnic solidarity. First, language. Unlike most Western European languages, Russian never had dialects; there are only insignificant differences in pronunciation. Russians, who lived thousands of miles apart in the largest country of the world, always shared a common idiom and could perfectly understand each other.

Second, religion. There have been no major religious divisions in Russia since the tenth century, when the population was baptized. For centuries, the overwhelming majority of Russians were Greek Orthodox. Thus, the dichotomy "us-them," which is the basis of ethnic self-consciousness, existed in Russia since the oldest times but in a peculiar "non-ethnic" form, with a clearly defined watershed between "Christians," which in reality meant Orthodox, and all the rest, including not only Muslims (infidels, *basurmany*) but also Catholics (heretics, *latiny*). So the Russian ethnos defined itself not in ethnolinguistic and cultural terms but in terms of religion and state belonging.

Third, a unitary and highly centralized state of their own, without any internal divisions of a federalist or autonomist type, and an absolutist state at that. The very strength of the Russian state, with its enormous degree of centralization, made for consolidating the population, rallying it, voluntarily or otherwise, to the idea of Mother Russia, with one state, one tsar, one faith, and one language.

To sum up, the ethnolinguistic dimension was by no means sufficient for a person to be qualified as "one of us"; what was vital was to be Orthodox and the tsar's subject. Much later, in the nineteenth century, a Russian statesman, Sergei Uvarov, coined a very concise formula: "Orthodoxy, Autocracy, People"; the translation is not quite correct because the last word (*narodnost* in Russian) really does not mean people as such (*narod*) but a derivative from this term, indicating a kind of ideology or way of thinking based on the people as a paramount value. This formula, fated to become quite famous, implicitly stipulates the existence of a community grounded on shared ethnicity that outweighs and overshadows class differences, thus bridging the gulf between the elite and common people. It is this last part of the triad that proved manifestly wrong. The Russian ethnic community, whose existence for almost a thousand years would be hard to deny, was not destined to grow into a national community, into a nation, precisely because of the lack of a shared culture and spiritual values. The gulf between the nobility and the "lower class," the peasantry, that fatal gulf which the Uvarov formula seemed to negate, was real at all times. It was never bridged, a genuine society was never formed, the task of nation-building was not accomplished. This historic failure can be regarded as one of the main causes of the crisis and eventual downfall of the tsarist autocracy in the twentieth century.

In Russian history, we can find neither of the two factors that gave a boost to the process of nation-forming in the West: the overthrow of monarchy followed by a proclamation of "all sovereignty residing in the nation" (France) and the integration of a number of local mini-states into a unified nation-state (Germany and Italy). Neither of those two processes were really necessary in Russia for developing ethnic consciousness; while the French, German, or Italian peasants as late as the eighteenth century can hardly be said to have possessed true ethnic consciousness, this was not the case in Russia at the same period. The Russians, probably since the time of the liberation from the Tatar rule, felt they belonged to a distinct community; there could be no doubt as to their ethnic identity. This made the effort of nation-building, or deliberately "erecting" a nation, virtually superfluous in the Russian case. Russia stopped at the threshold separating ethnos from nation.

The difference between ethnic and national consciousness can be formulated in this way: while the former is chiefly based on common language and territory, the latter also includes mentality, shared cultural values, and belief in a common destiny. In tsarist Russia, both the peasantry and nobility were perfectly aware of their "Russianness," as opposed to the people of alien languages and religions, but otherwise they represented two different communities. The main reason for this was the same autocracy that was at the centerpiece of the Uvarov formula, or, to be more correct, the age-old, awful Russian superautocracy. Of course, absolute monarchy existed in the West as well but no king, including Louis XIV with his famous motto "L'etat c'est moi," could claim such complete, total power, such mystical worship as the Russian tsar. The autocrat by the grace of God wielded immense powers unlimited by any form of control, and his authority was unchallenged over a huge territory that was extended beyond the Urals, to the heart of Asia. Thus, it was state power that was the cornerstone of the whole process of ethnonational development in Russia and, since Peter the Great, this absolute and ruthless power stubbornly tried to "Westernize," and in this way "civilize" the population. The result was the consolidation of two divergent communities that possessed the ethnic consciousness but lacked the national one. Indeed, no real nationalist ideology emerged in Russia. Even the famous Slavophile current of thought in the nineteenth century was focused not on the concept of a Russian nation forming a vanguard of a family of Slavic nations but on a messianic vision of Russia as "The Third Rome" (more about that later). It can be called pseudonationalist ideology in the sense that what was emphasized was not the idea of an ethnic nation but a historic mission of the Orthodox Russia with its unique spirituality.

Ethnolinguistic dimension as such had never been a cornerstone of Slavophile or Russophile trends; they rather focused on such themes as religion (Greek Orthodox church) and *derzhavnost* (the idea of a strong imperial Russia). Historically, Russia had for centuries resisted the onslaught of two powerful adversaries—Western Catholicism, headed by the papal Rome and practically represented by Poland, and Islam, represented by Turkey and the Crimean Tatars. The Poles were, of course, also Slavic and as such were sometimes included in the ''Slav family of nations,'' but the feeling was that they, unlike Orthodox Serbs and Bulgars, were somehow alien as an embodiment of that pernicious influence, the Catholic Rome. This attitude was, until the end of the eighteenth century, reinforced by interminable wars between Russia and Poland. Thus, Panslavism was always ambiguous as regards Poland. As to Muslims, they were regarded as infidels (*basurmany*) and treated accordingly, but only because of their religion and not on ethnic grounds. In fact, many baptized people of Turkic origin were co-opted into the imperial elite; by the way, that elite included a sizeable proportion of persons of Armenian, Georgian, and Lithuanian blood as well, not to mention many ethnic Germans. This Russian imperial tradition, largely indifferent to ethnicity and language, was later inherited by the Soviet regime, under which local Party bosses from Transcaucasia and Central Asia were able to rise as high as the Moscow Politbureau. As the British scholar John Barber stressed,

the concept of the Russian empire (*rossiiskaia imperiia*) was explicitly not one of an ethnic Russian empire, but of an autocracy whose citizens regardless of nationality owed allegiance to the tsar and could be employed in the service of the state. . . , Only in the late nineteenth century did an ideology of Russian nationalism develop, and with it the policy of the Russification of non-Russian provinces. The latter, however, was only selectively applied. Neither in theory or practice did the idea of Russia as a nation state have a significant political impact.[50]

Yet, the bulk and the hard core of the population of the Russian Empire had always been made of ethnic Russians perfectly conscious of their identity.

Historical memory is built on myths and legends, and there has been plenty of it in Russia's long history. Whole generations were brought up with respect for Russia's glorious past which, like everywhere else, is inseparable from military deeds, exploits, victories, and conquests. Every Russian schoolchild, both before and after the Bolshevik Revolution, knew by heart a poem by Pushkin exalting Peter the Great's victory over the Swedes and Lermontov's poem about the battle against Napoleon's army near Moscow. Military reverses also linger in historical memory, for example, the catastrophic defeat of the Russian army and navy in the Russo-Japanese war at the beginning of the twentieth century. This memory probably has something to do with the total rejection by most Russians of the idea of relinquishing Russia's rights on the Kuril Islands seized

from Japan after World War II. Somewhere, back in their minds, people seem
to have a recollection of that humiliation at the hands of the Japanese.

Naturally, as John Breuilly noted, "there is a general tendency for the initial
nationalist response to come from culturally dominant groups,"[51] or, in the
words of another author, "new middle-class intelligentsia of nationalism had to
invite the masses into history."[52] Anthony Smith, addressing this issue, calls the
intelligentsia "the new priesthood of the nation."[53] Krejci and Velimsky also
find it necessary to touch on this subject: "While the nationalist leadership of
territorial nations (and their civic nationalism) is increasingly recruited from a
bureaucratic and political class, demotic ethnie aspiring to form nations look to
their intellectuals and a wider professional stratum (or intelligentsia) for leadership and self-definition."[54]

Doing their best to shape national self-consciousness, scholars of history have
been in the business of creating their own version of events. Thus, in preparation
for a war against South Ossetians in 1990, Georgian historians and propagandists
treated Ossetians as just "guests" who had been provided with shelter by Georgians in a dark period of the formers' history; what they had in mind was the
Mongol invasion in the thirteenth century. Ossetian scholars retorted by pointing
out that traces of Scythian villages had been found in South Ossetia dating back
to the seventh century B.C. and, since Ossetians are regarded as descendants of
Sarmats-Scyths, the area in question rightfully belonged to them.

Another example is the controversy over the Nart epos, which is highly valued
by many ethnic groups in the North Caucasus. Georges Dumesil, a leading
French expert on ancient culture and mythology, came to the conclusion that
the epos had been basically Iranian in origin; it is known that the Ossetians are
an ethnos of the Iranian stock. In 1977, Dumesil's works dealing mainly with
the Nart epos were published in Moscow under the title "Ossetian epos and
mythology"; this produced an outrage in neighboring Ingushetia where people
had always regarded the epos as their own. What followed was a sharp deterioration of relations between the Ossetians and Ingush that added fuel to the
already existing conflict over a disputed territory; eventually, it came to a bloody
armed clash.

In Abkhazia, a local historian published a book in the mid-1970s claiming
that ancestors of the Abkhazians had in ancient times inhabited the whole of
the eastern and southeastern coast of the Black Sea, the areas populated at
present mostly by Georgians. This book, and a review of it, published in a local
newspaper, caused a real furor. Clashes between the Abkhazians and Georgians
in Sukhumi, the capital city of Abkhazia, an autonomous part of Georgia, were
so violent as to cause the Georgian authorities, in order to placate the Abkhazians, to open a university in Sukhumi with Abkhazian as a teaching language.
When, years later, as Georgia became an independent state, the nationalists in
power decided to abolish teaching in Abkhazian, the issue became one of the
main reasons for Abkhazia's secession from Georgia which, in turn, led to a
full-scale war.

NATION AND STATE

The ultimate aim of nationalism is to create a sovereign state. It demands a nation-state, it regards the state as the highest form of organized social activity. "Nationalism can be defined as the contention that the organizing principle of government should be unification of all members of a nation in a single state."[55] The very idea of nation was always linked to, and inseparable from, the notion of state. As Istvan Hont noted,

the pairing of the notions of "nation" and "state" makes sense when in people's imagination their nationality and their territorial official unit . . . becomes fused. The belief that a historically forged unitary state with a grisly past of war and coercion has become a true "nation" . . . provide it with the greatest political securuty which any power structure could ever aspire to, the supporting power of public opinion.[56]

"The most usual pattern of nation-building in Europe proceeded from a tribe (patriarchal organisation based on kinship) through a dynastic state (monarchic organisation based on feudal bonds of hierarchy of estates) to a nation-state (organisation by means of representative and/or bureaucratic institutions based on an enlarged, more or less linguistic kinship)."[57] To quote Istvan Hont again,

at the time of its inception the modern idea of the "state" could not be easily connected to the idea of the "nation," and despite the universal acceptance of the hyphenated term "nation-state" today, it would have been thought of as something of an oxymoron. The nation was mostly understood either as a pre- or non-political category or as a term on Christian political eschatology. It referred to people of common origin, like groups of students from distant countries and regions at universities, or social groups of a certain rank.[58]

In Europe, the statist idea was incarnated in the Roman Empire, and ever since the latter fell in the fifth century, a nostalgia was felt for the restoration of the great imperial entity. Suffice it to recall Charlemagne and, later, the Spanish monarchs. As the attempts to resurrect the grand cross-country empire failed, a more modest pattern emerged, that of establishing a viable state power in a specific, well-defined territory. This was realized in the fifteenth and sixteenth centuries in France, Great Britain, and Spain, while the other European peoples had to wait until the next two centuries. At its beginnings, the twin concepts of nation and state were focused on monarchy; the state was embodied in the person of the king.

The royal-national state collapsed in France as the Revolution abolished the monarchy and proclaimed the nation, not the king, as the bearer of state sovereignty. The nation-state came into being. In Istvan Hont's formulation, "the primary sense of the 'nation-state' is that it is the opposite of empire, defined as a kind of territorial state-system within which entire populations or nations . . . are also considered as either superiors or inferiors."[59]

Nationalism as a means of collective self-assertion spread over the whole of Europe. Gradually it largely took over the integrative role of religion and/or dynastic loyalties. The pace of this process varied from country to country and also with respect to social groups and strata, relative to the progressive secularisation of spiritual life. . . . In promoting the Sacred Fatherland in the place of the Holy Church, the nationalism of the romantic period was able to satisfy a deep socio-psychological need . . . the principle was promoted that any ethnic group is entitled to have its own state and that each state has to be based on one such ethnic group or nation.[60]

All those nations, and many others, have had an advantage of possessing not only an indisputable ethnic heritage but more or less clearly defined territory, a land of their own where they have never been a minority. This is a crucial issue. The Western concept of the nation is essentially territorial—a mass territorial nation. As Anthony Smith noted, nationalism is always "about the possession and retention of land."[61] What is at issue here is one's own land, "our land." A state built on this land does not need to be inhabited by a homogeneous population. After all, out of 180 states today only 20 can be called homogeneous. What is important is to have a clear and, if possible, overwhelming majority in the state population so as to be able unquestionably to call the country "our own." For many a state, it has never been a problem; there are, however, quite a few "difficult cases."

"States can exist without a nation," wrote Seton-Watson, "or with several nations, among their subjects; and a nation can be coterminous with the population of one state, or be included together with other nations within one state, or be divided between several states. There were states long before there were nations, and there are some nations that are much older than most states that exist today." In the case of many nations, he went on, a task for nationalists has been "to build a nation within an independent state, by extending down to the population as a whole the belief in the existence of the nation, which, before independence was won, was held only by a minority."[62] This is the case, for instance, in many African states and in some states of the former Soviet Union. They are clearly at a disadvantage compared to the old nations of a "classical" type mentioned earlier, where nations were "formed on the basis of pre-existing ethnie."[63] Anthony Smith differentiates between the *nation-state* (a nation with de facto territorial sovereignty and ethnocultural unity) and the *state-nation*, that is, a state which does not (yet) possess cultural differentiae and in-group sentiment, like Nigeria, Ghana, and others. "The introduction of the concept of the 'state-nation' breaks the . . . evolutionary pattern of the ascending sequence tribe-*ethnie*-nation-nation-state."[64] Whereas the nation-state, although polyethnic, is mostly dominated by "a single strategic *ethnie* which seeks to incorporate, or influence, the surrounding smaller or weaker *ethnie*," the state-nation faces tremendous difficulties in ensuring the supremacy of the strongest ethnic group, which usually appears dominant in the newly born state. Smith notes that some ethnic groups may have a headstart over others and, "any late-

comer ethnic identity will have great difficulties in gaining recognition.''[65] Almost inevitably, ''secondary'' nationalism, or even separatist counternationalism
emerges, fed by the huge disappointment which the minority ethnic communities
feel as they realize that independence and statehood have not provided them
with equality as a group within the state, the equality of access to political power
and economic resources. Many advocates of this ''secondary nationalism,'' reflecting the sentiments of a threatened and resentful minority community, would
agree with K. R. Minogue's opinion that ''it is a much worse fate to live as
part of a minority in a nationalist state than to be one people among many ruled
by a multi-national empire.''[66] The empire, after all, did not base its title to rule
on ethnonational grounds.

Indeed, complaints about the newly born state can be heard from many quarters. It claimed to treat all citizens and groups as equal members of the nation-
in-shaping, but in too many cases this claim only served to disguise the rule of
one ethnic group over another. In an atmosphere of frustration, bitterness, and
mutual distrust, it is extremely hard to forge a nation. Leaders of new African
states have been doing their best to create the ''state-nation,'' to induce people
to put overall national interest above ethnicity; the results, however, have been
mixed at best. The official slogan is: ''We are all Kenians'' (or Angolans, or
Nigerians) but in real life people feel at every step—or are made to feel—their
ethnic origins, their place in the new state hierarchy; mostly, they are not happy
with this place and resent their subordinate status. Of course, on some occasions
they feel what may be called ''state patriotism''; international crises or sporting
events may make them stand for their country, their flag. Otherwise, it is ethnicity expressed by tribalism that sets the tone.

The people of multiethnic states appear to have a complex, or mixed sense
of identity. For instance, citizens of India, when dealing with foreigners, regard
themselves as Indians, equally loyal to Mother India, while at home they clearly
see one another as Hindus, Bengalis, Tamils, and so on. The Arabs seem to
have three levels of identity and loyalties. At the macro-level, all of them consider themselves Arabs, and probably most of them believe in the existence of
''al-umma al-arabiya,'' the Arab nation. This applies mostly to the relations
with the outside world and can be seen as a manifestation of all-Arab nationalism and patriotism. At the next, or middle level, Arabs are citizens of particular
states, and at the third, or micro-level, it is the local, parochial loyalty based on
clan patronage and sect networks that is dominant. As state citizens, people
display what can be called local, or state, nationalism, as distinct from the ethnic
Arab nationalism. State nationalism could, however, better be called patriotism,
that is, love of *patria*, of homeland, of a specific country. On the other hand,
the term ''patriotism'' would not convey the true meaning of this particular kind
of loyalty because this world is traditionally associated with sentiments and not
with interests, while what matters most in the case of state identity is concrete
interests of large groups of the population. The sentiments bred on history,

myths, traditions, feeling of a shared destiny, remain in the "higher" sphere of Arab nationalism; real life interests demand the assertion of state patriotism.

The strength of Arab state patriotism can be explained by two factors. First, during the years of independence, a solid native state machine has been shaped. A huge state apparatus is functioning, with numerous officials having a vested interest in the preservation of the state. This applies as well to Party politicians of all levels, businessmen, managers, media people, university professors, and so on, all of them firmly entrenched in the state structure and prone to be apprehensive about possible implications of a disruption of the existing regimes and systems of relationships, a disruption which appears unavoidable in the event of a change in the country's status. And it is precisely these categories of the population that have the greatest opportunity to influence public opinion.

Second, people probably feel that an all-Arab nationalism is not sufficient for them, it being too general and abstract, to the point of vagueness, especially since all the projects of Arab unity in the form of political association have failed. What is needed is loyalty to something more specific and tangible. People want to belong to a sufficiently large and strong community placed somewhere in between the "global" Pan-Arab nationalism (so vague as to appear almost irrelevant) and the narrow local clan and sect loyalties. This desire seems to be met by state patriotism, which satisfies the need for a broad identity overriding purely local interests while at the same time offering a specific, clearly defined, and viable territorial dimension.

State patriotism, to the dismay of advocates of both "Arabism" and "Islamism," has proved a powerful force. During the Iran-Iraq War neither Khomeini nor Saddam Hussein were able to correctly evaluate the strength of this phenomenon. Khomeini hoped that the Iraqi Shi'ites, being coreligionists of Iranians, would not back the Sunni power in Baghdad while Saddam, on invading Iran, reckoned on the support of the ethnic Arabs of Khouzestan. In both cases, however, state patriotism proved to be stronger than common religion or the "call of blood." The Khouzestani Arabs took part in the defense of the Iranian state while the Iraqi Shi'ites fought on Saddam's side.

"Far from withering away," writes Gabriel Ben-Dor "the state in the Middle East today is stronger than ever."[67] Bernard Lewis draws attention to the "somewhat surprising phenomenon of the recent and current Middle Eastern world—the extraordinary persistence of states once 'created' "; he points out that the Arab states, in particular, "have shown—even the most improbable of them—an extraordinary capacity for survival and self-preservation, often in very adverse circumstances."[68] In the aftermath of the First World War, as "artificial states" in the Arab East were carved by the British and French, it could seem that those entities were not really viable and would disappear as soon as the European imperial forces leave the area. Surprisingly, not a single Arab state has collapsed to this day, in spite of all the turmoil and the change of political regimes. Even more amazing is the durability of African states, much more "artificial" than the Arab states since, unlike the latter, all of them are multiethnic and thus lacking a solid ethnic foundation which, in the case of the Arabs, has given rise to the "broad" Arab nationalism.

The state in its present form has emerged as a realization and culmination of the nationalist dream. While in the "nation-states" a large majority of the population is quite satisfied with their ethnic identity being legitimized and assured at the state level, in the "state-nations" at least the dominant ethnic group can be said to enjoy the fruits of independence (of course, strictly in the sense of ethnicity, otherwise there is a lot to be unhappy about). Paradoxically, however, it appears that nationalism, far from being in decline after having achieved its main goal—the creation of the state—is on the rise almost everywhere, in a more formidable form than ever before.

THE RISE OF MODERN NATIONALISM

"Modernity," says Alexander Motyl, "promotes nations, states and thus nation-states. . . . In short, modernity breeds nationalism."[69]

Violent upheavals, often endangering regional peace, largely occur in the case of *minority nationalisms*. In many countries it is mostly minorities that break the status quo; minorities which stand up to dominant nations or ethnic groups perceived as being oppressive and despotic. Also, in the Balkans and in the former Soviet Union, new states proclaimed on the ruins of the defunct federations are jockeying for positions, fighting over disputed territories and frontiers. Most of these new states are populated by former minority nations of the USSR and Yugoslavia: Georgia, Armenia, Moldova, Croatia, Bosnia. The mentality of these nations is still one of a minority struggling for its rights.

Why has minority nationalism in the old nation-states become more attractive and plausible lately? Anthony Birch suggests some explanations.

- The impact of television on cultural minorities has been different in kind from the impact of other media because it brings a majority culture right into the living room. Backlash reaction in defense of the minority culture becomes inevitable;

- Industrial rationalization—concentration of business headquarters in metropolitan centers—reduces peripheral people's control over regional economic affairs, strengthens the dominant community. This provokes minority protest; growth of political impatience. In an era when talk about the future is dominated by predictions of nuclear warfare, world famine, and the exhaustion of energy resources, people are no longer willing to accept a situation that displeases them in the hope that things will be better for their children or grandchildren;

- The changed nature of the international system has increased the security of smaller states. Secession has become less risky, the size of country is not so important;

- The supranational organizations—the World Bank, the International Monetary Fund (IMF)—can provide economic advantages, access to large markets, and so on.[70]

Still other issues can be added to this list. Ever since the First World War, slogans of self-determination of nations have been heard and actively propagated throughout the world. This idea has become an unalienable feature of the global politico-ideological landscape; it has really been introduced to the *zeitgeist*. The Second World War brought about the condemnation of totalitarian rule and racism; in the eyes of many, the struggle against domination of one ethnic group over others fits into the anti-totalitarian, anti-despotic pattern of human emancipation. The anti-imperialist propaganda widespread in the era of liberation movements in Asia and Africa has been also seen as related to "cultural imperialism."

All these factors largely account for the rise of nationalist sentiment that occurred even in the countries where there was no substantial deterioration in the material standard of life of the minorities. "Early diffusions of nationalism," notes Armstrong, "were well underway *before* the economic upheavals of industrialization had transformed the receiving countries. Hence Hayes and Kohn emphasize *contagion* by an intellectually and emotionally appealing ideology rather than economic explanations."[71] Krejci and Velimsky find little evidence that economic inequalities between cultural groups "do anything more than exacerbate preexisting grievances, antagonisms, and tensions."[72]

Indeed, it must be noted that those who are economically the worst off are generally not the most rebellious and adamant. Suffice it to look at the global history of mass discontent, uprising, and revolutions. Some of the poorest ethnic communities in Central Africa and South America have never found the will to rise against dominant ethnic or social groups; nor are inequality as such, or relative deprivation, or status discrepancies the critical precipitants of nationalism in ethnic groups but, as Paul Brass notes, "the relative distribution of ethnic groups in the competition for valued resources and opportunities and in the division of labour in societies undergoing social mobilization, industrialization, and bureaucratization."[73] The processes Brass mentions can be regarded as evidence of progress; even bureaucratization has to be seen as an unavoidable price to pay for the development of society. What is not in doubt is that more and more people are getting involved in affairs of the state; they get to know about things the previous generations had no notion of, and nationalist feelings certainly intensify with the increase of the number of people having a voice in politics.

"Markets," says Motyl, "place people into contact and competition. Nations that may have not known one another and thus, could not have been in conflict, are brought together under conditions that contribute little to peaceful resolutions of emergent problems. After all, it is in the very nature of market relations to reward efficient regions and to penalize inefficient ones."[74]

James Kellas suggests the existence of three elites making up the nationalist vanguard—political, cultural, and economic—and maintains that of those three, it is cultural nationalists who provide the backbone of nationalism.[75] Of course, what we now call mass media has a major role to play in this process of "national education" of the masses.

The leading role in the nationalist movements is played by the "intelligentsia of nationalism" and, at later stages, by a managerial, technical, and administrative middle class as well as young activists from the ranks of skilled workers. All of them see their prospects as potentially improving with the advent of an autonomous, if not independent, entity; and, as Breuilly suggested, "no nationalist movement is based on pure sentiment. All nationalist movements build upon a variety of interests."[76] Still, the *ideology* of nationalism focuses first and foremost not on interest but on sentiment, namely, on protecting national culture and fighting for the community's rights invariably perceived as being slighted by the ruling majority. It starts with culture and language. The emphasis on culture always strikes a chord with the broadest masses because the satisfaction provided by national culture, as Sigmund Freud noted, "can be shared not only by the favoured classes, which enjoy the benefits of this culture, but also by the oppressed, since the right to despise those that are outside it compensates them for the wrongs they suffer in their own unit. No doubt one is wretched plebeian, harassed by debts and military service; but, to make up for it, one is a Roman citizen."[77] The protection of culture and restoration of language provide a starting point for nationalist propaganda everywhere, from the first champions of Arab revival in the countries of Levant more than a hundred years ago, to the Ukrainian nationalists in the last few decades. It is a very serious issue in British Wales today. In the 1972 Manifesto of the Welsh Language Society, there is an interesting sentence: "To that astonishing question, 'Why do you want to keep up the Welsh language?', the true Welshman need only answer, 'That our fathers be not shamed.' "[78] It does not really matter how many people speak the language. In Belarus cities one can hardly hear the native language; everybody speaks Russian but it does not embarrass nationalist activists who relentlessly try to resurrect the local idiom. In some cases, progress is undisputable. Thus, the Yakut language in the autonomous republic of Sakha (formerly Yakutia), a part of the Russian Federation, just a few years ago was regarded as a joke; today, more and more people, ethnic Yakuts, are learning to speak it.

It is only when social and economic elites join the movement that it acquires a real strength. The elites in question are always urban. The bulk of the population in the countries in question, however, consisted of peasantry; sooner or later peasants, as well as the urban lower classes, had to be involved in the nationalist movement to give it a really mass character. This is the case not only with minority movements but also with campaigns aimed at mobilizing the masses of the ruling nation as the latter begins to feel threatened by the minority's mobilization. Thus, the nobility and clergy in Wallachia and Moldavia finally made an alliance with the peasants, whom they always despised, and mobilized them "around a Dacian myth and Rumanian language."[79] One of the typical cases of national conflict occurs when rural groups move into towns inhabited largely by other ethnic groups. The urban groups suddenly find their positions undermined.

Two processes of mobilization occur almost simultaneously, pushing both the majority and the minority toward conflict. Hetukar Jha describes this in the following terms:

Nationalism in a community possessing all the objective attributes of nation depends for its beginning on the subjective attribute or national consciousness. This national consciousness, in turn, depends for its evolution on the extent of mobilization of the masses by the organized and integrated elites. But this mobilization of people by the elites starts only when the elites get involved in a conflict . . . with the elites of the discriminating community. The more the conflict or contradiction between the two opposed groups of elites grows, the greater is the elites' effort towards mobilizing the masses, i.e., towards evolving national consciousness among the people.[80]

Evidently, we must differentiate between various types of nationalism. One of them can be called *victorious*, or *dominant nationalism*, that of a "happily settled" master-nation. This brand of nationalism—of the Germans, English, French, Americans, Chinese, and so on—does not appear to be a discontented and rebellious, much less a violent force. This can also be said, although with less certainty, about the nationalism of *dominant, ruling* ethnic groups in the new African states. Those groups have no cause to be defiant and violent; after all, they have a state where they are on top. Strictly speaking, this state has yet to be consolidated because its backbone, the nation, does not exist; the framework, however, is already there.

On the whole, it seems that some powerful wind of nationalism is sweeping the world. In totally dissimilar countries ethnonationalist movements have been surfacing lately with an amazing similarity of slogans and actions, as if orchestrated by some hidden force. From the Fleming in Belgium, Corsicans in France, Basques in Spain, French in Canada, Albanians in Serbia, Slovaks in Czechoslovakia, to Ossetians and Abkhazians in Georgia to Tamils in Sri Lanka, ethnoseparatist forces are on the march. Is it just *zeitgeist*?

Of course, in the last few years movements based on ethnic issues have been greatly strengthened and encouraged by the mere fact of the end of the Cold War and the collapse of a bipolar world. It would even seem that humankind, having breathed a sigh of relief at the end of global nuclear threat, feels free at last to turn its attention to the real business, that of settling old ethnic scores. This is partly true, by the way: bloc discipline gone, many nations can deal with problems closer to home without the fear of being punished by the Big Boss.

This, however, is only a part of the picture, albeit a major one. Even before the end of the Cold War, trends of the rise of nationalism were clearly discernable. In Western Europe and Canada as well as in Sri Lanka and India, ethnoseparatism has been steadily growing for decades, irrespective of the East–West confrontation. Today, in an athmosphere of "new world disorder," it seems easier to lump together various causes of nationalist upsurge; differentiations, however, have to be made.

Unfortunately, this effort is accompanied, more often than not, by nationalist paranoia, by what the Boston professor John Mack calls "the egoism of victimization," when there is no real empathy "for the suffering experienced by a group's traditional enemies, although it may be as severe as that of the group itself, or even worse."[81] The current fighting in former Yugoslavia provides the best example of horrible insensitivity for another group's suffering, an insensitivity displayed by people speaking the same language and very much alike in most respects. The same can be said about Rwanda or Tajikistan. Indeed, in some cases the differences between warring factions are so small that it almost seems that the enemies are shooting at themselves, or rather at the mirrored image of one's own bad and hateful features. It was Freud who coined the phrase "narcissism of minor differences": Enemies are seen as reservoirs for externalized bad aspects of ourselves.[82] Common origins and geographical proximity create negative reference points for each of the feuding communities. The point is, as noted earlier, that ethnic groups usually define themselves by reference to "out-groups." As the relations between unfriendly communities deteriorate to the point of confrontation, those negative reference points become a ready-made basis for hatred and intolerance.

It is inevitable that this hatred and intolerance begins to influence, in the most negative way, relationships, psychological climate, and political culture within the group. Militant nationalism breeds the spirit of exclusiveness and intransigence, encourages uniformity, and dreads differences of opinion seen as divisive and therefore treasonable. All those are typical traits of a totalitarian society. Indeed, suffice it to look at the "breakaway republics" of today: the Bosnian Serb entity, the self-proclaimed Dniester republic, Abkhazia, Nagorno-Karabakh, Tamil "mini-state" in Sri Lanka, and so on. None of them, to put it mildly, puts a premium on democracy. What we now see emerging is what the French author Edgar Morin calls a "*total-nationalisme*," with its obsession with *Lebensraum* and ethnic cleansing. "The legitimate patriotic aspiration to sovereignty has been transformed into nationalist virulence."[83]

Analyzing this aspect of nationalism, Ben-Israel stresses "the ambiguous notion of total sovereignty, from which nationalism was born. If the sovereign nation is the ultimate source of all laws governing its life, there is no limit to its freedom. Since total sovereignty of the people and the existence of a transcendent moral law are incompatible, nationalism, from the beginning, carried the potential for the tyranny of the majority or the historic nation."[84]

Nationalism always appeals to the heart, to emotions rather than reason. Essentially, nationalism, just like socialism and fascism, is an ideology of collectivism: An individual must dissolve oneself in a surpassing *ensemble*. The motto of Nazi Germany, "You are nothing, your people are everything," could just as well characterize the psychological atmosphere that "total nationalism" inexorably creates as it mobilizes the masses under the banner of that "supreme entity," the Nation.

Now, let us draw some conclusions.

1. The formation of *ethnies* appears to be a natural, unavoidable, and spontaneous process. Ethnoses can be regarded as the main form of the organization of society, a basic level of identity.

The building of nations is probably just as unavoidable but, different from ethnoses, it is not spontaneous; it requires a conscious effort. This effort is usually made by a vanguard represented by nationalist-minded intellectuals supported in the West by the middle class, and in the Socialist world by state-managerial elites.

2. There can be no uniform answer to the question: Which came first, state or nation? In France, a powerful state had already been in existence before the Revolution; so was, of course, the French *ethnie*. The Revolution and the Napoleonic wars gave birth to a genuine *national consciousness*. A national state was created which Fred Riggs defines as "a state whose citizens belong predominantly to a single ethnonation."[85] A parallel process was the rise of the middle class contributing to the formation of civil society. A net result of these two patterns was the formation of a *civic nation*, or a *state nation*, a concept opposed to that of an *ethnic nation*, just as state nationalism, or patriotism, can be called civic nationalism as different from ethnonationalism.

In Germany and Italy, unlike in France, not a social revolution but a movement born by a quest for unity became an instrument for promoting and asserting national consciousness. In these two cases, however, the middle class also played a major role: the nascent bourgeoisie desperate to destroy barriers between artificial statelets. Political centralization preceded the formation of ethnonations on the basis of preexisting *ethnies* and the birth of national states. In all the three cases—France, Germany, and Italy—two points have to be made: (a) ethnic foundations for nation-building had already been in existence before national consciousness took root in the population and before a national state was formed, and (b) the rise of bourgeoisie was a major factor contributing to the whole pattern: from nonethnic, although ethnically based, medieval states to ethnonational state to civic nation.

3. In Russia, an omnipotent, centralized state had existed since at least the sixteenth century, the same as, for example, in France, but, unlike it, ethnonational consciousness was already widespread and thus there was no need for the kind of ideological mobilization that was provided in France by a social revolution, and in Germany and Italy by a unification movement. There was, however, no significant development of bourgeoisie, of that middle class which usually becomes a driving force for the creation of civil society. The awesome power of the state, which later grew into an empire, prevented the middle class from becoming a genuine political force and destroyed all prerequisites for the formation of a civil society. Thus, what had been developing in Russia since the sixteenth century as territorial expansion was taking place, adding more ethnoses to the emerging empire, had been an *imperial supernation*. Ethnic Russians possessed first, a definite ethnic identity, and second, an imperial identity but no genuine national identity, no national self-consciousness, no national

mentality. It can be argued, therefore, that the Russians, in spite of being an old, deep-rooted, and well-defined ethnos, have not yet formed a real nation.

4. Under the Soviet regime, Russian ethnic consciousness was fading away under the impact of the ideology of proletarian internationalism; at the same time, a boost was given to the development of new ethnic nations, in some cases a veritable nation-building. A vanguard of this development was formed by native intelligentsia in alliance with managerial and party elites.

5. Both in Tsarist Russia and in the Soviet Union, no serious ethnic revolt was in evidence. Under the Soviet regime, the development of nations was actually sponsored and encouraged by the authorities. Just as in the British and French colonies, it was the intelligentsia educated in metropolises of colonial powers that was to become a gravedigger of the Empire, the difference being that in the Soviet Union the decisive blow to the Empire came from the center itself, and native gravediggers in the periphery just hastened to reap the fruits of the momentous events in Moscow in August 1991. In retrospect, it became clear that, by the 1980s, all the prerequisites for an explosion had already been at hand and all that was necessary for the breakup of the Empire was a mighty push from the center. Newly formed nations were ready to claim their rights while old nations, such as Armenians and Georgians, were ripe to reassert their once lost statehood.

6. In the post-Soviet Russia, beginnings of a civil society coupled with an assertion of national self-consciousness are manifest. Probably it is only now, after the dissolution of the Soviet Union, as a new Russian state slowly consolidates, that the Russians will be able to overcome the legacy of both the societal dualism of the pre-Bolshevik system and the false "internationalism" of the Soviet era. It is only then that the formation of the Russian nation in the strict sense of the term could be considered as accomplished.

NOTES

1. Karmela Liebkind, *Minority Identity and Identification Processes: A Social Psychological Study* (Helsinki: Societas Scientarum Fennica, 1984), 28.

2. Hans Kohn, *The Idea of Nationalism* (New York: Macmillan, 1958), 11.

3. Vamik D. Volkan, "An Overview of Psychological Concepts Pertinent to Interethnic and/or International Relationships," in *The Psychodynamics of International Relationships*, vol. 1, ed. Vamik D. Volkan, Joseph V. Montville, and Demetrios A. Julius (Lexington, Mass. and Toronto: Lexington Books, 1990), 36.

4. Anthony D. Smith, *The Ethnic Origins of Nations* (Oxford: Basil Blackwell, 1986), 49.

5. Anthony D. Smith, *Theories of Nationalism* (New York: Harper and Row, 1971), 141.

6. Louis L. Snyder, *The New Nationalism* (Ithaca, N.Y.: Cornell University Press, 1968), 364.

7. V. Reynolds, V. Falger, and J. Vine, eds., *The Sociobiology of Ethnocentrism* (London: n.p., 1987), 8, 22.

8. Paul R. Brass, *Ethnicity and Nationalism* (New Delhi and Newbury Park, Calif.: Sage Publications, 1991), 19, 21.

9. Smith, *The Ethnic Origins*, 32.

10. Ibid., 89.

11. John A. Armstrong, *Nations before Nationalism* (Chapel Hill: University of North Carolina Press, 1982), 5.

12. Cornelia Navari, "The Origins of the Nation-State," in *The Nation-State: The Formation of Modern Politics*, ed. L. Tivey and M. Robertson (Oxford: n.p., 1981), 14, 19.

13. Arnold J. Toynbee, *A Study of History*, abridgement of vols. 1–6 by D.C. Sommervell (New York: Oxford University Press, 1947), 14–20.

14. Carlton Hayes, *Essays on Nationalism* (New York: Macmillan, 1926), 26, 102.

15. Kohn, *The Idea of Nationalism*, 17.

16. Smith, *The Ethnic Origins*, 134, 143.

17. Anthony D. Smith, "The Ethnic Sources of Nationalism," *Survival* 35, no. 1 (Spring 1993), 52, 53; Smith, *The Ethnic Origins*, 119, 121.

18. Smith, *The Ethnic Origins*, 124.

19. Ibid., 115, 116.

20. Ibid., 146.

21. John F. Stack, Jr., "Ethnic Groups as Emerging Transnational Actors," in *Ethnic Identities in a Transnational World*, ed. John F. Stack, Jr. (Westport, Conn.: Greenwood Press, 1981), 17, 18.

22. Jaroslav Krejci and Vitezslav Velimsky, *Ethnic and Political Nations in Europe* (New York: St. Martin's Press, 1981), 38.

23. Smith, *Theories of Nationalism*, 186.

24. Smith, *The Ethnic Origins*, 2, 15, 214; Smith, *Theories of Nationalism*, 22.

25. Armstrong, *Nations before Nationalism*, 9, 16.

26. Vamik D. Volkan, "On 'Chosen Trauma,' " *Mind and Human Interaction* 3, no. 1 (July 1991), 13.

27. Brass, *Ethnicity and Nationalism*, 43.

28. Kohn, *The Idea of Nationalism*, 7.

29. Krejci and Velimsky, *Ethnic and Political Nations*, 78–79.

30. Hugh Seton-Watson, *Nations and States* (London: Methuen and Co., 1977), 5.

31. Krejci and Velimsky, *Ethnic and Political Nations*, 10.

32. Ibid., 22.

33. Ibid., 44.

34. Ibid., 44–45.

35. Ibid., 58.

36. Louis L. Snyder, *Varieties of Nationalism: A Comparative Study* (Hinsdale, N.Y.: The Dryden Press, 1976), 25.

37. Smith, *The Ethnic Origins*, 166.

38. Peter Sugar, "From Ethnicity to Nationalism and Back Again," in *Nationalism: Essays in Honor of Louis L. Snyder*, ed. Michael Palumbo and William O. Shanahan (Westport, Conn.: Greenwood Press, 1981), 69.

39. Dawa Norbu, *Culture and the Politics of Third World Nationalism* (London and New York: Routledge, 1992), 45.

40. Hayes, *Essays on Nationalism*, 23, 24.

41. Kohn, *The Idea of Nationalism*, 6, 8, 13.

42. Elie Kedourie, *Nationalism* (Cambridge, Mass.: Hutchinson University Library, 1960), 9.

43. Hedva Ben-Israel, "Nationalism in Historical Perspective," *Journal of International Affairs* 45, no. 2 (Winter 1992), 368–369.

44. Ibid., 377.

45. Ibid., 373, 374.

46. Gabriel Ben-Dor, "Ethnopolitics and the Middle Eastern State," in *Ethnicity, Pluralism and the State in the Middle East*, ed. M. J. Esman and Itamar Rabinovich (Ithaca, N.Y. and London: Cornell University Press, 1988), 80.

47. Paul R. Brass, "Language and National Identity in the Soviet Union and India," in *Thinking Theoretically about Soviet Nationalities: History and Comparison in the Study of the USSR*, ed. Alexander J. Motyl (New York: Columbia University Press, 1992), 100.

48. Istvan Hont, "The Permanent Crisis of a Divided Mankind: Contemporary Crisis of the Nation State," in Historical Perspective, *Political Studies*, Special Issue, vol. 42 (1994), 218, 217.

49. Ben-Israel, *Nationalism*, 379.

50. John Barber, "Russia: A Crisis of Post-Imperial Viability," *Political Studies*, Special Issue, vol. 42 (1994), 35.

51. John Breuilly, *Nationalism and the State* (New York: St. Martin's Press, 1982), 90.

52. Tom Nairu, *The Break-up of Britain: Crisis and Neo-nationalism* (London: New Left Books, 1977), 340.

53. Smith, *The Ethnic Origins*, 157, 160.

54. Krejci and Velimsky, *Ethnic and Political Nations*, 60.

55. John A. Armstrong, "The Autonomy of Ethnic Identity: Historic Cleavages and Nationality Relations in the USSR," in *Thinking Theoretically about Soviet Nationalities*, ed. Alexander J. Motyl (New York: Columbia University Press, 1992), 29.

56. Hont, "The Permanent Crisis," 182.

57. Krejci and Velimsky, *Ethnic and Political Nations*, 36.

58. Hont, "The Permanent Crisis," 183.

59. Ibid., 172.

60. Krejci and Velimsky, *Ethnic and Political Nations*, 61.

61. Smith, *The Ethnic Origins*, 163.

62. Seton-Watson, *Nations and States*, 1, 3.

63. Smith, *The Ethnic Origins*, 137.

64. Smith, *Theories of Nationalism*, 189.

65. Smith, *The Ethnic Origins*, 150, 223, 224.

66. K. R. Minogue, *Nationalism* (London: B. T. Batsford, 1967), 137.

67. Ben-Dor, "Ethnopolitics," 80.

68. Ibid., 81.

69. Alexander J. Motyl, "The Modernity of Nationalism," *Journal of International Affairs* 45, no. 2 (Winter 1992), 322–323 (emphasis in original).

70. Anthony H. Birch, *Nationalism and National Integration* (London: Unwin Hyman, 1989), 70–71.

71. Armstrong, "The Autonomy," 30.

72. Krejci and Velimsky, *Ethnic and Political Nations*, 62.

73. Brass, *Ethnicity and Nationalism*, 47.

74. Motyl, "The Modernity," 316.

75. James J. Kellas, *The Politics of Nationalism and Ethnicity* (London: Macmillan, 1991), 80, 81.

76. Breuilly, *Nationalism and the State*, 81.

77. Sigmund Freud, *The Future of an Illusion* (London: Hogart Press, 1962), 9.

78. Birch, *Nationalism and National Integration*, 67.

79. Smith, *The Ethnic Origins*, 166.

80. Hetukar Jha, "Stages of Nationalism: Some Hypothetical Considerations," in *National and Ethnic Movements*, ed. J. Dofny and A. Akiwowo (Beverly Hills, Calif.: Sage Publications, 1980), 197.

81. John E. Mack, "Foreword," in V. D. Volkan, *Cyprus-War and Adaptation* (Charlottesville: University Press of Virginia, 1979), ix, xxi.

82. Volkan, "An Overview," 38.

83. Edgar Morin, "Le surgissement du total-nationalisme," *Le Monde*, March 11, 1993.

84. Ben-Israel, "Nationalism," 389.

85. Fred W. Riggs, *Turmoil among Nations, A Conceptual Essay: Ethnonationalism, Authoritarianism, Anarchy, and Democracy*, paper prepared for the International Studies Association Conference in Chicago, February 22–25, 1995, 20.

3

On Some Aspects of Ethnic Conflicts

THE BACKGROUND

Ethnic conflicts are not exactly a new phenomenon. It is only since World War II, however, that ethnopolitical conflicts of all kinds have sharply increased. Nonviolent political action more than doubled between 1950 and 1990, while violent protest and rebellion quadrupled. Most of the conflicts stem from minorities' grievances; if the first period after the war can be called an era of liberation of the colonies, it would be appropriate to call the next period an era of rising minorities.

Henry Tajfel, in his excellent study *The Social Psychology of Minorities*, suggested that

the development of the relations between large-scale social groups (ethnic, national, cultural, social, etc.) since World War II has been profoundly affected by two continuing processes which seem to pull in opposite directions and yet—paradoxically—complement each other. This is the simultaneous growth of interdependence and differentiation between social groups. There has never been a time before when economic and political interdependence has been so clearly present and visible in our everyday affairs, nor has there ever been before such widespread awareness that decisions taken or conditions prevailing at great distance from our own backyards are likely to affect directly and, at times, immediately the fabric of our daily lives. . . . This growing awareness of interdependence has evolved together with a world-wide push towards differentiation originating from minorities which are often at great distances from each other geographically as well as in their cultural and historical diversity. There is one crucially important element which is common to many of these movements towards differentiation: the new claims of the minorities are based on their right to decide to be different (preserve their separateness) as defined *in their own terms* and not in terms implicitly adopted or explicitly dictated by the majorities.

Speaking about the transition of minorities from acceptance to rejection, Tajfel noted that "the prime condition for the maintenance of a status quo of inequality, formal or informal, is the unequal distribution of power—political, economic or military. Two major psychological correlates of this unequal distribution of resources help to ensure the maintenance of its stability: the perception of the system of inequalities as being *stable* or *legitimate* or both simultaneously."[1]

Thomas Friedman makes another penetrating observation:

Indeed, to some extent, the changing world economy can also sharpen ethnic conflicts in this sense: The more people are asked to integrate with distant, impersonal economic structures, the more they want to assert their own particular local or national identity. The more the world beckons from one side, the louder the call of the tribe, the family, the neighborhood from the other. . . . In Yugoslavia, it seems that a yearning to make up for years of suppressed personal identity is, for the moment, overriding the lure of the global economy.[2]

Both Tajfel's and Friedman's analyses are helpful in understanding the nature of the ethnopolitical conflicts in industrial countries, well integrated into world economy. It is relevant as well, although probably to a lesser extent, to Third World countries and newly independent states in the southern tier of the former Soviet Union. In these two cases, one can also notice such phenomena as "the simultaneous growth of interdependence and differentiation between social groups," although in a regional, rather than global, context, as well as "the new claims of the minorities," "the unequal distribution of power," and "a yearning to make up for years of suppressed personal identity." The problem is to understand precisely why conflicts explode at a particular moment, what has triggered them, what is the critical mass of discontent piling up to the point when ethnoses that had been living side by side for centuries more or less peacefully suddenly feel their patience exhausted?

A typology of conflicts according to their historic background is clearly necessary. It is possible to distinguish between: (1) conflicts marked by *old antagonisms* just waiting to erupt into violence at a certain point (Armenians-Azerbaijanis, Serbs–Bosnian Muslims, Iraqi Kurds–Arabs, the opposing sides in Northern Ireland); in these cases, there is a kind of "blood legacy"; (2) conflicts characterized by a *long mutual estrangement* that had, however, never before reached the level of open violence (the opposing communities in Canada, Belgium, Nigeria, Sri Lanka as well as Abkhazians versus Georgians, Ossetians versus Georgians); and (3) conflicts between communities with *no apparent feud legacy* (Ossetians versus Ingush, Uzbeks versus Kyrgyz, Russians versus Moldavians in the "Dniester republic").

A classification along these lines may be helpful in attempting to evaluate the relative difficulties of settling conflicts. Apparently, those marked by long-standing animosities and mutual hatred, especially when "blood legacy" is involved, are the hardest to deal with. Thus, in Northern Ireland ethnic communities have for centuries "confronted one another over the classical and interrelated questions of agrarian society: political power, the distribution of land, and the definition and worship of God"[3]; divided by their languages, dialects, religion, and political status, they have resorted to violence, especially in the last few decades; mutual distrust and hatred have been steadily growing, and the legacy of blood has become a major issue. This applies to many other ethnopolitical conflicts as well; "how can we live side by side with those butchers after so much blood has been shed?" was the question I often heard in the Caucasus. In former Yugoslavia "today's horrors are woven from strands of an entire tapestry of history since the sixth-century Slavic invasion of the Balkans, with the subsequent religious division between Catholicism and Orthodoxy and, from the fifteenth century on, Islam . . . over the long run the fighting between Serbs and Croats in Croatia and Slovenia has been fueled by culturally derived feelings of 'otherness' between Catholic and Orthodox."[4] Even worse is the attitude of Serbs toward Bosnian Muslims: while the Croats "see the Muslims merely as heretics," the Serbs "see them as traitors as well as heretics. Scratch a Muslim, they believe, and you will find a Serb whose ancestors went over to the Ottoman side four or five hundred years ago, in order to keep his land."[5]

Another way to classify ethnopolitical conflicts would be to differentiate between (a) old, long-standing conflicts of the *"open,"* well-known and acknowledged type (Canada, Northern Ireland, Belgian and Spanish separatisms, etc.), (b) old, long-standing conflicts of the *"hidden"* or latent type (former Yugoslavia, Nagorno-Karabakh, Abkhazia, Kurdistan, Rwanda, Sri Lanka) and (c) *new* or not previously anticipated conflicts deriving from abruptly changed situations (South Ossetia-Georgia, Northern Ossetians-Ingush). Of course, sources of potential flare-ups were in existence for a long time in all these types of conflicts; the difference between (a) and (b) is that the conflicts of the former type have been in the open for quite a long time and have created a routine pattern of their own, whereas those of the latter type broke out suddenly, thus taking the world by surprise, although, strictly speaking, they could have been anticipated in view of the known long-standing differences between the parties concerned. The difference between (b) and (c) is that the latter, although not devoid of a historical background of mutual dislike, flared up mainly due to unreasonable and irresponsible actions of political leaders who had been deliberately and somewhat artificially stirring up ethnic passions. For example, it has always been open knowledge that there was no love lost between the Georgians and Abkhazians and that, given appropriate circumstances, things could come to a head while the relations between the Georgians and Ossetians had been quite peaceful, devoid of a hate legacy, with no hint of violence to come.

Looked upon from yet another angle, the conflicts in question can be classified according to the *immediate aims of antagonists*, particularly the aims of rebellious minorities, since it is they that usually initiate the conflict; it is minorities that desire to change the status quo which, as a rule, appears satisfactory to majorities. Of course, an overall aim in these cases is the creation of an independent state or, at the very least, the heightening of status within a federation; for example, the Tatars have finally found it quite sufficient to establish a "state" within the framework of the Russian Federation. What seems to have mattered to them most—at least in the legal sphere—was just to change the Soviet term "autonomous republic" to "sovereign state"; the Tatar authorities withdrew their objections to the federal arrangement as such.[6] The Northern Ossetians were at first willing to upgrade their legal status within Georgia from an autonomous *oblast* to an autonomous republic; the Georgian authorities, however, would have none of it, and a bloody conflict ensued. In all these cases, statehood is the bottom line. The underlying motives of the players, however, have not always been the same. While some of the disputes seem to originate mostly from conflicting claims on land, on a particular territory, others derive from grievances based on alleged unequal treatment and distribution of resources. The former can probably be termed *land demarcation conflicts* (Armenian-Azerbaijani, Ossetian-Ingush, Uzbek-Kyrgyz, Ossetian-Georgian, potentially Uzbek-Tajik, and interethnic disputes in Daghestan), and the latter *conflicts of separation* (Abkhazia, Nigeria, Czechoslovakia, Canada, Belgium, Sri Lanka, the so-called Dniester republic, Lezgins in Azerbaijan, Kurds in Turkey and Iran). In the case of the Iraqi Kurds, both types seem to merge.

The difference between the two types of conflicts is rather subtle. Sometimes, it is virtually nonexistent. For instance, the war between the Azerbaijanis and Armenians over Nagorno-Karabakh was caused as much by a dispute over a concrete territory as by long-standing grievances of the Karabakh Armenians, who have felt all along that they were being discriminated against in the Republic of Azerbaijan. Finally, it came to the idea of a total separation of Karabakh from Azerbaijan. In this case, we see a deadly combination of land dispute and long-standing mutual animosity. Generally, however, the difference does exist. In conflicts of the first type ("land demarcation") what is at issue is a piece of land to which both sides lay a claim, regarding it as their own. Both Azerbaijanis and Armenians would give you the same line about Karabakh: "This is our land from times immemorial; our ancestors had lived there for centuries before 'the others' came; Karabakh is the cradle of our civilization," and so on. The main argument in this type of conflict is history: "we were the first to settle here, the others are newcomers and usurpers of our land." Thus, Thomas Butler writes about Bosnian Serbs that they are "sick from history, from half-truths and ethnic prejudices passed from one generation to the next, through religion, political demagoguery, inflammatory tracts, and folklore. More recently, the books of unscrupulous writers and the deliberately inaccurate speeches of unprincipled leaders have further contaminated the athmosphere."[7]

This observation is very important. As noted in the preceding chapter, humanitarian intelligentsia have always played a major role in awakening and fostering nationalist feelings. It is especially the case with historians. In the previous chapter, some cases were noted dealing with the impact of historical writings on the political situation in the former Soviet republics, particularly in the Caucasus.

As regards the second type of conflicts, the difference is that both ethnoses involved possess a more or less clearly defined and acknowledged core territory of their own, and neither side denies the other's right to live in that territory as a compact majority. Czechoslovakia is probably the best example: The Czechs always recognized the Slovaks' rights to an autonomous existence in the eastern part of the common state and there were no territorial disputes. Fleming and Walloon nationalists in Belgium acknowledge that, in most areas of the country, either one or the other community predominates. This is also the case in Canada where the English-speakers do not try to prove that the province of Quebec is their English realm. Ibos in Nigeria as well as Tamils in Sri Lanka have their own territory not claimed as such by the dominant ethnic groups. In all of these cases, what is at issue is not a dispute over a particular piece of land claimed by the conflicting sides as their own, invaded or usurped by "the others," but the principle of "keeping the state in a whole piece," of not dismembering the country. Yet, sometimes this principle has to be sacrificed in order to prevent a violent interethnic struggle or even an armed confrontation, as happened, for example, in Czechoslovakia where it has been possible to reach a "peaceful divorce." This outcome, however, is more likely in the countries with just two communities involved in conflict. In addition to Czechoslovakia, the peaceful breakup of the union between Senegal and Mali can be mentioned. Unlike these benign solutions of the crisis, events in Nigeria in the 1960s have proved that in those countries where not just two but many ethnic groups are engaged in a conflict, secession is extremely difficult for any one of them to achieve. It is easy to see the reason for this: The federal authorities in Nigeria evidently feared that, if Biafra were to be allowed to stay as an independent state, Yorubas could have come with claims of their own. Likewise, the government in Moldova is clearly apprehensive that, should it accede to the Russian separatists' demands in the Transdniester area, it would have to grant a sort of independence to the other rebellious ethnic community, the Turkish-speaking Gagauz.

Of course, there are borderline cases. The situation in Abkhazia, briefly mentioned earlier, is typical of these. Georgians acknowledge that the Abkhazians, unlike the Ossetians, are no newcomers to the land they inhabit; nobody would deny that an Abkhazian kingdom did exist in the Middle Ages. The point is different: In the eyes of the Georgians, Abkhazia is homeland to both nations and should stay as an autonomous entity within the framework of the Georgian state. The situation of the Iraqi Kurds is another case in point: The Arab majority of Iraq recognizes that Kurdistan is basically the land of the Kurds but feels that, at the same time, it must remain a part of the Iraqi state.

It can be suggested, therefore, that *conflicts most difficult to settle are those combining age-long animosity, dispute over territory, and minority grievances caused by real or perceived injustice, unequality, and discrimination.* The obvious cases are: Armenia versus Azerbaijan, Bosnian Serbs versus Muslims, Iraqi Kurds versus Arabs. In all these situations, it is the mentalities of the conflicting sides that seem to be totally different and almost incompatible; the perception of "the other" is that of a hereditary enemy; coexistence under the same roof is ruled out. In some other cases, this feeling had not been particularly strong up to the outbreak of violence but became a major factor once blood had been shed. For example, the Georgians and Abkhazians, although ethnically not very close, have always had a similar mentality and way of life; as a result of the 1992–1993 war, however, the relations between the two communities have grown hostile to such an extent that at present you can hear: "After all this bloodshed, it is hard even to imagine that we can live together." The same goes for Ossetians and Georgians, Ossetians and Ingush, Tamils and Singalese, although with a vital difference: in the two former cases, both sides claim the same piece of land which cannot be divided, whereas each of the warring communities in Sri Lanka possesses a territory of its own. Thus, the conflict between the Tamils and Singalese appears easier to settle, at least theoretically, than that involving the Ossetians, because Sri Lanka can physically be divided into separate states, or a mutually acceptable form of Tamil autonomy can be worked out. This can also be the case in Bosnia if its territory could be divided into separate entities to the satisfaction of all the parties concerned, although the legacy of blood and the mutual enmity will continue for long. In Northern Ireland, however, the partition of land is practically impossible, and the country can only exist as a single entity.

Krejci and Velimsky make an important point: "Whether an ethnic minority lives in a completely settled territory or not is most relevant for its aspirations. With a completely settled territory there is a case for national independence or at least a territorial autonomy. When the minority is scattered, it strives primarily for equal opportunities with the dominant ethnic majority/equal access to better jobs and higher rewards. The need for autonomy, if any, is reduced to the cultural-personal sphere."[8]

All of these observations, however, do not provide an answer regarding such a vital issue as the timing of conflict: why is it precisely at a given moment that the relations between ethnic communities went sour to the point of open confrontation? Evidently, some other issues have to be taken into consideration.

First, global factors, some of which have been noted by Tajfel, namely, "the simultaneous growth of interdependence and differentiation between social groups."[9] This is just a part of a certain *zeitgeist* of our epoch. Both World Wars powerfully contributed to the spread of the ideas of freedom and independence. People throughout the world grew less tolerant of oppression; freedom movements were springing up everywhere; the spirit of independence, of "throwing off the yoke," of asserting national identity was in the air. It was a kind of chain reaction. Suffice it to recall "the Year of Africa," 1960. The independence achieved by one nation or ethnic community triggered liberation movements elsewhere; a successful example was contagious. Likewise, in the Soviet Union after the collapse of the Communist rule, one nation after another started to proclaim independence; the fall of a political regime led at once to the disintegration of an empire under the slogan of national emancipation. What followed was the emergence of competing nationalisms, most of which came into conflict not so much with the collapsing central power as with the authorities of the newly independent republics. This phenomenon was aptly called by Ray Taras "matryoshka nationalism," after the famous Russian "dolls within dolls."[10] Ethnic Russians and Gagauz in Moldova, Ossetians, and Abkhazians in Georgia, Lezgins in Azerbaijan came out with claims of sovereignty. In some cases, the problem was exacerbated by the sensitive issue of the deported communities; for instance, the Chechens and Ingush, deported by Stalin to Central Asia back in 1944, returned to their homeland only to discover that parts of their territory had already been taken over by their neighbors. Claims and counterclaims followed, sometimes culminating in open conflicts.

Second, a major reason for the growth of nationalist feeling is, as noted in the preceding chapter, the rise of the two social forces that most vigorously promote it, namely, the intellectuals and the middle class. In this respect, as Marxists say, sooner or later quantity turns into quality; at a certain point, a critical mass is reached, and the people who seemed to be reconciled to their fate start to rebel against the status quo. The motives of the two standard-bearers of nationalism are not quite the same: While the intellectuals, scholars, university professors, lawyers appear to be interested mainly in reviving and fostering national culture, language, and tradition, the business community is trying to gain stronger positions in the domestic market. Stalin used to say that market was the first school where the bourgeoisie learned its nationalism. This simplistic notion which disregards "pure," idealistic national sentiment, contains nevertheless a grain of truth. Competition against the ethnically dominant commercial and financial community inevitably requires raising nationalist slogans which contribute to the awakening of the masses of the minority group. The combined effort of the intellectuals and the middle class, made extremely powerful by the spread of education and the steadily growing role of mass media, helps create a strong and organized nationalist movement proclaiming statehood, or at least substantial autonomy, as its goal.

Third, what is crucial to the growth of nationalist movement is the appearance of highly motivated or just ambitious and power-hungry political leaders and warlords. Gareth Evans argues that while

ethnic and religious differences are not in themselves causes of conflict, they may become so when historical grievances—sometimes as much imagined as real—are exploited by unscrupulous political leaders. That is especially so in periods of economic decline. In almost every case of major intrastate violence, from the former Soviet republics to Rwanda, ethnic and religious conflict has been associated with significant periods of declining per capita gross national product, the rise of demagogic politics, and the intensification of chauvinistic myth making. Contemporary ethnic violence stems as much from deliberate government policies as from traditional communal antagonisms.[11]

Thus, in the former Soviet Union it is easy to see a whole generation of new republican leaders who have no card to play in the struggle for power but the ethnic one. They are unable to cope with the huge economic, social, and environmental problems of the new republics; they cannot offer any real solutions but are quite adept at raising nationalist passions. President Yeltsin's adviser on national issues Emil Pain believes that ethnopolitical conflicts serve these nationalist leaders as, first, the means of struggle for power; second, the means of clinging to power; and third, as an instrument of political hegemonism.[12] In the self-styled "Dniester republic" as well as in North Ossetia, for instance, local leaders, according to the opinion of knowledgeable observers, have successfully exploited nationalist sentiment in order to keep virtually intact the old Soviet political and economic system, while in Abkhazia, South Ossetia, and Crimea new elites have sprung up, eager for power and privileges and skillfully using ethnic issues in the struggle against old central elites of Georgia and Ukraine.

It is precisely in the zones of "new conflicts" that the negative role of political leaders is particularly strong. Long-standing conflicts of the "open" type have been going on in the West within the framework of a civil society; they are subject to certain "rules of the game" of a democratic political culture. Thus, separatist or autonomist movements have moderate and extremist wings, and even the latter, conscious of the importance of public opinion and the ever-vigilant eye of mass media, have to be concerned about their image. Although the extremist wing can be, and often is, intransigent, brutal, intolerant of dissent, and essentially totalitarian, the movement as a whole cannot escape some characteristic features of the open, democratic civil society in which it operates. As to the ethnopolitical conflicts that have suddenly flared up on the ruins of empires, colonial or socialist, the politics in the areas of these conflicts bear all the unmistakable traits of totalitarianism. Both sides are driven by extremism, neither tolerates dissent or even pluralism of opinion; all the parties concerned resort to crude and one-sided propaganda, to straitjacketing of public opinion and brainwashing of the population. Once a nationalist movement is set afoot, it is extremist factions that invariably come to the fore, moderates being branded as traitors. The central authorities act in the same way. Suffice it to look at the warring clans in Somalia, the Tamil Tigers, or the conflicting parties in Abkhazia and Ossetia.

In attempting to assess the relative weight of various factors in the process of the eruption of ethnopolitical conflicts, it can be argued that: First, as regards the "old, open" conflicts in the West, what appears to be crucial is the accumulation of objective factors. These include the processes noted by Tajfel: the simultaneous growth of interdependence and differentiation between social groups and the new claims of the minorities, and more generally—the *zeitgeist*, the chain reaction of liberation movements. All of the above is closely linked to the gradual but inexorable growth of the social forces instrumental in awakening and fostering mass nationalism. Second, in the latent and the "new" types of conflicts, mostly in the Third World and the post-Socialist areas, a key factor appears to be a drastic and radical change of the status quo. Indeed, a question can be asked: What fundamental, objective changes have occurred in the situation of the minorities in Yugoslavia since Tito's death, or in the republics of the southern tier of the Soviet Union since the collapse of the Communist rule? Arguably, if the old regimes in both cases still existed today, no outbreaks of violence could have occurred. The cumulative objective factors mentioned in regard to the first, "European" type of conflict did not pertain in Africa, Yugoslavia, or the Caucasus, although the professional classes and modern, educated elites were slowly growing there as well. Eventually, this growth would have created the conditions that Tajfel had in mind when he described the social-psychological sources of conflicts in more advanced countries. Sooner or later, this would have triggered an outbreak of militant nationalism. The whole process, however, might have taken a long time, primarily because of the character of the old regime. The point is that in the empires, both colonial and Communist, the authorities claimed to be a kind of arbiter, standing above particularist ethnic interests; the regimes in power were doing their best to look neutral and unbiased regarding ethnic issues. The British authorities in Ceylon and the Communist leaders in Moscow or Belgrade, all the fundamental differences between them notwithstanding, tried to maintain a balance of ethnic forces; an all-powerful "center" was overshadowing, and sometimes actually suppressing, the ambitions of ethnic majorities. Tamils did not feel that they were politically dominated by Singalese, nor did Croats and Bosnian Muslims regard themselves as subjects to Serbs, although ethnic grievances deriving from perceived injustices did exist and were inevitably piling up. It must also be added that both the colonial and Communist authorities were known to be strong and tough, not hesitating to use force to quell any manifestation of discontent.

Once the colonial or Communist rule had been removed, the old balance of ethnic forces was totally disrupted. Overnight, old differences and grievances surfaced. What was more or less acceptable to ethnic minorities under the old regime suddenly became intolerable within the framework of independent governance, as majority groups set out to assert their dominant position. Here again, it would be appropriate to quote Tajfel, who noted the minorities' perception of the existing system of inequalities in the state "as being *stable* or *legitimate* or both simultaneously."[13] After the downfall of the Communist regime in Moscow, for instance, both the legitimacy and stability suddenly disappeared. Regardless of the actual degree of national consciousness and of the prerequisites for independence, ethnic minority groups started to claim sovereignty. As always happens in this kind of situation, ambitious extremist leaders began to spring up from nowhere. Moderates were squeezed out, crude nationalist slogans, often tainted with chauvinism, fast became an *idée-fixe* which captured the masses. Nationalist movements acquired a momentum of their own.

ETHNOPOLITICAL CONFLICTS IN THE FORMER SOVIET UNION

The Ethnopolitical Research Center established in Moscow soon after the collapse of the Communist rule published a report entitled "Interethnic Conflicts in Post-Soviet Society." Excerpts from this document deserve to be quoted.

Interethnic conflicts are most acute in multiethnic states, in which the struggle of peoples for their ethnic self-determination as a rule outstrips restructuring of society's economic, political and legal institutions. It seems that it is precisely this contradiction which has mainly given rise to the two principal conflict tendencies; on the one hand, the emergence in a number of republics of authoritarian nationalist regimes of various political hues, and on the other, the consolidation (concealed or overt) of pro-empire political forces. Despite the seemingly opposite nature of these two tendencies they complement each other, driving the flywheel of uncontrolled, painful disintegration of a unified human space. But it was in fact unified despite the fact that in the former Union official statistics alone listed 125 peoples, the majority of which had "their own" compact ethnic territories.

This refers not only to the 65 million people living outside the bounds of their ethnic regions (just name any other place in the world where a comparable number of people suddenly, from one hour to the next, found themselves foreigners), but also to the 12.8 million ethnically mixed families (one family in six), which have around 50 million members. If one adds to this the families that have relatives in other independent states of the Eurasian Commonwealth, then one finds that a majority of the population has a blood kinship (in the literal sense of the term) with many of its parts. That alone indicates how painful the process of destroying a unit such as the Union could be. . . . During the 1988–1991 period a total of over 150 conflicts erupted, including over 20 involving deaths and injuries.[14]

The authors of the report distinguish among three types of conflicts: (1) those of "unbridled emotions," (2) those of "ideological doctrines," and (3) those between "political institutions." As noted earlier, there are many ways of classifying conflicts, and this is certainly one of them. The first type is characterized by the vagueness of the goals of those who initiate the unrest. Thus, neither scientists nor members of law enforcement organs can explain with any certainty why, during the Fergana events in the summer of 1989, pogroms were directed specifically against the Meshketian Turks and none of the other ethnic minorities who inhabit the Fergana valley. Equally unclear are the causes of the anti-Armenian sentiments which marked the beginning of the Dushanbe events of 1990. Most likely, in all these cases, the ethnic community which was subjected to attack served as a scapegoat, while the real reasons that huge masses of people got involved in the unrest were connected with social and economic disorder:

the acute housing shortage in Dushanbe, and the acute shortage of land in Fergana, Osh, and other places. The most powerful social detonator for a conflict of this type may be rising unemployment.

Conflicts of "ideological doctrines," according to the report, can be roughly divided into four basic categories:

1. Conflicts over historically disputed territories which each side regards as its own historical homeland (Nagorno-Karabakh, Ossetia).

2. Conflicts over the administrative status of an ethnic territory (disputes over the right to be an autonomous area or an independent state). This includes the events in Abkhazia, Gagauzia, the Dniester region, Chechnya, and many other regions.

3. Conflicts caused by a change in the ethnodemographic situation in a number of regions, with an increase of new arrivals of a different ethnic group. The threat of losing status as the ethnic majority, or efforts to restore that status, give rise to demands for "protection for the rights of the native ethnic group," say, for instance, through the introduction of special advantages for that group. Such demands meet with understandable resistance on the part of the "nonnative" nationalities, giving rise to various forms of interethnic confrontations in the Baltic republics, Moldova, some republics in the Russian Federation, and elsewhere.

4. Conflicts of an ethnoterritorial nature created as a historical echo of the deportation of many of the USSR's peoples in 1937–1944.[15]

This typology, while extremely helpful in understanding the causes of ethnopolitical conflicts in the former USSR, can be subject to some qualifications. For instance, the difference between the first and second types of the "conflicts of ideological doctrines" is not quite clear; in Abkhazia, just as in Karabakh and Ossetia, the two issues which are presented in the report as being characteristic and specific features of either one or the other type, are really intertwined. In all these cases, what is at the bottom of conflicts is both "historically disputed territories which each side regards as its own homeland" and "disputes over the right to be an autonomous area or an independent state."[16] Abkhazians and Georgians alike regard Abkhazia as their "historic homeland" and, in this respect, should be included in the first category, while South Ossetia is in confrontation with Georgia precisely "over the right to be an autonomous area or an independent state,"[17] which the authors of the report consider as characteristic of the second category. Thus, the difference as formulated in the report seems to be rather blurred if not artificial, which is not to say that the authors have been wrong in pointing out this difference as such. The two categories mentioned by them do exist in reality; it would just be more correct to make a distinction along somewhat different lines, to wit, as noted earlier in this chapter, between the conflicts involving territories which are claimed by both sides and could not possibly be divided (Nagorno-Karabakh, South Ossetia, Vladikavkaz's Prigorodnyi Rayon) and those in which the existence of a specific core territory of "the other ethnos" is acknowledged by the majority group. In the latter case, a crucial difference between the conflicting sides is not the recognition of the right of a given ethnic group to inhabit the territory in question, but the majority's insistence on preserving this territory within the framework of an already existing state dominated by that majority.

Reasons for making a fundamental distinction between "ideological conflicts" and those deriving from the confrontation of political institutions also appear doubtful. A conflict of the latter type, according to the report, is based "not only on ideological doctrines, but also on the power of political organizations: parties, political blocs and institutions of state authority."[18] Clearly, all the organizations listed above are playing a major role in the "ideological conflicts" as well. Suffice it to look at Abkhazia, Karabakh, or the Dniester region. What the authors of the report seem to have in mind are interstate conflicts as opposed to intrastate ones. The former certainly deserve to be put in a category of their own; obviously, the current or potential disputes between Russia and Kazakhstan or between Moldova and Ukraine, specifically noted in the report, ought not to be mentioned in the same breath with the conflicts inside Moldova, Ukraine, or Georgia. The difference, however, lies not in the participation of political organizations in the conflicts—this phenomenon can be observed everywhere—but in the formal status of the parties concerned. Whereas Russia, Ukraine, Georgia, Moldova, and Kazakhstan are universally recognized sovereign states, Abkhazia, Karabakh, or the "Dniester republic" are just self-styled entities which, from the point of international law, still form a part of sovereign states. If, eventually, they succeed in gaining recognition on the part of the world community, no formal difference will exist between the "conflicts of ideological doctrines" and those of "political institutions."

The Russian scholar N. Petrov has made a detailed analysis of ethnic conflicts in the territories of the former Soviet Union. He lists 168 various ethnic claims that had been made public by the time the Union disintegrated; in the Caucasus alone, which accounts for just 2% of the territory and 9.8% of the population of the former empire, the number of state-national entities of all types is disproportionally high: 26.4% of all the units of this kind in the former Union. The Caucasus also accounts for 34.8% of all the ethnic claims and conflicts in the territories that used to be Soviet republics. As to the reasons for ethnoterritorial claims, Petrov points to some of them: the existence of compact areas populated by a particular ethnos at present, 36%, or in the past, 12%; the consolidation of kindred ethnoses, 7%. In thirty-four cases territorial claims derive from border changes: 26% from the changes that were made prior to 1945; 11% prior to 1924; only 5.5% prior to the Bolshevik Revolution. Analyzing the course of conflicts, Petrov suggests four consecutive stages of making claims: potential claims, latent claims, open claims and, finally, open conflict.[19] Another Russian expert on ethnic questions, Galina Starovoitova, suggests the following scheme of the development and course of ethnopolitical conflicts: first, some essential prerequisites must exist before demands for self-rule are made. An ethnic group must feel threatened or at least jeopardized by such processes as

creeping assimilation; the influx of nonnative labor force; the adoption of laws
on language perceived as discriminatory; restrictions on teaching or broadcasting
in the native language; and so on. The threat is felt most strongly by those
ethnic groups which only recently became minorities within a state, or found
themselves separated from the bulk of their ethnos that stays elsewhere. Spontaneous movement then shapes up, and its leaders are very soon condemned by
the authorities as conspirators with links to outside forces. A vicious and cari-
cature image of the enemy is certain to be projected by both sides and spread
by media. At the next stage, the party claiming self-rule takes steps to upgrade
its area's status or even to create a new quasi-state. Then, a "war of decrees"
follows, with each center of authority insisting on the priority of its juridical
acts. The group seeking secession tries to minimize its contacts with the Center,
calls on the area's population to boycott elections to the legislative bodies of
the state, looks for a "big brother" outside state borders. The central authorities
respond by disbanding local self-governing bodies and depriving the rebellious
region of its former autonomous status. In some cases, direct rule from the
Center is introduced. Leaders of the separatist movement are forced into exile
or underground; the previously legitimate phase of the confrontation is being
abruptly and artificially ended. For awhile, the local leaders lose control over
their followers and a spontaneous protest movement begins, laying ground for
direct action. The Center reacts by setting up an economic blockade which in
turn prompts some of the separatist leaders to call for more energetic, forceful
actions; armed struggle is proclaimed to be a justifiable means of self-defense;
the Center's behavior is increasingly seen as deliberate provocation. At some
point, terrorist acts occur and first victims appear, the guilty never found. The
situation goes out of control, armed confrontation is practically inevitable. Those
who failed to take a seat at the negotiations table at the outset of the conflict
find it increasingly hard to do so anytime soon.[20]

This scheme can be seen as an apt and accurate description of the course of
major ethnopolitical conflicts in the successor states of the Soviet Union. Of
course, not all of the conflicts can be pigeonholed; some just do not fall under
any category. For instance, some of the lesser conflicts in the post-Soviet space
have been mixed together with really important ones and generalized under the
same heading—ethnic conflicts. In reality, they can be called quasi-conflicts.
For example, some intellectuals of the Karachaev ethnic group have laid claim
to the Russian city of Kislovodsk on the ground that centuries ago the Karachai
had inhabited the areas around the piece of land on which, much later, Kislovodsk was to be built. The Nogai national movement "Birlik" is not happy
because in the last few decades Dargin and Avar ethnic groups settled in the
Nogai steppe. In the Nenetz national *okrug*, in the North of Russia, separatist
noises have been heard; there, grievances have actually been voiced not by
Nenetz ethnics but by Russian administrators who, masquerading as protectors
of national rights of the local ethnos, seek more independence from the central
Russian authorities for purely selfish ends.

Generally speaking, the scale and scope of ethnic conflicts in the post-Soviet space have proved not so great as many had anticipated. In the aftermath of the collapse of Communism, dire forecasts could be heard in Russia and abroad; a veritable avalanche of ethnic wars was predicted; total disintegration of Russia was feared. Fortunately, the gloomier scenarios have not materialized. Of course, dozens of ethnic claims and counterclaims are being listed by experts but only a small percentage of those can be considered full-bloodied conflicts. So far, it is only the southern tier of the former Soviet Union that has experienced real upheavals. It has been possible to avert the most dangerous and disastrous of all the potential conflicts, namely those between Russia and Ukraine and between Russia and Kazakhstan. Contrary to some expectations, the Yugoslav tragedy has not been repeated in the post-Soviet states. Russians and Ukrainians, Tatars and Bashkirs, and numerous ethnic groups in Daghestan did not take advantage of the Soviet Union's collapse in order to start killing each other.

The question is: Why? What are the reasons for this remarkably smooth and peaceful transition to independence?

In this writer's view, three basic reasons can be suggested as an explanation.

1. The lack of blood legacy, the lack of tradition of interethnic strife both in Tsarist and in Soviet Russia.

Both the Tsarist and Bolshevik regimes were harsh and oppressive, the latter, of course, immeasurably more so. They did not tolerate any upheavals or rebellions against authority. Any independently initiated attempts at setting intercommunal differences were nipped in the bud. Violence could be of only one kind, that sanctioned from above. This pattern held even during the 1917–1920 civil war, when authority crumbled; violence was unleashed, but of a class, not ethnic, nature. Horrible atrocities were committed on all sides but they were not ethnically motivated (except for Jewish pogroms in Ukraine). Moreover, both the Imperial idea in Tsarist Russia and the ideology of proletarian internationalism in the USSR did not encourage the growth of ethnic nationalism. In fact, even relationships between Orthodox Russians and Muslims, although not exactly friendly, were reasonably quiet and devoid of hostility and hatred.

2. Aversion to violence as a backlash against the Soviet regime's violent practices.

The seventy-odd years of the existence of a brutal and inhuman system could conceivably create a type of person insensitive and inured to violence. In fact, the opposite happened. The endless struggle against all kinds of "class enemies," "enemies of the people," traitors, saboteurs, imperialist agents, and so on succeeded only in making people disgusted with all forms of violence. Decades of arbitrary rule and ruthless oppression resulted in a general reluctance to resort to force. It is revealing that, with the exception of the events around the Moscow White House in August 1991, and again in October 1993, there has been no violence and bloodshed in Russia's turbulent recent history. People are reluctant to take to the streets, to build barricades or attack the police, even to strike. University students, unruly and rebellious throughout most of the world, are remarkably quiet and apolitical in the former Soviet republics. It seems that, after all the horrors of civil war, the nightmare of the Stalinist collectivization of the countryside, the purges and the Gulags, people are just tired of violence and blood.

3. Privatization of social life.

This phenomenon requires some explanation. The point is that in the Soviet Union, everything was to be subordinated, at least officially, to the interests of the collective. A song we used to sing as "Young Pioneers" had these words: "There is a lot of pretty girls in the *collectif* but you fall in love with just one of them." Individualism and selfishness were to be eradicated, personal interests sacrificed to the altar of the Great Common Cause. This tendency was typical of the so-called socialism everywhere; it was the famous Cuban revolutionary Ché Guevara who said: "The fundamental goal of Marxism is to eliminate individual interest as a psychological motivation." In fact, something totally opposite has occurred: the Soviet people, sick and tired with an artificially enforced and hypocritical collectivism, have become probably more individualistic and self-centered, if not outright egoistic, than any. From the thoroughly collectivist and statist Soviet regime, people emerged as totally oriented to private life. It may be regarded as completely natural and logical. What is evident here is not only the inevitable backlash against the excessive emphasis on grand common values and virtues, not only the rejection of the loathsome Communist ideology, but also a peculiar, typically Soviet pattern of adjusting to reality. After all, in the Soviet era people had to make constant and enormous efforts to improve the quality of life. Of course, the state cared for citizens and ensured their security; everybody knew just to what salaries, pensions, social benefits, and privileges he or she was entitled. If you wanted to have something extra, however, you had to learn all kinds of tricks in order to bypass the law or, at the very least, to find some unorthodox ways of making life less ugly, more tolerable. The most widespread saying was: "You want to live, you learn to work the system." Incidentally, the ingenuity acquired by the Soviet people in the years of a parallel, shadowy economy, when it was necessary to resort to ruses and machinations a Western person has no notion about, helps today to explain the "achievements" of the Russian mafia abroad.

Thus, a Soviet person had to spend an incredible amount of time and energy in order to live a more or less decent life. Paradoxically, personal concerns were probably more vital for a member of the ideology-driven and collectivist society than for a citizen of a democratic capitalist state where the law is both a rule and an inevitable restraint. Contrary to the intentions of Soviet ideologues, the "new human being" they attempted to create, the *Homo Soveticus*, has proved eventually a thoroughly non-collectivist, non-ideological, totally "private" person. Weary of over-politization and over-ideologization during the Soviet era, engrossed in private life, people are not prepared to fight, to kill and die for any Great Cause, for any "ism." Even the issue of ethnic identity, which for many has become the only remaining spiritual value in the current vacuum, does not appear crucial. Of course, things could change overnight if some really serious discrimination against Russians in the "near abroad," or ethnic cleansing, or clashes in other republics were reported (and confirmed by television, not just by rumors). So far, however, my own observations, not only in Russia but in Ukraine and Central Asia as well, have led me to believe that for most people the newly-found and never-dreamt-of opportunities to achieve something, to improve their lot (and for many, just the need to survive), are a great deal more important than common or state interest. The Soviet system has ended in an ultimate defeat: it has succeeded only in effectively inoculating people against all sorts of collectivism, including its ethnic variety.

NOTES

1. Henry Tajfel, *The Social Psychology of Minorities* (London: The Minority Rights Group, 1992), 7.

2. Thomas Friedman, "A Peace Deal Today Really Is a Bargain," *New York Times*, September 11, 1994.

3. Brendan O'Leary and John McGarry, *The Politics of Antagonism: Understanding Northern Ireland* (Cambridge: The Athlone Press, 1993), 57.

4. Thomas Butler, "Yugoslavia Mon Amour," *Mind and Human Interaction* 4, no. 3 (August 1993), 124.

5. Ibid., 125.

6. Krejci and Velimsky note the difference between federation and autonomy: "federation is a composite state superimposed on *de jure* equal partners—member states of the federation. Autonomy is a special status of a region within an otherwise unitary (non-composite) state. This difference is symbolised by the respective names: a federation bears a name different from the member states (in the case of only two members it may be a composite one); a state containing autonomous regions keeps the name of the dominant nation." See Jaroslav Krejci and Vitezslav Velimsky, *Ethnic and Political Nations in Europe* (New York: St. Martin's Press, 1981), 58

7. Butler, "Yugoslavia," 124.

8. Krejci and Velimsky, *Ethnic and Political Nations*, 39–40.

9. Tajfel, *The Social Psychology of Minorities*, 7.

10. Ian Bremmer and Ray Taras, eds, *Nations and Politics in the Soviet Succession States* (New York: Cambridge University Press, 1993), 513.

11. Gareth Evans, "Cooperative Security and Intrastate Conflict," *Foreign Policy*, no. 96 (Fall 1994), 5.

12. Emil Pain, "Intranational Conflicts in the Game of Politics," *Nezavisimaia Gazeta*, July 10, 1992, 5.

13. Tajfel, *The Social Psychology of Minorities*, 7.

14. Vladimir Mukomel, Emil Pain, and Arkadiy Popov, "The Union Has Disintegrated—the Interethnic Conflicts Remain," *Nezavisimaia Gazeta*, January 10, 1992, 5.

15. Ibid.

16. Ibid.

17. Ibid.

18. Ibid.

19. N. V. Petrov, "What Is Polyethnism," *Polis*, no. 6 (1993), 7, 9.

20. Galina Starovoitova, "Tavrida Anxieties," *Nezavisimaia Gazeta*, July 19, 1994, 5.

4

The Caucasian Cauldron

Of course, the Caucasus and Transcaucasia are two separate areas. For Russians, however, the word "Kavkaz" (Caucasus) means the whole large region to the south of the Don River, including Krasnodar and Stavropol provinces of the Russian Federation, several autonomous republics, which are also constituent parts of the Federation (Adygeia, Kabardino-Balkaria, Karachaevo-Cherkessia, Chechnya, Ingushetia, North Ossetia, Daghestan) and the three republics—Georgia, Armenia, and Azerbaijan—that used to be Union republics of the USSR and have become independent states.

The three latter republics, situated to the south of the Caucasian ridge, are properly called Transcaucasia, while the regions of the Russian Federation lying to the north of the ridge belong to the North Caucasus. In the eyes of the Russians, however, all those areas on both sides of the ridge are commonly called Kavkaz.

No other area of the former Soviet Union is so ethnically heterogeneous, so conflict-laden, so potentially explosive as the Caucasus. The number of ethnic groups there is truly staggering. For example, Daghestan alone is inhabited by ethnic groups speaking as many as twenty-six different languages, not to mention local dialects. Relationships between nations and ethnic groups in the Caucasus throughout history have been extremely complicated, in many cases quite tense, if not outright hostile. Ancient feuds and land disputes abound in many regions. Under the Soviet regime, old passions were held in check by the tight control of Moscow authorities. Now, old grievances and latent animosities have surfaced, and the Caucasus has become one huge area of instability.

There are numerous specific conflict situations in the Caucasus, namely: the war between Armenia and Azerbaijan over Nagorno-Karabakh; the Abkhazian and South Ossetian wars in Georgia; the armed conflict between Northern Ossetians and Ingush; the strained relations, sometimes verging on open conflict, between different nations in the autonomous republics of the North Caucasus as well as between native peoples and Cossacks in the same area. In all those disputes, the role of Russia, which has recently become quite assertive, is very important if not decisive.

THE ARMENIAN-AZERBAIJANI WAR

It would be superfluous to describe the origins of this war, since it has been widely covered by the press. Not all the coverage, however, has been quite fair and objective. Some explanatory remarks, therefore, appear necessary.

Under the Soviet regime, Nagorno-Karabakh was an integral part of the Azerbaijani Soviet Socialist Republic, an autonomous *oblast* (province) within that republic. It was largely inhabited by ethnic Armenians (123,100 Armenians as opposed to 37,200 Azerbaijanis in 1979). An area of 1,700 square miles, it was separated from Armenia by a narrow corridor. Both the Armenians and the Azerbaijanis claim this piece of land and are convinced that, by historic right, it belongs to them. Who is right and who is wrong?

Historically, the area in question, while being for the most time largely Armenian-populated, was an autonomous entity, ruled by local Armenian princes who offered fealty to Muslim khans. Under the Tsarist regime, it belonged neither to Armenia nor to Azerbaijan for the simple reason that such entities officially did not exist; if the term "Armenia" could be used at that time, it was only in a historical context, and the name "Azerbaijan" was unknown altogether. After the Bolshevik Revolution, Nagorno-Karabakh at first became a part of Armenia but, under the influence of Kremlin intrigues, and the intricate combination of domestic and foreign policy considerations, it was finally decided to make it an autonomous part of Azerbaijan. The Armenians never reconciled themselves to this decision.

The whole conflict must be regarded against the background of the whole history of a nation persecuted for centuries, conquered and subjugated over and over again by powerful neighbors. Particularly, it has to be seen in the context of the massacres committed by the Turks during the First World War, and of the plight of the Armenians in Karabakh and Nakhijevan in the Soviet era; Nakhijevan is another autonomous province of Azerbaijan where the number of Armenians decreased from 53,700 in 1914 to a mere 3,400 in 1979. Armenians call Azerbaijanis just Turks, and this tells it all. Lacking the means to get back the historic heartland of Armenia captured by the Turks, Armenians were all the more determined to put an end to what they feel to be the other injustice: the Azerbaijani rule in Karabakh.

I remember a colleague of mine in the Soviet Academy of Sciences, Gregoriy Akopian, an old Armenian who was one of the founders of the Young Communist League in Armenia back in the 1920s. He was a native of Karabakh and used to go to his home country each year for vacation. Coming back to Moscow, he always looked terribly confused, bewildered, and depressed. This was because of the sad stories his relatives and friends back home kept telling him: stories of unending humiliation and discrimination against Armenians on the part of the local Azerbaijani authorities in Karabakh, mainly in the field of culture, religion, and job opportunities. An old Communist—which, of course, meant "internationalist"—Akopian just could not comprehend how it was possible for his "Azerbaijan comrades" to behave in such a "chauvinistic" way. He used to tell me (his boss at the department) those nasty stories in a confidential manner, taking precautions so as not to be overheard by anybody else, almost whispering in my ear. He was to die just as the Armenian-Azerbaijanian war began, a completely broken man.

Of course, there is another side to the picture as well: All the Azerbaijanis firmly believe that Nagorno-Karabakh is an inalienable part of their motherland. I was repeatedly told by my colleagues in Baku that Karabakh had been the cradle of the Azerbaijani civilization, their culture, art, and craftmanship. Yet, the feeling is that, basically, Karabakh does not matter to Azerbaijanis as much as it does to Armenians. Probably, this is why young volunteers from Armenia proper have been much more eager to fight and die for Karabakh than the Azerbaijanis have.

At first, the Karabakh Armenians opted for incorporation into Armenia which still was a part of the Soviet Union, already weakened by Gorbachev's *perestroika*. A decision to that effect was taken by the *oblast* soviet in February 1988, after grandiose mass manifestations and strikes both in Yerevan, the capital of Armenia, and Karabakh. The Azerbaijani government, of course, declared this decision to be null and void while Moscow, reluctant to consider any border changes in the Union, effectively sided with Baku. Faced with Moscow's refusal to acknowledge their "secession," the Karabakh Armenian leaders changed their tactics and decided to proclaim a de facto independent entity. While not denying the considerable assistance they have been receiving from Armenia, the Karabakh Armenians claim that they must be regarded as one of the sides to the conflict, as an actor distinct from Armenia. The point is that, if this claim came to be generally acknowledged, the border conflict between the two states, Azerbaijan and Armenia, would automatically become one in which three sides are involved. In other words, the Karabakhans demand to be recognized as a legitimate party to any future negotiations aimed at solving the conflict, which is precisely why Baku rejects their claim and insists on talking only to Yerevan.

In the meantime, the Karabakhans have managed to set up impressive armed forces of their own. Just to what extent the Republic of Armenia's military is involved in the actual fighting is anybody's guess, though there is no doubt that Armenian officers have been training the Karabakh armed forces. Military supplies, of course, have been arriving mainly from Armenia.

It is known that on the eve of the breakup of the USSR, about 5,000 ethnic

Armenians served as officers in the Soviet army, as opposed to approximately 300 Azerbaijanis in the same capacity. It would be a fair guess that most of those officers of Armenian origin are now serving in the Armenian army and quite a few of them are on combat duty in Karabakh. A high-ranking Russian official told me that of all the armed forces in the Commonwealth of Independent States, Russia included, the Karabakh army was the best as regards morale, training, and combat experience. This assessment is certainly borne out by the impressive performance of the Karabakh army in the war against Azerbaijan. Having driven the Azerbaijani troops from Karabakh, they invaded Azerbaijan proper and have succeeded in capturing sizeable pieces of Azerbaijani territory along the border with Iran, obviously hoping to use it as a bargaining chip in future negotiations with Baku.

The Karabakh conflict can be called a classic example of the clash between two principles of international law: the right to self-determination and the inviolability of borders. In accordance with the former, the Armenians, constituting an overwhelming majority of the population of Karabakh, have a right to secede from Azerbaijan while the second principle denies them this right, since juridically the area is just a part of a sovereign state. Those principles contradict each other in many areas of the world, and this contradiction has become a matter of intense debate. So far, it is hard to see how they can be reconciled. In the territories that used to be parts of the Soviet Union, this problem is particularly acute. Besides Karabakh, conflicts of this kind exist in Georgia (with Abkhazia and South Ossetia) and in Moldova (with the "Dniester republic"). More can emerge shortly.

What are the prospects of solving the Karabakh conflict at present? In principle, the Karabakh situation appears to be deadlocked. No regime in Baku could survive for twenty-four hours if it dared to rescind the present official stand, namely, that Nagorno-Karabakh is an integral part of Azerbaijan. Nor can any government in Yerevan survive if it demonstrates its indifference to the fate of the Karabakh Armenians.

This does not mean that the two nations are destined to wage incessant war. True, it is all but impossible to envisage a document, terminating the conflict, that would be satisfactory to both sides; however, a permanent cease-fire arrangement is possible. It can only be based on a tacit Azerbaijani recognition of Karabakh's de facto autonomy, while not forcing Baku to formally renounce its claim on the territory. In this case Azerbaijan will consider Karabakh, for years and decades to come, as its integral part, temporarily occupied by Armenia and bound to be liberated some day. There are historic precedents for this kind of pseudosolution: Vilnius was part of Poland between the two world wars but Lithuania officially considered the city its capital. Bessarabia was a part of Rumania but on all the Soviet maps it was painted in Soviet colors as a territory unlawfully occupied by a foreign power. Israel's occupation of the Golan Heights has not prevented Syria from regarding the area as its own. Of course, it would be hard for Azerbaijanis to swallow the loss of Nagorno-Karabakh; the alternative, however—an interminable war—would bleed the nation.

As to the external forces influencing the course of events, a direct intervention by either Turkey or Iran does not seem likely. But what about Russia? One thing to be always borne in mind is the Karabakh Armenians' total dependence of fuel supplies from Russia. Their main combat units are tank and mechanized forces which could not move without being constantly supplied with fuel from Batumi via Georgia, and every mile of the route is under Russian military control. The tap can be turned off at any moment. It was reliably reported in Moscow that in 1993, the Russians deliberately gave the Armenians a green light for their offensive aimed at capturing the Azerbaijani provinces bordering on Iran. Moscow's aim was to make the Azerbaijan authorities more amenable to pressure over the issue of Azerbaijani oil. It is alleged that, as a result of this pressure applied by supplying the Karabakh army with additional fuel, Russia has succeeded in obtaining its share of the oil concession, along with a British firm.

In the meantime, the Karabakh conflict remains the gravest not only in the Caucasus but in the whole territory of the former Soviet Union, except for Tajikistan. It is the only real full-scale war between former Soviet republics, now independent states, and, as such, it has acquired the character of an international conflict. It is bigger than just an armed conflict over a piece of land; it bears the mark of a genuine clash of civilizations, using Samuel Huntington's term. The question is—what civilizations? Christianity versus Islam? Certainly not. The fact that the Armenians are Christian and the Azerbaijanis Muslim is, of course, important but no more so than that the Israelis are Judaists and the Arabs Muslim. The Arab-Israeli conflict can hardly be called a religious war. The Abkhazian war in Georgia, to be discussed later, has nothing to do with religion, although the intransigence of both conflicting sides rivals that of the Armenians and Azerbaijanis.

Probably, it would be more correct to call this conflict a clash of subcivilizational communities. Why not assume that, alongside great civilizations that have shaped world's history, other, lesser, modest civilizations exist that only partially belong to the larger ones? Let us take, for instance, Japan. Some historians, including Toynbee, believed that Japan never gave birth to an independent civilization. Admittedly, the Japanese civilization is not of the same scope as the Judeo-Christian or the Islamic or the Buddist ones, and Toynbee rightly pointed out its Chinese roots. Yet, although starting from an "offshoot of a continental civilization," Japan gradually developed distinct and specific civilizational features of its own. It may be argued that, while belonging to the greater Far Eastern civilization, according to Toynbee's classification, Japan has become a subcivilization. In this case, a parallel with Armenia is worthy of consideration. Undoubtedly a part of the great Christian world, Armenia, as regards its culture, tradition, mentality, possesses some unique civilizational features. While not necessarily incompatible with, or hostile to, the Islamic civilization, this Armenian subcivilization, represented in the case at hand by the Karabakh Armenians, has found it impossible to exist under the rule of a nation closely related to the Turks, who are regarded as perpetrators of the biggest massacre in Armenian history.

The widespread protest which had been growing and accumulating for decades finally resulted in a tremendous outburst of nationalist and patriotic feeling. Seen in this light, the Karabakh conflict was probably unavoidable.

Of all the former Soviet republics, with the exception of Tajikistan, the three Transcaucasian states are in the worst shape. There are, however, important differences both in the origin of their plight and in the way they bear their crosses. So far, it is only Armenia that has faced the challenge with courage and dignity, displaying stamina, determination, and discipline. The morale of the Armenian nation is incomparably higher than that of its neighbors, and its internal stability is remarkable.

To a large extent, this is due to the very cause of all Armenia's misfortunes to begin with, namely, the Nagorno-Karabakh issue that triggered the war with Azerbaijan, followed by economic blockade and tremendous suffering of the Armenian population. It may be argued that the Armenians practically asked for it; if they had not stirred up trouble over Karabakh in the first place, women and children in Yerevan would not be starving and freezing now. This argument, however, must be weighed against the undisputable advantage that the Karabakh issue has brought to Armenia. It rallied and mobilized the whole nation, provided a cause for patriotic unity against a common enemy and thus probably prevented a bitter internal strife of the kind to be seen only too often in the post-Communist states.

THE GEORGIAN-ABKHAZIAN CONFLICT

The second major Caucasian conflict, the one between Georgia and Abkhazia, seems to be just as hard to settle as the Karabakh dispute. Again, who is right and who is wrong in the Abkhazian conflict? It was Hegel who said: "The true tragedy is not a conflict between right and wrong but between right and right." Both the Georgians and Abkhazians have quite plausible cases. The piece of land on the Black Sea coast can be said to be a motherland to both communities. The Abkhazian kingdom, born in the eighth century A.D., was incorporated into Georgia some two hundred years later. Both peoples were for centuries fighting off foreign invaders, mostly Turks in the Abkhazian case. In the early nineteenth century Abkhazia followed the rest of Georgia into the Russian Empire. The two peoples are quite close as regards their appearance and way of life but their languages are completely different. Under the Soviet rule, Abkhazia was an autonomous republic within Georgia. From time to time, differences arose and there were periods of tension; by and large, however, both communities lived in peace. The Abkhazians, numbering little more than one hundred thousand people, made up just 17% of the whole population of the autonomous republic but had a majority in the local parliament, this arrangement being a major concession on the part of Tbilisi.

The Abkhazian majority in the local Supreme Soviet (parliament) proclaimed the republic's sovereignty as early as August 1990, but at that time nobody paid much attention; that was a time of a "parade of sovereignties," with many Union and even autonomous republics enjoying the opportunity to use the magic term. Things changed in a fundamental way when the USSR disintegrated and Georgia became an independent state. The old Soviet-imposed constitution of Georgia was abolished and thus the legal ground for Abkhazia remaining an autonomous part of Georgia virtually disappeared. The Abkhazian majority in the local parliament, led by a Moscow-educated professor of ancient Oriental history Vyacheslav Ardzinba, moved to restore the constitution of 1925 which had postulated Abkhazia's autonomous status within the framework of the Soviet Union, but outside Georgia (it was not until 1931 that Abkhazia, remaining an autonomous republic, became part of the Georgian Union republic). To Georgians, it was clearly a provocation: Abkhazia was turning independent, thus seceding from Georgia. No Georgian could accept this.

It was at that point, in August 1992, that the Georgian national guard, under a pretext of ensuring the safety of a railroad linking Georgia to Russia and setting free some Tbilisi officials held as hostages in Abkhazia by unknown persons, entered the capital city of Abkhazia, Sukhumi. This action marked the beginning of the war. The Abkhazian nationalists, with Ardzinba at their head, fled into neighboring Russia and quickly formed their armed forces on the Russian territory, with the assistance of some blood-related ethnic groups in the North Caucasus—Cherkess, Chechens, and so on. The Abkhaz side was also joined by quite a few ethnic Russians, professional military men who came to be called volunteers by the Abkhazians and mercenaries by the Georgians. In a few months, the newly born coalition forces mounted a successful offensive and finally drove the Georgian national guard out of Abkhazia. The Georgian side has lost the battle.

The Abkhazian version of the story runs like this: We are a small nation, Abkhazia is the only place in the world for us to live, we have nowhere else to go while Georgians have the whole land of Georgia all to themselves. Let them leave us alone.

The Georgian version: there is no denying that an Abkhaz kingdom did exist many centuries ago and that ethnic Abkhazians are not Georgians; for hundreds of years, however, Abkhazia has been a homeland for Georgians as well. It is a land of two nations. How can an ethnic group making up just 17% of the population of a given area claim to be this area's sole master and owner? The Abkhazians may have cultural and even administrative autonomy but they have no right to secede. Abkhazia is a home for both peoples but a part of Georgia.

Both versions are right, and both cases are just. What is more, they are not basically incompatible, albeit only theoretically. Peaceful coexistence of the two ethnoses could still be saved prior to the summer of 1992. It is infinitely more difficult, if at all possible, after blood has been shed. At present, most Abkhazians probably regard Georgians as vicious and bloodthirsty enemies, and this is precisely how they are being seen by the Georgians. The parallel with the Karabakh issue is evident: Some of my colleagues—artists, scholars, intellectuals, friends for decades, now would not give one another the time of day. The reason is quite simple: They have been divided by the ethnic issue, they are not on speaking terms anymore.

Which side is most to blame for the rupture? It would be futile to hope to get a mutually acceptable version of events. This is not the Iraqi invasion of Kuwait. No clear and definitive facts can be established as to the guilt of the one side in triggering the explosion without the other side liable to be accused of having set in motion a chain of events that had given the first side an excuse for action. This action would be described, naturally, as "counteraction," or reaction to an impending threat, or a preemptive move. As to the atrocities, they have been committed by both sides.

What is really striking is the incredible amount of blunders and stupid moves on both sides, a truly amazing shortsightedness demonstrated by Abkhazian and Georgian leaders alike. Thus, there could have been no doubt in any Abkhazian's mind that their move to change the status quo, no matter what the official formulations were, would have been unanimously interpreted by the Georgians as secession and, as such, rejected and combatted by all means. In other words, Ardzinba and the rest of the Abkhazian leaders must have known perfectly well that they were provoking a war and that, given the correlation of the military forces, a Georgian occupation of Abkhazia followed by a tremendous suffering of civilians would be inevitable. Likewise, the Georgian authorities, by ordering their troops into Sukhumi, must have known that this would not be the end of the story, since the Abkhazians were certain to find impressive allies both in the North Caucasus and beyond, notably in Russia. Yet, knowing all this, neither side took the most elementary precautions to protect the very population whose rights and interests were ostensibly at stake to begin with.

As a result, the Abkhazian leaders could offer no resistance to the Georgian national guard in Sukhumi and fled north to Russia, leaving their civilian population at the mercy of unruly and marauding invaders. As if to mirror this cynical insouciance, the Georgian authorities, a couple of months later, failed dismally to foresee and forestall the Abkhazian counterstrike from across the Russian border and lost all their gains in just a few days. This time around, Georgian civilians fell victim to the advancing Abkhazian-spearheaded coalition forces burning with a fierce desire of revenge.

What looks at first sight like mere bungling and ineptness, however, acquires a more sinister meaning if we take into consideration ulterior motives of leaders of the conflicting sides. The matter at issue is not only Abkhazia but other areas of interethnic conflicts in the post-Soviet republics, from the Moldavian-Dniester confrontation to the Tajik civil war. Of primary importance here is the existence of powerful political forces strongly committed to instigating ethnic strife as the means to protect their vested interests or to gain political and economic dominance. To those forces, civilian suffering is essential; it is both useful and desirable for mobilizing "their" ethnos, for rallying "their" population around the leadership, for raising a battle cry. Blood is what cements ethnic hatred, creates nationalist myths, and ensures loyalty to "The Cause."

This is not to imply that the Abkhazian leaders, for example, deliberately planned the whole operation, including a temporary retreat and Georgian occupation of their territory, in order to have a pretext for a "war of liberation and revenge." When making their fateful decision, they could not predict the exact form of an inevitable Georgian reaction; they did not know details of the complicated relationship between the new Georgian leader Shevardnadze and his Minister of Defense Kitovani, who actually gave the orders to march into Sukhumi. Probably, Ardzinba and his followers hoped they could get away with their de facto secession without a war. Yet, it is hard to believe that the eventuality of a brutal Georgian military response, with all its awesome implications, was something they could never imagine; they were not that naive, nor were they ignorant of the warlord mentality of the people who had real power in Georgia. Most likely, the Abkhazian leaders tacitly acknowledged that if this was to be the price they would have to pay for independence, so be it. The ensuing suffering of their people would only strengthen the growing anti-Georgian feeling and make their own positions as true national leaders more assured than ever. This is exactly what happened.

The leadership on both sides has given many proofs of its incompetence and ruthlessness. The Abkhazians appear to have played their cards more skillfully. Their leadership also seems to be much more united, determined, and single-minded than the Georgian one. Still, to many an observer it would appear rather odd that the tiny Abkhazian community could not only hold its own against seemingly overwhelming odds but win the decisive battle for Sukhumi and establish its control over all of Abkhazia, thus achieving a de facto secession from Georgia.

The point is that the outcome of the battle was not just the result of a direct confrontation between the two communities and their armed forces on the territory of Abkhazia. It was heavily if not decisively influenced by some other factors, the most important of them being:

Georgia's Internal Weakness

Georgians are a very old community with a rather complex composition. The nation is not ethnically monolithic, like, for instance, Armenians; it comprises diverse groups: Kartveli, Kakhetians, Mingrels, Imeretins, Ajarians, Svans, and so on. The first two groups inhabit a large area in Central Georgia around the capital Tbilisi and are considered a "core" of the Georgian nation. They, as well as Ajarians and Imeretins, speak the classic Georgian. Mingrels and Svans at home speak a colloquial idiom of their own but are being educated in Georgian, which is also the official language of the country as a whole. These differences usually do not count for much; certainly, they do not prevent various groups of the population from feeling that they belong to a nation. The lack of homogeneity, however, can acquire some significance at times of crisis; clan and parochial trends may suddenly surface.

The first leader of independent Georgia, Zviad Gamsakhurdia, was a Mingrel. A well-known freedom fighter, son of a famous writer, Gamsakhurdia was elected President in May 1991. In a few months' time, however, it became clear that the popular choice had been wrong. The president failed dismally both in his attempts to initiate a healthy economic development and in his bid for political stability and national consensus. Accused of political manipulations, suppression of the opposition, arbitrary and even despotic style of governing, megalomania, and economic mismanagement, Gamsakhurdia managed, in a remarkably short time, to alienate the bulk of the Georgian political class, intelligentsia, and the military. The man he made the chief of his national guard, a certain Kitovani, betrayed him and staged a mutiny. A typical representative of a new breed of warlords, Kitovani became a major figure in the opposition camp which succeeded, after bloody street battles in the center of Tbilisi, in overthrowing the Gamsakhurdia regime in January 1992. Soon afterwards, the former Soviet Foreign Minister Shevardnadze (who had once been the first secretary of the Georgian Communist party) was invited by the victorious faction to become Head of State. This move was prompted not so much by the new leaders' genuine respect and admiration for the old politician as by their desire to gain international recognition for the regime that could not boast legitimacy, since it had ousted by force a constitutionally elected president. The warlords who had come to govern the republic failed to create a viable leadership. The new regime degenerated into a reign of gangsters and racketeers fighting among themselves for spoils and privileges, pillaging and bullying the population. Yet, their calculation as to Shevardnadze's usefulness for them on the plane of foreign relations proved to be correct: the regime was recognized by the world community.

At once, new series of intrigues began, this time aimed at Shevardnadze. The warlords never wanted him to become a real leader of Georgia; they just intended to profit by his international reputation. They actually were apprehensive of Shevardnadze, probably believing him to be too smart for them. And when the Abkhazian leaders made their imprudent secessionist move, it was the same Kitovani who, under a clumsy pretext, ordered the national guard into Sukhumi. One plausible version is that he intended in this way to set up Shevardnadze: the veteran politician, true to his reputation, could be counted upon to raise objections to the use of force in Abkhazia, thus losing his patriotic credentials in the eyes of the Georgian public infuriated by the Abkhazian ''treachery.'' Shevardnadze, however, chose to acquiesce. Anyhow, he probably was unable to prevent the military move even if he wanted to, since the upsurge of nationalistic feeling in Georgia was already too strong to be calmed down. Besides, the Georgians unanimously believed at that point that it would come to no more than a walkover; the revolt of the unarmed Abkhazia would be subdued in a matter of days.

In the meantime, Gamsakhurdia, who had fled to his native Mingrelia, was becoming active again, and his support was growing. It was at that point that the ethnic dimension of the domestic crisis came to the fore. The collapse of Gamsakhurdia in the capital city was not followed by a decline of his popularity in Mingrelia, where the largely rural population did not feel as strongly about his undemocratic ways as did the Tbilisi elite. Moreover, many people there were convinced that the main reason for their fellow-countryman's downfall had been his Mingrelian background. Dislike of the Tbilisi political and intellectual elite had historic roots in Mingrelia; it became reinforced as news of the national guard's ugly behavior began to spread. The policy of the new regime was increasingly regarded as anti-Mingrelian. Pro-Gamsakhurdia forces were growing daily, all the preconditions for a civil war were shaping up. By the summer of 1993, newly formed armed forces loyal to the ex-president were openly challenging government troops in western Georgia.

So it came about that just as the government forces were engaged in the last, decisive battle in Sukhumi against the hostile coalition troops, they had to face another enemy in the rear. Whether or not rumors of collusion between the Abkhazian forces and the pro-Gamsakhurdia insurgents were true, there is no doubt that the government troops' lines of communications were severely disrupted and they had a serious supply problem. Finally, having to fight simultaneously on two fronts proved too much for the inadequately armed and poorly led Georgian army.

The morale of Georgian soldiers undoubtedly suffered, because the country in general seemed to be breaking apart. By that time, South Ossetia had virtually seceded from the republic, and Ajaria had become a de facto independent entity. (Ajaria, bordering on Turkey, has a largely Muslim population, although of a pure Georgian stock; since 1990 this former autonomous republic has effectively become a state within a state, its leadership taking no orders from Tbilisi. A very knowledgeable Russian official recently told me that, if worse came to worse, the Ajarians would probably prefer merger with Turkey to being ruled by an agonizing gangster regime in Tbilisi.) To many, Georgia at that moment looked like a basket case; the situation looked hopeless.

A Surprisingly Powerful Anti-Georgian Coalition

There had never been such a thing as an Abkhazian army. Of course, Georgia had no army either but Gamsakhurdia managed to set up a surrogate—the national guard. Poorly trained and lacking combat experience except for having stormed the president's headquarters in Tbilisi, the guard, however, was an armed unit of sorts, which was more than could be said of the Abkhazian haphazard volunteer militia. Hardly any resistance was offered to the Georgians as they marched into Sukhumi and then northward up to the Russian border. Considering the expedition over, the guardsmen indulged in looting and drinking. The enemy's counteroffensive came as a complete surprise. The only battle to speak of took place at the charming sea resort of Gagra; soundly beaten, the guardsmen hastily retreated all the way down to Sukhumi. The siege of the capital of Abkhazia lasted for almost a year, interrupted by cease-fires and negotiations with Russian participation. Finally, a peace arrangement seemed to be in the making, withdrawal of the armed forces of both sides was agreed upon, and the Georgian troops were actually pulling out. It was at that point that the Abkhazian-led coalition broke the truce and the assault on Sukhumi resumed. Shevardnadze personally took command of the defense of the city but failed to save the day. Sukhumi fell in September 1993 and the whole of Abkhazia was lost to the advancing secessionist forces. Ethnic cleansing followed at once, with tens of thousands of Georgian civilians fleeing to the mountains, many only to meet their death from cold and diseases.

When asked about the causes of the disaster, most Georgians would maintain that their side was defeated not by the pathetic Abkhazians but by the Chechens and Cherkess armed and backed by Russia. This version of events, merciful and face-saving for Georgian pride, is largely correct. The Abkhazian irregular guerrilla detachments, hastily formed after the Georgian attack, may have been fighting with courage and even fanaticism but they were no match for the national guardsmen with their modern weapons taken over from the Soviet army arsenals. In just a couple of months, however, Georgians were to meet a completely different enemy, armed with Soviet-made weapons, including the newest type of tanks. Where had all this weaponry come from? The standard Abkhazian explanation has since been "war trophies," arms captured from Georgians. Of course, it cannot hold water, although a certain quantity of arms may actually have been captured from the enemy. The bulk was undoubtedly provided by the Russian army for reasons to be discussed later. What is necessary to note here is that hundreds if not thousands of quite professional soldiers suddenly emerged from nowhere, ready to fight the Georgians. Some were ethnic Russians, veterans of the Soviet army turned mercenaries, with the experience of Afghanistan behind most of them. The majority, however, came from an area closer to home: They were Caucasus-born just as the Abkhazians and Georgians. Volunteers from the North Caucasus, largely Chechens and Cherkess, obviously played a decisive role in the outcome of the battles for Gagra and Sukhumi.

The ethnic factor proved paramount in this situation. Contrary to some assertions, religion was not an issue; Georgians are Christians, but so are many Abkhazians. For centuries, Abkhazia has been inhabited by Muslims and Christians alike. The North Caucasian volunteers did not come to Abkhazia to defend Islam; they came to the aid of their ethnic brethren.

Of all the ethnic groups in the North Caucasus, at least three undoubtedly belong to the same "family"—Adygeians, Cherkess, and Kabardinians; their languages are related, all three groups call themselves "adyghe," and regard the Abkhazians as their relatives. It is natural, therefore, that these groups were the first to provide volunteers for Abkhazia. As to the Chechens, they belong to a different linguistic group but it is precisely they who seem to have made a majority of the North Caucasian volunteers. Reasons for this would be hard to find in any historic legacy of hostility between Chechens and Georgians. Probably, what prompted Chechens to enter the war, apart from their notorious warlike mentality and natural readiness to fight, was Caucasian solidarity and feeling for the underdog, which was how the Abkhazians were generally regarded at the moment. Of course, there were a lot of adventurers and mercenaries as well.

It is difficult to gauge the proportion of Abkhazians and North Caucasians in the army that drove the Georgians out of Abkhazia; there is no doubt, however, that without outside help it would have been impossible for the Abkhaz troops to defeat the Georgian forces, even though the latter were not exactly formidable. Most observers seem to believe that it was not so much the Abkhazians who won the war as the combination of Chechen-Cherkess manpower, Russian officers, and Russian heavy weapons.

Moscow's Game

The cynical role the Russian military played in Abkhazia in 1993 is obvious. While proclaiming themselves honest brokers and mediators, the Russians were at the same time supplying the Abkhazian side with weapons and ammunition. No direct proof of this has ever been offered, but it would be more than naive to believe that the tanks, rockets, howitzers, pieces of ordnance, and other heavy weapons that the anti-Georgian coalition forces were increasingly using in the war had been captured from the enemy. Even though some of this weaponry may have been bought from Russian army arsenals, the bulk of it must have been given over to Abkhazian commanders by their Russian counterparts on orders from somewhere in Moscow.

Regardless of who exactly was pulling the strings and at what level decisions were made, the overall aim of those who masterminded Moscow's policy in the Georgian-Abkhazian conflict was simple enough: first, to establish Russian military presence in a geopolitically vital area and second, to prevent an upsurge of anti-Russian feeling in the North Caucasus that would have been inevitable had Moscow allowed the Georgians to crush the Abkhazian independence movement. By their Machiavellian tactics the Russian military leaders, with or without an actual "green light" from the Kremlin, got precisely what they had wanted all along. Assuring Russian military presence in the Abkhazian coastal area would have been impossible if it came under Georgian control, as anti-Russian sentiment in Georgia in 1992–1993 was extremely high. "Russians out!" would have been the motto, and any idea of Russian military bases in Georgia, including Abkhazia, would have been out of the question. Moreover, Chechens, Cherkess, and the rest of North Caucasians would have condemned Russian policy as plain betrayal of the Abkhazians, and tension in the relations between those nations and ethnic Russians residing in the North Caucasus could have risen to a dangerous level. On the other hand, with Ardzinba and his people in control of Abkhazia, Moscow can be assured of its military forces permanently staying in the area, if only because the tiny Abkhazian nation will live forever in fear of the Georgians' return and will regard Russia as the sole guarantor of its newly won independence.

Securing a military foothold in Abkhazia was, however, just the initial part of the Russian strategy. Even more ambitious was the goal of reasserting a measure of Russian control over Transcaucasia as a whole, first and foremost over Georgia as a bridge to Armenia and Azerbaijan. At the first glance, this goal would seem to be incompatible with backing the Abkhazian separatists against Tbilisi, thus antagonizing the Georgians and hurting their national pride. But here we must remember the second war, already mentioned, that was going on simultaneously with the fighting in Abkhazia, namely, the civil war between the forces of ex-President Gamsakhurdia and those of the new regime led by Shevardnadze, Kitovani, and the rest of them. In this war, the Russians were ready to back Shevardnadze who, after the loss of Abkhazia, appeared to be facing total disaster, since the Georgian military machine had all but broken down. At one point, just after the fall of Sukhumi, pro-Gamsakhurdia forces in Mingrelia felt strong enough to actually threaten Kutaisi, the second largest city of Georgia. Shevardnadze had to admit in public that the Georgian army had virtually disintegrated.

It was at this hour of dire need that the Russian military came to the rescue of the Shevardnadze regime. The veteran Georgian leader who, but a few days earlier, had bitterly accused Moscow of duplicity and betrayal, now felt it necessary to take the offered hand. The Georgians realized that it was only Russia, perfidious as its role had been all along, that could help them out of their predicament. The Russians, as if willing to make up for their treacherous behavior in the Abkhaz war, rapidly started to give the government forces substantial military aid and, more importantly, sent their troops to guard the lines of communication in western Georgia, thus effectively blocking Gamsakhurdia's forces and stemming their advance. It was the Russian military intervention that tipped the scale in the civil war. Swallowing their pride, the Georgians had to come to terms with Moscow. Georgia joined the CIS, and Russia will have its military bases in Georgia proper and in Abkhazia, whatever the eventual status of the latter.

This status will be extremely difficult to define, the positions of the protagonists being diametrically opposed. It would be hard to find a single ethnic Georgian who would agree with the idea of Abkhazia becoming an independent state just like the other neighbors—Russia or Armenia. Equally difficult at this point would be to convince the Abkhazians that the solution is Abkhazian autonomy within the framework of the Georgian republic. People who have gone through so much suffering find it very difficult to forgive and forget, nor can they be sure that the other side could forgive and forget, either. A major issue with the Abkhazians now is the fear of Georgian reprisals. Numerically inferior, the Abkhazians would hate to have to live in constant fear of Georgians' eventually reasserting themselves as a dominant nation in Abkhazia. They believe that an irreversible step has already been taken, that a historic parting of the ways is an accomplished fact. At the same time, it is hardly conceivable that either Russia or the world at large would formally recognize Abkhazia as a sovereign state. Thus, at the time of this writing, the situation remained wholly confused.

THE SOUTH OSSETIAN CONFLICT

According to the 1989 census, Ossetians made up only 3% of Georgia's population of about 5.4 million. Most of them were concentrated in the South Ossetian Autonomous *oblast* (province) in the north of the republic where the Great Caucasian Ridge lies. To the north of the ridge is North Ossetia, part of the Russian Federation. Thus, the Ossetian nation is administratively divided. The issue of North Ossetian will be dealt with later. The Georgian-Ossetian conflict is one that has been going on within the confines of the Georgian republic.

Ossetians are an ancient nation of Iranian origin. Their ancestors, called Alans, migrated widely, and their traces were found as far away from the Caucasus as Western Europe. Finally, Ossetians settled in the area around the Great Caucasian Ridge. Tens of thousands of them found their home in the territory that later became a part of the Georgian Soviet Republic

When asked about the difference in their approach to Abkhazians and Ossetians, most Georgians would explain it in this way: The former had, in ancient times, a kingdom of their own (although on Georgian territory) and therefore are naturally entitled to have an autonomous status, while the latter are relative newcomers with no historic roots in Georgia. One widespread version is that Ossetian peasants who used to live to the north of the Ridge were invited by Georgian landowners to work their fields and later became a majority in an area of northern Georgia. Sure, they were granted autonomy, but of a lower grade than the one accorded to the Abkhazians.

In 1989, in the midst of Gorbachev's *perestroika*, as the power of the Center was beginning to crumble, the Ossetians decided to demand that their autonomous status be raised to equal that of the Abkhazians and Ajarians. This request was rejected by the republican authorities, and militant nationalists in Tbilisi mounted a "peaceful march" on Tskhinvali, the capital of the autonomous region. This, in turn, provoked an outburst of anti-Georgian feeling among South Ossetians.

In September 1990, the local Soviet of South Ossetia voted for a "declaration of sovereignty," and on the same day Tbilisi, not unexpectedly, declared it null and void. The authorities in Tskhinvali, however, refused to comply, and elections to the parliament of a "South Ossetian Soviet Republic" were held on

December 9. Two days later the Supreme Soviet of the Republic of Georgia moved to abolish the South Ossetian autonomy altogether. The region officially became just another province of the republic, the autonomous *oblast* formally ceased to exist. A state of emergency was introduced, followed by the formation of Ossetian military units. Fighting started, on a small scale at first, but everybody felt that escalation of the conflict was inevitable. Things came to a head in June 1992, when Georgia was already an independent state under President Gamsakhurdia, a former dissident and freedom fighter turned leader of extreme chauvinistic forces. Units of the Georgian National Guard entered North Ossetia (just as, two months later, other units of the same formation marched into Abkhazia) and captured villages surrounding the Ossetian capital. From there, Georgian artillery began shelling Tskhinvali. Soon, the city became an "Ossetian Sarayevo." It was only a few months later that, with Russian mediation, cease-fire was arranged. An uneasy truce took effect and is still holding, with Tskhinvali a ghost city, half destroyed.

The political situation in South Ossetia remains deadlocked, just as it is in Abkhazia. With so much blood shed during the siege of Tskhinvali, and with hostile feelings so high on both sides, a compromise solution is hard to envisage. In fact, Georgia does not control most of the area of its former autonomous region, and South Ossetian nationalists say that the area will never again be a part of Georgia. Russia's stand is just as ambiguous as in the case of Abkhazia. Officially, Russia is committed to respect Georgia's territorial integrity but it would be difficult to see Moscow pulling its peacekeeping forces out of South Ossetia and letting Georgians recapture the area by force.

In retrospect, it can be said that the Georgian authorities, with their chauvinistic and ill-conceived actions, have only themselves to blame for the series of events that have led to a de facto secession of both Abkhazia and South Ossetia. Here, however, we have to come back to what was mentioned earlier, namely: new elites coming to power in newly independent states of the former Soviet Union are doing their best to assert themselves by playing the only card they have at their disposal—the ethnic one. They just have to posture as supreme patriots and nationalists; otherwise they will be accused of neglecting national interests. And, as ethnic minorities within the new republics grow restive and, in their turn, demand greater autonomy if not independence (a phenomenon aptly called "matryoshka nationalism"), new republican leaders feel they have no choice but to forcefully reject those claims. If they fail to take vigorous action against the minorities, they will look much less capable of preserving the integrity of their states than the old Soviet regime was, which, after all, had managed to check separatist trends.

On the other hand, self-proclaimed leaders of new nationalist, or separatist, movements rapidly shaping up among ethnic minorities cannot afford to look weak and irresolute in the eyes of their followers. The public feels that, the empire having fallen apart, the hour has struck for the creation of their sovereign entity. If Georgia has become an independent state, why not Abkhazia? The genie is out of the bottle, and it is not for leaders of ethnic minorities to calm down the population; if they do, they will be swept away by more energetic and ruthless rivals, plenty of whom can be found in every autonomous area. And so it happens that, bent on holding to power at any cost, new minority leaders have to appear as patriotic and intransigent as possible. If it comes to bloodshed, this can even be a blessing in disguise for the leaders, as explained earlier: Nationalist myths will be created, martyrs' blood will cement national unity. Seen in this light, there is really little difference in the motivation and behavior of both central and local elites in ethnic conflicts. The mentality of new leaders is virtually the same.

Who are those leaders constituting a new political class that has emerged on the ruins of the Soviet Empire? Broadly speaking, they fall into two categories. The first is the traditional party-state *nomenclatura*. An innumerable army of party secretaries of all levels, chairmen and members of local executive and legislative bodies, chiefs and officials of provincial departments of the former KGB and the Ministry of Interior, managers of big industrial and agricultural enterprises—the whole vast elite feels its legitimacy undermined after the disintegration of the old regime. Overnight, their vested interests, their privileges appeared threatened, ready to crumble. Their only chance of survival was to jump on the nationalist bandwagon. Those people have only one card to play— the ethnic one.

The second group may be called new nationalistic intelligentsia. University professors, journalists, writers, academics, petty functionaries, state employees— those people, unlike the first category, did not hold any positions to speak of under the old regime. Now they feel that their hour has come. They see power and privileges ahead.

Both groups sometimes challenge each other, sometimes merge. On a recent visit to Vladikavkaz, the capital of North Ossetia, I had a chance to learn something about both kinds of the new indigenous political class. While in North Ossetia, with its long tradition of semistatehood, this class is represented exactly by the type of *nomenclatura* described above, the one in neighboring Ingushetia is predominantly of the second category, with an addition of Islamic elements. Both republics, members of the Russian Federation, are locked in a bitter conflict over the issue of land. The Ingush, who came from a mountainous Muslim nation, were deported by Stalin to Asia along with several other nations in 1944 on charges of a massive collaboration with the invading German army during the war. When they were rehabilitated after Stalin's death and, much later, got a chance to return home, a part of their land was already inhabited by (mainly Christian) North Ossetians. What the Ingush claim at this point is nothing less than half of Vladikavkaz, the capital of North Ossetia. During the fighting in October–November 1992, close to a thousand people were killed. I saw hundreds of destroyed Ingush houses outside Vladikavkaz.

The conflict between the North Ossetians and Ingush is probably the only ''neat'' case of a confrontation on ethnic ground involving both types of elite;

on the part of the Ossetians, an old party and managerial elite establishment; on the part of the Ingush, a nascent leadership group of mixed background. More often, some combination of both kinds of elites can be found in ethnic conflicts. Practically in all of them, people mainly responsible for the flare-up of passions belong to the already mentioned new political class, all those power-hungry politicians of the typical Soviet mold claiming to be "genuine patriots." Next to blame are field commanders, warlords, local gang chieftains of the kind described by the British journalist Michael Ignatieff: "short, stubby men who in a former life had been small-time hoods, small-town cops or both. Spend a day with them and you'd hardly know that most of them are serial killers. These are the modern warlords. They appear wherever nation-states disintegrate. . . . With their carphones, faxes and exquisite personal weaponry, they look post-modern, but the reality is pure early medieval."[1]

It is precisely in the Caucasus, with its dozens of ethnic groups, that the soil for this kind of conflict is particularly fertile. Altogether, there are no less than sixty "core" peoples, or large ethnic groups, in the whole area, including the three Transcaucasian republics. In Daghestan alone, twenty-nine basic ethnic groups are listed; including smaller ones, the number is eighty-one. Of course, not all of them are hostile to their neighbors. The most dangerous potential trouble spots are: (1) Ossetians and Ingush, already mentioned; (2) Chechen-Akkin and Lak and Kumyk in West Daghestan (Chechens had been deported to Central Asia during the war and later were allowed to return but, as in the case of the Ingush and North Ossetians, another ethnic group was already living on their territory, namely Lak; now, the authorities intend to move the Lak out of the Chechen areas and settle them in another territory which, however, is being claimed by yet another ethnic group, Kumyks, as belonging to them); (3) Lezgins in South Daghestan who demand the creation of their own state, Lezgistan (at present, 44% of the Lezgins live in Daghestan, 37% in Azerbaijan); and (4) areas of Chechnya and Cherkessia bordering on Stavropol province and populated by ethnic Russians (Cossacks). Conflicts between "native" Caucasians and Cossacks are potentially some of the most dangerous in the territory of the former Soviet Union.

These conflicts can be properly understood only against the historic background. The great Caucasian War was one of the major events of Russian history. For almost one hundred years mountainous peoples of the North Caucasus resisted the onslaught of the Russian army. The Tsar's generals waged the war of colonial conquest with utter ruthlessness and brutality; villages, crops, and cattle were being destroyed, civilian population, including in many cases women and children, slaughtered in cold blood. To crush the resistance of the unbelievably stubborn and valiant highlanders who were fighting the "holy war" against the "infidels" under the banner of Islam, large-scale deportation of population was carried out. Whole ethnic groups were forced to leave for Turkey. One of the mountainous peoples, the Adygeia, suffered a particularly cruel fate: out of almost one million people, little more than 100,000 remained in the mid-1860s, after a few years of mass deportations to Turkey, and more were forced out in the next thirty years. At present, Adygei number just 125,000 in their own autonomous republic (22% of the population) while ethnic Russians outnumber them by three to one. Another ethnos, the famous Cherkess, number just 60,000, with Russians outnumbering them by four to one. Even worse has been the fate of smaller ethnic groups; Shapsugi, for example, have all but vanished, only 9,000 remaining in a mountainous area close to the Black Sea resort of Sochi.

Spearheading the Russian military expeditions in the Caucasus were the Cossacks, a trusted and loyal component of the Russian army throughout centuries. Cossacks are not easy to define in usual ethnographic terms. They are certainly not an ethnic or national group. They are ethnic Russians and speak only Russian. Largely the descendants of serfs who had fled from feudal landowners some centuries ago, the Cossacks were gradually co-opted into the state structure and became a special, privileged community in Tsarist Russia. There were thirteen Cossack *voisko* (armies) on Russia's periphery, mainly in southern areas (Don, Kuban, Terek, and others), but also in Siberia, the Far East, and Kazakh steppes. The term *voisko* could be misleading in translation, however; each *voisko* was a large agricultural area inhabited by Cossack peasants who cultivated some of the best, most fertile land in Russia. Male Cossacks, while not different from ordinary peasants in peacetime, constituted a special army elite formation. They were generally regarded as irregulars, although the term is doubtful in this case: the Cossacks did regular military service, mostly in the cavalry, and were instantly mobilized in wartime. A highly respected and privileged military elite, the Cossacks, notorious for their redoubtable professional skill, courage, and unbounded loyalty to the throne, possessed a formidable esprit de corps and a manifest superiority complex vis-à-vis the common Russian peasantry. In peacetime, Cossacks served as frontier guards, also taking part in punitive expeditions and repressive actions against "enemies of the monarchy."

The hostility that the conquered mountain peoples felt for Cossacks was thus deep-rooted, and it was amply demonstrated during the civil war that followed the October Revolution. This anti-Cossack feeling was encouraged by the Soviet authorities, since the Cossacks largely fought against the Reds in the civil war. One of the first to suffer was the Terek Cossack *voisko*: the Bolshevik commissars promised to give the Cossack land to the Ingush, who immediately started driving the Cossack population out of their villages; later, they were joined by the Chechens who, too, gladly took part in the deportation and, in some cases, massacre of the Cossacks. More than 70,000 Terek Cossacks were either driven out or killed.

Under the Soviet regime, Cossacks fared ill. Their privileged status as well as the Cossack military formations were abolished, their traditions trampled down, their pride humiliated. It is only after the fall of Communism in Russia that a revival of the Cossack community began. Their *voiskos* have by now been restored, led again by their traditional chieftains, the *atamans*, the time-honored

Cossack military uniform drawn out of oblivion. And, inevitably, old disputes and grievances resurfaced. For example, the Terek Cossacks officially claim three administrative districts that had once been a part of the Stavropol province and were later transferred to Chechnya and Daghestan. The reaction of the Chechens and Ingush was predictable; harassment of the Cossacks residing in the disputed areas was reported; hundreds of Cossack families had to leave.

The point is that it is extremely difficult if at all possible to separate the Cossack settlements (*stanitsa*) from Muslim villages, since the areas of residence are wholly intermixed. In the meantime, both sides appear adamant in their demands. To quote an American expert, Jane Ormrod, "In Chechnia and in Daghestan, Terek Cossack populations have threatened to transfer their settlements to the Russian Republic. . . . The Terek Cossacks have declared their support for 'a single united Russia' and 'the widening of Russian boundaries.' In response to the departure of 2,773 ethnic Russians from the Sunzhenskii region of Ingushetia, the Terek Cossacks announced their intention to establish a new settlement (*stanitsa*) in the territory. Vocal pro-Russian sentiments and aggressive actions serve to draw the Cossacks further into conflict with the neighboring North Caucasian groups."[2]

After a temporary eclipse under the Soviet regime, a resurrection of Cossackdom is in progress, fraught with grave dangers in the Caucasus.

THE CHECHEN TRAGEDY

Of all the conflicts in the former Soviet Union, the Chechen war has been the most prominent in world media. Not that it was the bloodiest of the post-Soviet conflicts; the civil war in Tajikistan, for instance, claimed more victims. But it has been, so far, the only one where the Russian army has been openly and directly involved.

The Chechnya tragedy can hardly be called an ethnic conflict, at least not in the way ethnic conflicts are usually meant to be. It was not a war between rival ethnic groups disputing territory, nor was it a movement of national liberation whereby a small nation tries to break free from a dominant power. At the same time, the central question was undoubtedly independence, protection of national sovereignty.

Chechens are an ancient ethnos. By the way, they do not call themselves Chechens; this word was a Russian invention derived from the name of the first conquered settlement. In their native language, this ethnos calls itself Noxcijn, and the name of their republic in Noxcijn Republika Ickeriy (Chechen Republic Ichkeria). Together with their neighbors and half-brothers, Ingush, with whom they lived until recently in a dual Chechen-Ingush Autonomous Republic, they belong to the Vainakh nation. Chechens are Muslims; Islam came to them from neighboring Daghestan in the fifteenth century. Later, Islam in its Sufi variety played a major role in the long saga of Caucasian resistance to the Russian imperial expansion which began at the end of the eighteenth century.

It was in 1785 that the legendary Chechen hero Sheikh Mansur launched his campaign against the advancing Russian forces. Seven years later, his revolt was crushed and some Chechens were deported from their homeland. In the following decades, more Chechens were driven out of their homes after the collapse of two rebellions (1831–1832 and again in 1836–1837). Russian general Yermolov, who began a new drive into Caucasus in 1817, founded the city of Grozny and built a fortified line along the river Sundzha; it was on the banks of this river that Dudayev's fighters made their last stand in Grozny against Yeltsin's troops in January 1995.

A real full-scale war began, however, after Yermolov's death. The Great Caucasian War lingers in the historic memory of both Caucasians and Russians as Shamil's war, after the name of that famous leader of Chechens, Daghestanis, Cherkess, and other North Caucasian peoples, Imam Shamil. He was not a Chechen but an Avar from neighboring Daghestan, but many Chechens to this day believe that he was one of their blood. Shamil became a part of mythology, a great and powerful charismatic leader, a fearless and legendary freedom fighter.

In 1834, Shamil founded an Imamate in Daghestan, and Chechnya joined it six years later. The Imam was an undisputed religious, political, and military leader, a truly mediaeval combination of king and warrior. At times, his forces counted as many as 25,000 armed men. To defeat Shamil, Russia had to send to the Caucasus an army of almost 200,000 strong. It was only in 1859 that Shamil was forced to surrender. Chechnya was finally conquered, although the Cherkess continued the struggle until 1864. A large-scale deportation of Caucasian highlanders, including the Chechens, followed Shamil's defeat; this time, people were deported to the Ottoman Empire. One more deportation of Chechens, Avars, and Dargins was carried out in 1878 after a new revolt had been crushed. Finally, in 1913, after the suppression of one more Chechen revolt, thousands of Chechens were deported to Siberia. All these deportations, however, counted for nothing compared to the horrible fate which befell the Chechens and some other Caucasian ethnoses under the Soviet regime.

After the Bolshevik Revolution, Chechnya was initially a part of the short-lived Mountain Republic, then an autonomous district. Finally, Chechen and Ingush autonomous districts were amalgamated in 1934 and a Chechen-Ingush Autonomous Republic was created. A few years later, Hitler attacked the Soviet Union, and in 1942 the North Caucasus was in German hands. After the German army had been driven out of the Caucasus, Stalin decided to punish some Caucasian peoples for their alleged collaboration with the enemy during the occupation. On February 23, 1944, the entire Chechen population was deported to Kazakhstan. Their republic was dissolved and their land given away to new settlers, mostly Russians. "New inhabitants moved into the houses of the deported, others fell into decay. Graveyards and national monuments were destroyed and the names of the collectively punished peoples were deleted from maps, streets, documents, and public memory. It was forbidden to enquire on their fate. . . . All deportees came under severe surveillance, with up to 20 years in labour camps if they left their assigned place of settlement. Wherever they settled, the local population was told that they were bandits, traitors and criminals.''[3] One-quarter of the Chechens died during transportation or deportations. It was only in the late 1950s that the deported people were allowed to return; the nation was officially rehabilitated and the republic restored.

Thus, Chechen history in the last two hundred years has been one of rebellion and punishment, struggles and deportations. Caucasian highlanders have always been known as proud and warlike, the Chechens probably being more so than the others. ''The Chechens are characterized by their aggressive nationalism and strong sense of national identity. As early as the 1960s and 1970s, the Chechen national intelligentsia was active. Its more vocal and nationalist elements called for respect for Chechen ethnic and religious practices, an enhancement of Chechen language education.''[4] Also, the mountain traditions put high premium on family honor, respect for elders, loyalty to the local community, military prowess, honesty, and hospitality. During the Caucasian War, the Russian military invariably regarded Chechens as their most formidable adversaries; truly legendary warriors, they were noted for their fearlessness and contempt for death. A Russian officer in the nineteenth century, asked what he needed to help win a battle in the Caucasus, replied: ''One Chechen.'' At the same time, unwritten tradition demanded of a Chechen man to be able to ensure his family's subsistence by any means, including those that in most countries would be regarded as legally dubious: If unable, for some reason, to earn his living by work in field or town, a Chechen could go for highway robbery. These brigands used to be called *abreki* and were held in high esteem, especially if they robbed the rich in a Robin Hood fashion or successfully defied the authorities. Respect for official law certainly has not been one of the highest priorities on the Chechen society's scale of values. After all, they never had statehood of their own; the state for them has always been something quite alien and hostile, an external force imposed on them by Russia. On the micro-level, however, Chechens have had for centuries a well-organized pattern of local self-rule based on a network of territorial-kinship units called *teip*. Representatives of each *teip* made up *Mekhk-khel*, a kind of supreme council of elders. The *teip* system persists to the present day and, not unlike the caste system in India, plays a major if not officially recognized role in the country's life. Some *teips* and more important and influential than others; a person belonging to a particularly ancient, prestigious, and wealthy *teip* would be certain to command higher respect and have easier access to top positions in every walk of life than his fellow countryman from a smaller and poorer *teip*. There are about one hundred mountain *teips* and more than seventy valley *teips*, the former being regarded as more prestigious and ''pure-blooded''; the standing of highlanders is generally higher than that of valley people.

Chechens as a rule have no dislike for ethnic Russians on a personal level but traditionally despise the Russian authorities. Practically the whole urban population is bilingual, with many village people, especially men, also speaking passable Russian. Ethnic Russians accounted for 22% of the population of the Chechen-Ingush Autonomous Republic estimated at 1,338,023 in 1989; Chechens made up 55%, and Ingush 12%. The density of the population—66 per square kilometer —yields only to the Moscow and St. Petersburg regions. The oil industry has been the main branch of the economy all along, accounting for 80% of the industrial output. Overall, local resources can provide subsistence for just 20% of the population, and this helps explain why, in recent years, one-fifth of the Chechens resided in Russia while more than 100,000 of those living inside the republic had no permanent jobs.

It is against this background that the dramatic events of the last few years have to be analyzed: Chechnya's bid for independence after the collapse of the Soviet regime in the fall of 1991, the emergence of General Dudayev as the first president of the new Republic, the divorce from Ingushetia, the creation of a sovereign Ichkeria and, finally, the Russo-Chechen war in 1994–1996. In breaking out of the Russian Federation, Chechnya has become the only autonomous republic to have done so.

There is a belief in Russia that it is precisely Chechnya's bad luck in having chosen an adventurist warlord as its leader that predetermined the fatal course of later events. This opinion seems superficial. There was no shortage of Afghan war veterans in other republics as well; in fact, the president of the neighboring Ingush Republic, General Aushev, is an even more prestigious figure than Dudayev, a Hero of the Soviet Union (the highest military award). Yet, it is only in Chechnya that a real Third World–type military strongman has emerged. Even so, the total break with Russia and the ensuing war could have been averted. Dudayev was no Saddam; though undoubtedly quite ambitious and power-hungry, he could hardly be called a mad fascist dictator bent on war, aggression, and destruction. Obviously, some deeper causes of the tragedy have to be found and, on reflection, it seems that, unfortunately, it can be seen as a logical, if crazy, consequence of the interrelation of totally rational objective factors. Dudayev's figure was incidental; the underlying issues are crucial for understanding the problem.

On the Chechen side, two issues seem to be of major importance. The first is rooted in the Chechen mentality which combines a fierce spirit of independence and a surprisingly strong penchant for enterpreneurial activity, mostly of a not-quite-legal variety. The former, shared by the other Caucasian highlanders, can be traced back to an age-long pattern of virtually autonomous community life without any overall state authority; it has been strengthened by the bitter memories of prolonged suffering at the hand of the Russians. The latter is more difficult to comprehend; most probably, it has to do with the scarcity of resources, the poverty and unemployment which for decades has been driving Chechens to Russia in the search of means for survival.

Chechnya has never been able to provide the population of one million with jobs. One or two hundred thousand of them have always been looking for jobs all over Russia. Seasonal teams of builders working on the side, as well as middlemen in deals travelled from Kamchatka to the Baltics and found refuge there. A Russian author wrote: "Once I heard an old woman's tale about a geologist walking through the taiga forest thinking he was the first man there. But then he hears the hammer click to see a Chechen completing a shed. An American landed on the moon and said: 'How do you do!' This greeting is in keeping with the Chechen phrase: 'Is it hard for you here?' The Chechen crawls out of the crater and says: 'It is hard but one can keep going.' This is how people described the habit of a Chechen to wander aimlessly, be 'everywhere,' earn his living throughout the world."[5]

While many of the newcomers found jobs in legitimate spheres of the economy, more and more young people became involved in black market and shadow business networks. Then, after the collapse of Communism, followed by disorder and a total economic mess, fabulous opportunities opened up for unscrupulous operators in a chaotic money market. In Moscow and other major cities, a powerful Chechen Mafia shaped up.

While it would be grossly unfair to depict Chechens as a gangster nation, it is a fact that their share in criminal activities in Russia has by far exceeded their proportion in the population. According to official data, one of every three people charged with counterfeiting has been a former resident of Chechnya, as well as 42% of the persons involved in embezzlement and machinations in the sphere of finances and credit operations. The protection racket was thriving, murders and kidnappings became a regular feature of life; of course, Chechens were far from representing the main body of criminals; lots of various mafiosi groups have been active as well, but somehow Chechens were the most conspicuous. A Moscow acquaintance of mine, owner of an auto repair shop dealing with BMW cars, told me in 1993 that about 60% of his clients belonged to Chechen Mafia, most of their cars having been smuggled from Germany.

While Chechen mafiosi in Moscow have been largely indifferent to politics and could not care less about Dudayev, they had strong links to powerful *teips* in the home country and, according to press, were smuggling billions of roubles to Chechnya using forged documents and lavishly bribing Moscow bank officials. Taking advantage of the economic near-anarchy in Russia, Dudayev's entourage rushed into business in a big way, trading in arms and oil products, privatizing wealthy neighborhoods in Grozny. Profitable spheres of Chechnya's economy came to be controlled by clans; the most powerful *teips* virtually appropriated the oil industry.

Oil may be called the second major issue determining the formation and viability of the Dudayev regime. By 1980, Chechnya produced 7.4 million tons of crude a year but its refining capacity was 20 million tons, so crude oil was usually transported from Russia, mainly from western Siberia, for processing. After independence, oil deliveries from Russia continued until November 1992, but in the absence of any real control it became possible for local businessmen to export both oil and oil products, thus earning handsome profits. In addition to oil, a new, fabulously lucrative business was fast spreading, namely, "shuttle flights" to foreign countries. The "flying merchants" in Chechnya, just as in Russia, have been called "shuttles." It was reported that every passenger in this category, on boarding the plane, had on the average as much as $10,000 in cash, and on the return flight the plane was packed with goods; the monthly profit of all the "shuttles" was estimated at $40 million, or 40% of Chechnya's yearly budget.[6] According to 1993 statistics, Grozny boasted of more luxury cars per capita than Moscow or St. Petersburg. Thus, powerful vested interests in possession of immense sums of money were directly interested in the existence of the Dudayev regime.

It appears, therefore, that it is this peculiar and paradoxical combination of love for freedom and the newly acquired enterpreneurial talent as a basis for the rapid growth of (largely illegal) business that can, at least to a degree, explain the Chechens' stubborn resistance to the restoration of their former status as an autonomous province of Russia. It is the convergence of both factors that has made Chechnya distinct from the other autonomous republics within the framework of the Russian Federation. Chechnya's neighbors in the North Caucasus may be no less freedom-loving than the Chechens but they lack a socioeconomic base for independent statehood. Also, the Chechen military tradition of adamant resistance to Russian domination is probably stronger and more deep-rooted than that of the neighboring ethnoses.

Could Chechnya really stay independent? From the juridical point of view the answer would seem to be an unequivocal yes. Even under the old Soviet constitution the difference between Union and autonomous republics consisted mainly in the former's right of secession due to their having a common border with foreign states; of course, it was just a theoretical possibility. Anyway, Chechnya after 1991 had a common border with a foreign state, namely Georgia. Chechens could ask a perfectly legitimate question: "If, for instance, Turkmens or Azerbaijanis are entitled to a sovereign state of their own, why should we be deprived of this right? In what way are we inferior to them?" Indeed, the historical fate of most nations of the former empire's southern tier was largely identical; as to geographical proximity, it was not a vital issue. Economically, of course, Chechnya could hardly survive without Russia, but this applies to most other republics, too.

The official Russian argument that if Chechnya were allowed to secede other autonomous republics would automatically follow suit does not hold water. The most dangerous moment for the existence of the Russian Federation was in 1991–1992, right after the disintegration of the USSR. Especially disquieting were Tatar nationalists. The storm passed, and by 1994 there was no sign that any of the republics was eager to imitate Chechnya.

With the passage of time, the economic situation in the breakaway republic was steadily deteriorating. The Grozny oil refinery was working at 50–60% capacity as early as 1993; the slump of production made 80%. There were 200,000 unemployed in the republic with a population of one million. There were districts where the unemployment rate was 80–90%. The regime's popularity plummeted while the opposition led by Dudayev's former lieutenants was growing in strength. Many observers believe that it was possible to stifle the Chechen gangsterland by economic measures.

What tipped the scales in favor of war was Moscow's irritation at its own inability to topple Dudayev by proxy, acting through the opposition. Now, the question arises: Why was it necessary for the Kremlin to try to put an end to Chechnya's independence in the first place?

Economic considerations played a certain part but not inasmuch as Chechnya's proper economy was concerned. The oil extraction in the republic accounted for less than 1.5% of Russia's total output. What was of genuine concern to Moscow was the railway linking Russia to Daghestan, its farthest-located republic, and from there to Azerbaijan. According to the Russian Interior Ministry, during the first eight months of 1994 about 2,000 goods wagons were pillaged on the Chechen territory, with loss of more than 11 billion roubles. The authorities had to close that part of the railway line altogether. Probably even more important was the issue of the potential pipeline which would link the newly found Azerbaijani oil fields to Black Sea terminals. The Russian company Lukoil had a stake in the exploitation of the new oil fields and was anticipating huge returns. The pipeline had to cross Chechnya's territory.

Yet, it was the political dimension that eventually presented a rationale for the decision to invade Chechnya. From the very beginning, Moscow leadership has been unhappy about Chechnya's successful bid for independence. It has been a flaw in the pattern. As soon as Dudayev was elected president and declared Chechnya a sovereign state, Yeltsin proclaimed a state of emergency in the republic and sent in paratroopers who were quickly surrounded by local militia and then had to be ignominiously flown back. This was in the fall of 1991, a preview of things to come: a rag-tag band of poorly armed volunteers, without a shot being fired, had inflicted a defeat on the armed forces of Russia; the Russian military have been smarting ever since. But on the whole, Yeltsin's government had more serious things to attend to in the next two years, and the Chechnya situation was put on hold. Moreover, as the Russian army withdrew from Chechnya by mid-1992, huge quantities of arms were left behind, including 108 armored vehicles, 590 anti-tank rockets, 153 artillery pieces, 41,538 rifles and machine guns.[7] It has been proved by now, however, that about three-quarters of these weapons had simply been stolen by Chechens by the time the last Russian units left the area. As to the arms that were left behind, 50% of them had to be returned to Russia according to an agreement concluded between Dudayev and General Grachev, the Russian Defense Minister. Nothing ever came out of it, and when, two years later, Russian forces moved in, they were shot at with the very Soviet arms the Chechens had appropriated as the result of the negligence of the Russian high command. Some sources indicate, however, that a sizable share of the military equipment had not so much been stolen or just left behind as bought by Chechens from local Russian commanders only too willing to give them to Dudayev's men in exchange for hard currency.

Things came to a head in 1994. By that time, many of Dudayev's companions had deserted him and established bases of their own outside Grozny. So-called "liberated zones" were created, a Provisional Council was formed which, on August 1, issued a decree removing Dudayev from office. Of course, all these actions had no practical effect, and only strengthened Dudayev's resolve to hold on to power, if only to avoid a certain punishment in the case of defeat. Actually, Dudayev, by the fall of 1994, seemed to be on his last legs. He was saved by his enemies' ineptitude.

The majority of the Chechens, while thoroughly disillusioned by Dudayev, did not feel terribly enthusiastic about the opposition, either. Certainly, very few people were committed to a real civil war. Tradition forbids Chechens to kill each other; moreover, it legitimizes vendetta in the cases when one Chechen is murdered by another, so everybody knew that blood vengeance on the part of the victim's relatives would be unavoidable should killings occur, even if they were politically motivated. In fact, one of the opposition leaders, Labazanov, swore merciless vengeance to Dudayev precisely because his brother had been killed, allegedly at the president's orders.

The opposition was divided; two of its best-known leaders, Avturkhanov and Labazanov, were highly apprehensive about the sudden emergence from no-where of Ruslan Khasbulatov, a former speaker of the Russian parliament. Just back from a Moscow prison where he had been jailed after his defeat in the historic confrontation between President Yeltsin and parliament, Khasbulatov, an ethnic Chechen, now out of the Moscow political scene, appeared ready to assume the role of savior of his home country while, for tactical reasons, joining hands with the opposition leaders. By far the more intelligent of the whole lot, Khasbulatov favored a political solution, proposing to outmaneuver Dudayev and eventually edge him out of power. But this was precisely what the opposition leaders were reluctant to do, probably suspecting that in this scenario it would almost certainly be Khasbulatov who would come out on top.

In the summer of 1994, Avturkhanov and his friends approached the reformed Russian KGB and probably told them that everything was ready for Dudayev's ouster and all that was needed was a swift military push. They were sure it would be a walkover but they still needed tanks and planes. Money and arms were given to them in quite sufficient quantities; the problem was that the opposition had neither pilots nor tank crews. It was at this juncture that an unfortunate decision was made (it is not clear whether Yeltsin himself was involved at that stage) to commit several dozens of Russian "volunteers."

This was a critical and decisive mistake. Once military planes appeared over Grozny, just for reconnaissance purposes, the populace immediately realized that Russia had become involved in the confrontation, because everybody knew that the opposition had neither planes nor pilots. Worse was to follow: After a humiliating collapse of the ill-planned and badly executed attack of the opposition forces on Grozny on November 26, captured Russian tank crews were paraded on the streets for all to see. From this moment on, for most Chechens the power struggle between Dudayev and the opposition was transformed into a patriotic war between independent Chechnya and imperialist Russia. And when, a few weeks later, the Russian army openly moved into Chechnya, Dudayev, who had called for resistance, became overnight a national hero. As to the opposition, it virtually vanished. Now, it was a war against the same invaders who have been killing and deporting Chechens for two centuries.

What were Yeltsin's reasons for this fateful decision? The most compelling of them seems to be his intention to capture the Russian public apparently swayed by the wave of nationalism which had been so vividly demonstrated during the parliamentary elections of December 1993. Zhirinovsky's success coupled with a drastic decline of the president's popularity, as evidenced by numerous polls, clearly prompted Yeltsin to commit himself to the new nationalist line; it was necessary to show that he was no less concerned about Russia's territorial integrity and grandeur than "the patriots." Also, a swift and victorious military campaign is always helpful for an embattled leader. Lastly, Yeltsin seemed to feel that his forceful action would enjoy a wholehearted support of the Russian population, biased as it was against the ubiquitous Chechen Mafia.

Yeltsin certainly did not anticipate that the military operation, instead of being a glorious *blitzkrieg*, would turn out to be a humiliating disaster. He was obviously misinformed and misled by his military and intelligence chiefs. As Jim Hoagland put it, "Yeltsin has been the victim of any military establishment's ability to render any situation FUBAR—a military acronym gently translated as Fouled Up Beyond All Recognition."[8] Later on, he tried, with mixed success, to cut his losses.

The often expressed fears of a new, large-scale war in the whole area of the North Caucasus have proved groundless. The solidarity with Chechens has not been translated into an anti-Russian revolt, one of the reasons being that the people of most republics making up the Russian Federation have reluctantly come to the conclusion that, their contempt for the Elder Brother notwithstanding, the economic hardships they were experiencing have made it imperative to continue an uneasy but unavoidable coexistence.

NOTES

1. Michael Ignatieff, "Warlords Rule in a Hobbesian World," *The Observer*, April 4, 1993, 21.

2. Jane Ormrod, "The North Caucasus: Fragmentation or Federation?," in *Nations and Politics in the Soviet Successor States*, ed. Ian Bremmer and Ray Taras (New York: Cambridge University Press, 1993), 468.

3. Helen Krag and Lars Funch, *The North Caucasus: Minorities at the Crossroads* (Minorities Rights Group, 1994), 13.

4. Jane Ormrod, "The North Caucasus," 456.

5. Ninel Loginova, "The Billiards of Dzhokhar Dudayev," *Moscow News Weekly*, no. 50 (1992), 8.

6. Lev Arkadiev, "V Groznom rasporiazhalis bandity i ugolovniki" (Gangsters and felons were calling the Shots in Grozny), *Segodnia*, December 22, 1994.

7. "Chechenski uzel: na poroghe voiny?" (The Chechen Knot: On the Eve of War?), *Izvestia*, December 3, 1994.

8. Jim Hoagland, "Yeltsin's Chechnya Gunmen," *Washington Post*, February 7, 1995.

5

Central Asia

A new area has emerged in the world—Central Asia. It seems paradoxical, since Central Asia is actually one of the world's oldest inhabited areas and home to an ancient and highly developed civilization. And yet, until recently, in the eyes of the world community it was a faraway, godforsaken place of no serious interest to anybody.

The collapse of the Soviet Union has brought about the emergence of new independent states on the ruins of the multinational empire. This process is accompanied by confusion, stresses, and conflicts. Up to now, Central Asia has been neither the quietest nor the most restive of the former Soviet territories. What about tomorrow?

TRADITIONAL SOCIETY AND THE SOVIET RULE

The territories of Central Asia were conquered by Russia in the late nineteenth century and became the Empire's backyard. Except for violent uprisings and a protracted guerrilla war in 1920s, it was the least troublesome part of the USSR; it was its colonial periphery, its source of raw materials (primarily cotton); in short, it was the Soviet Third World, lagging behind the industrial center in economic and social development. Traditional patterns of beliefs, lifestyles, behavior, and attitudes toward work successfully resisted Soviet-style modernization. In fact, it is totally incorrect to consider Central Asian societies as Sovietized by Communist rule and the Central Asian peoples as no more than just regular Soviet people speaking Oriental languages. A unique society managed to preserve its identity, although not quite intact.

Resistance was only one side of this relationship, the other side being coexistence. The Communist rule was superimposed on traditional social structures that were sometimes called feudal (though there has never been true feudalism in Central Asia). Communism and traditional society proved to be quite compatible, since both have an authoritarian base. Central Asian scholar Boris Rumer maintains that clan and tribal consciousness "not only survived but [became] even stronger in the Soviet era. . . . A majority of the national cadres remain[ed] loyal to their clan and tribe."[1]

Central Asia's client-patron relationships persisted from generation to generation and its clan and communal group mentality fit easily into a Soviet system built on the absolute rule of omnipotent Party first secretaries. In every locality there was only one official worth talking to, one man who decided everything— the Party first secretary. In Central Asia the first secretary also symbolized and took the place of the traditional clan leader; he was the local chieftain and all-powerful patron, a Godfather figure lording it over an entrenched network that often resembled the corporative structures of the Mafia. Loyalty to him was paramount, and hardly related to Communist ideology.

The native *nomenclatura* played a dual role: first, party and state officials were Communist apparatchiks just like their colleagues in Moscow, Leningrad, or Kiev; and second, they were traditional local bosses and patrons. Thus, their system of rule was vertical, and they always had the valuable feedback from the grass roots, allowing them to gauge the mood of the populace. This is why they, unlike their counterparts in Russia, have retained their positions after the collapse of the Soviet system.

These elites held sway over a society that was predominantly Muslim. Of course, within atheistic Soviet ideology, Islam was, if not banned, at least not encouraged. But people knew they were Muslims, and observed religious practices such as circumcision, marriage, and funeral rituals. They had a rudimentary knowledge of the basic tenets of Islam; some performed their prayers and respected the region's few mosques and mullahs.

With independence came an inevitable religious revival. Overnight, Islam became a common denominator, a powerful vehicle (alongside ethnicity) for asserting identity. People instinctively felt it was Islam—which, of course, is not just a set of religious beliefs but a way of life and a civilization—that made them different from the Russians, whose rule they had never accepted as legitimate. Now openly proclaiming themselves Muslims and asserting their Islamic identity, they have found at last what makes them a community distinct from all the others.

Before the Bolshevik Revolution, ethnicity was not a reference point for Central Asian communities, which historically were divided not along ethnolinguistic lines but by their sedentary or pastoral origins. For centuries, sedentary, land-cultivating peoples lived in this huge area side-by-side with nomads, the main language of the former being Persian (Farsi) and of the latter, dialects of Turkic languages. The sedentary civilization was mainly concentrated in the great cities of commerce—Samarkand, Bukhara, Khojent, Tashkent, Kokand; Farsi was the language of culture throughout the area (one of its local variants is Tajiki). At some time, before the Bolshevik Revolution, literate Uzbeks even used to speak Farsi at home. All in all, it was a multiethnic region with a common Muslim culture and with two classical written languages—Farsi and, to a lesser extent, Chagatay Turki. This Chagatay language that some scholars call Old Uzbek, was the foundation of the modern Uzbek (which also has the Kipchak dialect).

Farsi has never been the language of just one ethnic community but rather a universal language of Islam culture and civilization, a Central Asian lingua franca. Local Muslims were divided, first, by the pattern of life and occupation, and second, by the place of residence. For the Russian Tsarist government, "religion formed the basis for distinguishing natives from infidels. . . . The term 'nationality' in its modern meaning did not exist in this period."[2] The oases identities were of primary importance. People were Samarkandis or Tashkentis but not Uzbeks or Tajiks. History never knew such state formations as Uzbekistan, Tajikistan, or Turkmenistan. As late as 1921, people, when asked about their nationality, answered: "Muslim."

Under the Soviet regime, this unique and quite viable polyethnic community was torn to pieces and replaced by a completely new setup based on the quasi-scientific Stalinist theory of nations and on a typically Bolshevik, rigid hierarchy of Union and autonomous republics, *oblasts*, and *okrugs*. A rich Islam-based civilization was smashed by the Stalinist hammer forging new, ethnic nations. The Soviet regime, having discarded religion as an identity factor, made the national-linguistic issue the cornerstone of its neoimperial policy. New political units were created based on nationality, which was rigidly linked to the issue of territory. The republics created in this manner were formed around a "core" nationality, which was the largest or the dominant ethnic group in an area. The jewels of the old civilization, the famous cities Bukhara and Samarkand, ended up in Uzbekistan, although even now the majority of the population there seem to be Tajiks, many of them registered in their passports as Uzbeks. On my recent visit there, I heard only Tajik and Russian.

True, inhabitants of Samarkand or Bukhara, and Northern Tajiks in general, do not care about language or ethnic origins. Had history gone in a different direction, Uzbeks and Northern Tajiks, people of a common civilization and—or so it seemed—common destiny, could have merged into a single community or nation. The time for this, however, is lost.

Interethnic relations in Central Asia are not exactly smooth or harmonious. Traditionally, there has been an ethnic hierarchy of sorts in the region. Tajiks, of course, are acknowledged as the people with the oldest and richest culture; they represent the largest non-Turkic Muslim community in Central Asia. Turkmens are considered by both Tajiks and Uzbeks to be seminomadic, and much less cultured. The Kazakhs and Kyrgyz are looked on by other Central Asians as gruff nomads only recently converted to Islam. Particularly bad are relations between Uzbeks and Kyrgyz; one need only recall the bloody massacres in the largely Uzbek city of Osh in Kyrgyzstan in 1990. The most dangerous conflict of the region, however, may flare up between Uzbeks and Tajiks, largely because of the issue of Bukhara and Samarkand, but also as a result of a certain turn in the Tajik civil war.

Many an observer believes that because ethnicity is a divisive rather than a unifying force, only religion can bring the Central Asian nations together. The newly formed Islamic political parties in the region tend to play down identification with ethnic groups and nationality, stressing the irrelevance of these. And the idea of creating an Islamic commonwealth is gaining ground in certain Muslim quarters that are anxious to put an end to ethnicity-based nationhood. It may be too late. Ethnicity was given a tremendous boost by the Soviet regime: ethnic identity was enshrined as nationality, and areas that had been bilingual and nonethnic were split up into separate nation-states. The consolidation of the nation-states appears to be the most likely scenario in Central Asia. The emergence of a Greater Turkestan or an Islamic community in the area does not look like a realistic proposition.

But even if the present boundaries of the Central Asian countries remain unchanged, interethnic conflicts cannot be ruled out. And Uzbekistan is likely to be at the center of these conflicts, since the Uzbeks are the most powerful and dynamic people in the area. Uzbek assertiveness is a source of anxiety for neighboring states.

The situation in Central Asia is unique, since people look for and assert their identity in terms of both ethnicity and religion. The countries of the area have no traditions of statehood whatsoever and rather feeble religious traditions. The role of Islam has been exaggerated and overestimated by some Western writers and scholars even after the collapse of the Soviet Union. The term "Muslim republics" has often been used, and there has been talk of an imminent emergence of "Islamic republics."

In fact, there are different facets of Islam in Central Asia. A strong, deep-rooted, though rather vague, feeling of belonging to a Muslim community can be sensed practically everywhere in the area. Interest in Muslim countries is undeniable. It is becoming customary for the young people to emphasize their "Muslimness." In some cases, however, there seems to be an element of something artificial about it all, or possibly of a reaction to the old times when religion was all but banned. This applies particularly to the young, while elder people seem to be genuinely religious, although ignorant about Islam. It appears that, for the majority in this "new Muslim world," Islam has not become—so far, at least—what it is in the "old," traditional Muslim world: a set of beliefs presenting a wholesome, total, comprehensive, and all-encompassing view of the world; a way of life and a key to human behavior. Rather, it can be regarded as a means of asserting identity.

Not all of the Central Asian peoples can be said to be in search of identity. The inhabitants of valleys and oases, agriculturalists, merchants, and artisans had always had an identity. When the Russians came, later to be replaced by Soviet Russians, what separated the natives from those alien intruders was locality identification first, culture second, religion third. Or, probably, it would be better to say that culture and Islam were inseparable. Linguistic ethnicity was not an issue. It is precisely the culture based on Islam and defining a distinct identity that was being destroyed under the Soviet regime. But the second layer of identity remained—the locality identification; local consciousness which in practice meant largely clan and tribal consciousness. This lowest level of identity/loyalty became the only one that could survive the onslaught of Bolshevism. It was there, at clan and kinship level, that the preservation of identity became possible, thus compensating, at least partially, for the demise of the larger, Islamic and cultural identity.

Usually, nations or ethnic groups that have had to submit to foreign invaders have found a point of resistance to assimilation and loss of identity in sticking to their religion, or cultural-linguistic community, or both. Suffice it to recall the history of Greeks and Bulgars enslaved by the Turks, or Poles under the Russian and German rule, or Czechs threatened by Germanization. In Central Asia, communities which are now being called Uzbek, Tajik, and Turkmen nations had neither the Church nor ethnolinguistic unity to protect their identity. This was achieved, nevertheless, by clinging to the only remaining bulwark—clan and tribal identity. Islam, of course, was also part of this identity. It was not eradicated; it stayed throughout, somewhere in the background of the clan-kinship mentality, adding to it, enlarging and ennobling it. Without the Islamic element—vague and distant but ever present—family, clan, locality would have been the only reference points of identity. Islam was something bigger; it was transcendental, a symbol of higher authenticity. And, of course, Islam was not so severely and brutally persecuted in the Soviet Union as was Christianity.

What we see now in Central Asia is a rather complex interplay of three different factors of identity: (1) local, parochial, clan loyalties; (2) Islamic-civilizational identity; and (3) ethnic nationalism. Of the three, the first is the most solid and deep-rooted, having survived both the Tsarist and Communist rule; the second is more fragile, likely to be overshadowed by the two others, especially by the rise of ethnic nationalism—a completely new phenomenon, a product of the Soviet era, but already possessing a powerful momentum of its own. This is not to say that the Islamic factor is totally unlikely to surge up. Deterioration of the economic situation, coupled with the impossibility of venting popular frustration through legitimate opposition channels can make Islamism the only pattern of revolt against the authority in Uzbekistan and Tajikistan. Turkmenistan with its neo-Stalinist regime and stable economy seems to be the only country immune to this scenario.

As to ethnic nationalism, purely ethnic hatred is hard to detect in Central Asia, except for the ugly mood in the relationships between the Uzbeks and Kyrgyz in the bordering area. But ominous signs of deterioration of relations between Uzbeks and Tajiks have already been in evidence due to Uzbekistan's role in the Tajik civil war. This role is largely regarded by Tajiks as a direct intervention pointing at Tashkent's hegemonic trends.

As the overwhelming majority of the area's population are Sunni Muslims, intercommunal feud on religious ground can be effectively ruled out. The deadliest scenario would be a combination of ethnic or communal rivalry with Islamic extremism. This is what has happened in Tajikistan. Neither Islam nor ethnicity has had anything to do with the outbreak of the Tajik civil war, although Islamists have been a component part of one of the rival coalitions. Then, as the conflict intensified, Islam did become a factor. Islamic slogans greatly facilitated the mobilization of large sections of the population which had been concerned with quite different issues to begin with, but later found it psychologically much easier to justify their hostility for the opponents by appealing to basic, fundamental values.

In Kazakhstan and Kyrgyzstan neither purely ethnic nor Islamic nationalism is likely to play any serious role in potential upheavals. What is certain to surface there is clan rivalry in the broadest sense of the word, involving class differences (jobs, privileges, spheres of the Mafias' influence, and so on). Ethnicity and Islam would, in this case, mostly be used as propaganda weapons or camouflage of real intentions.

UZBEKS AND TAJIKS

Uzbekistan is the heart of Central Asia—the most populous republic with the strongest economy. Its population numbers about 20 million, with ethnic Uzbeks accounting for approximately 70% and Russians almost 11%. Uzbeks are a people of mixed Turkic-Mongolian origin. In the fifteenth and sixteenth centuries nomad tribes of Mongolian descent came into Maverannahr, inhabited by sedentary Farsi-speaking people, and later formed a new population. As noted earlier, history knew no such things as an Uzbek nation or an Uzbek state; currently, however, the official Uzbek historiography dates Uzbek statehood from the era of Tamerlane, the famous founder of a great empire stretching from Delhi to Damascus. Tamerlane, whose body lies in a magnificent shrine in Samarkand, is increasingly regarded at this point as a great precursor of Uzbek statehood, a kind of Founding Father figure, although he could hardly be called ethnic Uzbek.

The Uzbek Soviet Republic, which preceded today's independent Uzbekistan, was born in the mid-1920s, at the time of the so-called "national delimitation" that, according to the foremost expert in the field, Donald Carlisle, "lumped together within republic borders diverse, sometimes divergent, and certainly different communities. Some groups were declared to be the 'Uzbek nation' and were territorially delimited within the boundaries of an entity called 'Uzbekistan'—which had never previously existed. . . . What took place in 1924–25 was political engineering and boundary delineation, not national delimitation. In 1925, Uzbek national consciousness did not exist, and the process of national consolidation had barely begun.''[3] By that time, the three major Khanates into which Central Asia had been divided—Kokand, Khiva and Bukhara—were liquidated, and in their place, Turkestan Autonomous Soviet Republic was set up in 1922 as a part of the Russian Federation which was itself part of the USSR. It was two years later that the "delimitation" followed (actually, the title of the Politbureau resolution was "On the National Redistricting of the Republics of Central Asia"). The Uzbek and Turkmen Soviet Socialist Republics were formed as well as the Kyrgyz Autonomous Republic and the Karakyrgyz Autonomous Oblast, the two latter as parts of the Russian Federation. As Gregory Gleason notes,

ethnic Uzbeks fared very well in the division of land in the original districting of Central Asia. They captured the most agriculturally productive region in Central Asia, the Fergana valley. In addition, they gained the watersheds and the associated agricultural areas of the Chirchik river (which runs through Tashkent), the Zerabshan river (which runs through both Samarkand and Bukhara) and the Surkhan-Doria. . . . The big losers in the division were the Tajiks and Kyrgyz.[4]

Later the Uzbeks increased their share of the minority group by gradually accumulating the Turkic-speaking tribal groups and assimilating them into the Uzbek ethnos. At present, Uzbeks in Central Asia number close to 20 million people, the largest population of any republic except Russia and Ukraine. They have the second highest birth rate in the former Soviet Union. Uzbeks account for 23% of the population of Tajikistan, 13% of Kyrgyzstan, and 9% of Turkmenistan. However artificial its creation had been, the existence of an Uzbek nation, very much aware of its identity, is not in dispute. This is not the case with Tajiks, although they are a people with an ancient and rich culture. Tajiks, as Barnett Rubin notes, "had never ruled an empire or identified themselves as a group. The centers of Persian-speaking culture in Central Asia, Bukhara and Samarkand, had been ruled by Turkic dynasties, and their inhabitants had never called themselves 'Tajiks,' a term mainly applied to mountain-dwelling peasants."[5] Before the Bolshevik Revolution, the word "Tajik" meant Persian-speaking Sunni Muslim living in the southern mountains. Even now, the overwhelming majority of the Tajiks inhabiting Tajikistan are those who live in the mountainous villages and their progeny who had moved to other areas of the republic. Centuries ago, their ancestry did not even speak Tajik Farsi, which is a western Iranian language; they spoke eastern Iranian languages—Yaghnobi and Pamiri. Farsi replaced those idioms much later, and even now some, not very numerous, ethnic groups in the mountainous areas retain their ancient languages.

The mountainous Tajiks, the majority of whom at present speak Tajiki Farsi, are what the Russian expert Yuri Kobishchanov calls "peripheral Tajiks," as opposed to "central Tajiks" who inhabit both the northern plains of Tajikistan (Fergana, Zerashan, and Gissar) and the adjoining regions of Uzbekistan.

Strange as it seems, those ethnic Tajiks who live in Uzbekistan (more than one million) outnumber their compatriots—"central" Tajiks inhabiting Tajikistan— by four to one. The main cities inhabited by the "central Tajiks" are Bukhara and Samarkand in Uzbekistan and Khojent (former Leninabad) in Tajikistan. As noted earlier, those Tajiks virtually belong to the same community and to the same sedentary Islamic civilization as "central" Uzbeks. They live side by side, mostly bilingual people, in those big historic cities as well as in the countryside. Ethnic Uzbeks make up about one-fourth of Tajikistan's population. In Khojent and Kurgan Tyube areas Uzbeks constitute more than 31% of the population, in Gissar about 45%. In Tursun Zade region almost 60% of the inhabitants are ethnic Uzbeks. Less clear is the number of ethnic Tajiks in Uzbekistan. The official figure is about 5% of the population, but some unofficial estimates put the Tajik population of the republic at 3 million at least, or almost 15%.[6] The discrepancy in figures is not due to any mystery. The point is that many ethnic Tajiks (although nobody knows just how many) voluntarily listed themselves as Uzbeks in their internal passports. I recall being driven once from Tashkent to Samarkand by a local journalist; by the end of our night's journey, after a long and friendly talk, the man admitted that he, a born Samarkandi, was actually a Tajik. "If I had not registered myself as an Uzbek," he told me, "it would have been rather difficult for me to make a really successful career in Uzbekistan."

According to the 1920 census, ethnic Uzbeks constituted just 4% of the population of Bukhara. The share of Tajiks in the population of Bukhara and Samarkand was estimated at about 75%. The well-known French expert Olivier Roy describes what happened later:

When Tajikistan was created by Stalin, the historical "Tajik" cultural centers, Samarkand and Bukhara, were not included in Tajikistan; the small city of Dushanbe . . . was artificially promoted Capital of the Republic. Few of the traditional persian-speaking intellectuals and "*litterati*" left Samarkand and Bukhara for Dushanbe. . . . By depriving Tajikistan of its cultural capitals, Stalin has undermined the building of a Tajik intelligentsia; today, Dushanbe's university is still far behind Tashkent. Finally, the birth of the Soviet Republic of Tajikistan was painful: the present Tajikistan was first divided into the Soviet Republic of Turkestan (created in 1918) and the Soviet Republic of Bukhara (1920); in 1924, Tajikistan was established as an Autonomous Region of the new Republic of Uzbekistan, then as an Autonomous Republic still included in Uzbekistan (1925); it has been upgraded to a full Soviet Socialist Republic only in 1929.[7]

Eden Naby notes that, in Bukhara and Samarkand under the Soviet rule, "the tendency has been to force Uzbek identities upon the population. In a campaign led by the first Tajik association to exist in the contemporary period, 35,000 Uzbeks reregistered as Tajiks in Samarkand within one month in 1991."[8]

Another problem, already mentioned, is that of the Pamiri highlanders, the peoples inhabiting the Western Pamir (the autonomous region of Gorno-

Badakhshan) and speaking eastern Iranian languages distinct from Tajik. Unlike other Tajiks, who are Sunni Muslims, the Pamiris are Ismailis, followers of the Ismaili sect headed by the Agha Khan. The official policy of the Tajik Soviet authorities denied the Pamiris the right to ethnic identity; efforts were made to assimilate them. Most observers have noted that there is no love lost between plainsmen (the "central Tajiks" of the north) and "peripheral" Pamiri highlanders. Many of the former regard the latter as little more than savages, due to their cultural and religious characteristics. Certainly, there is no feeling of belonging to the same nation; this is an important difference between Tajiks and Uzbeks.

The less than friendly feelings between different Tajik groups were exacerbated by the transfer of a large number of highlanders to the plains in the late 1940s and early 1950s. It was done in order to bring additional labor force to Kurgan Tyube area where great expansion of cotton farming was planned. As noted earlier, about one-third of that region population were ethnic Uzbeks. The newcomers were not Pamiris but people from Gharm and other mountainous areas. "The new settlers lived in their own villages within mixed *kolkhozes*. Rather than integrating with the local population (including local Tajiks), these settlers became a separate subethnic group, called 'Gharmis' by their neighbours."[9] It was precisely here that some of the first shots in the Tajik civil war were to be fired later. People outside Tajikistan were wondering what was going on: peasants from one *kolkhoz* were murdering their neighbor peasants. The point was that the old dislike for the outsiders, the newcomers, flared up as the central authority disintegrated. This phenomenon is by no means exceptional; suffice it to recall, for example, the bitter feud between the indigenous population of West Pakistan and the *muhadjirin*, Muslims who had fled from India at the time of the subcontinent's partition.

The situation in the Vakhsh valley, where the Kurgan Tyube region is located, was further complicated by the fact that some of the people who had been transferred to the area many years ago along with the Gharmis were peasants from Kulab area, with a traditional plainsmen's dislike of highlanders. It is also important to note that in the eyes of the Kulabis, the Gharmis represented the hated "commercial Mafia." As soon as the indigenous Kurgan Tyube Tajiks and Uzbeks clashed with the Gharmis, the Kulabis joined the former. The Kulabi-Gharmi confrontation rapidly became the focal point of the civil war.

This confrontation, however, was just a manifestation of a deep malaise of the Tajik society bitterly divided along local and clan parochial lines. Under the Soviet regime, there was a traditional system of partition of top rank posts between different local groups. The first secretaries of the Central Party committee in Tajikistan invariably came from Khojent (formerly Leninabad). Also from the North came the president as well as the ministers of agriculture, commerce and economics, while the chairman of the Supreme Soviet and the ministers of the interior, education, and culture were always southerners. The Leninabad province was usually getting amost 60% of all the subsidies that

Tajikistan received from Moscow while Kulab's share did not exceed 6% and Pamir was getting 0.6%.

By the time of the breakup of the Soviet Union, four main clans were clearly distinguishable in Tajikistan: Leninabad (Khojent) in the north; Kulab to the southeast of the capital, Dushanbe; Gharm, a mainly mountainous area around the capital; and Pamir (Gorno Badakhshan) in the east. The Leninabadis, including local ethnic Uzbeks, were the most powerful; in the 1970s, the Kulabis became their clients. And in the civil war, two major coalitions were acting: the first, Khojent-Kulabi faction (known as the "pro-Communist" bloc); the second, Gharm-Pamiri faction (the Islamic-Democratic alliance). The political and ideological affiliations of the two coalitions were rather relative; it would be wrong to suppose that the adherents to the first bloc supported a return to the Communist rule while the people behind the second coalition backed the idea of an Islamic state or a Western-style democracy.

The bulk of the "pro-Communist" coalition consisted, first, of the people who supported the powerful traditional Leninabad *nomenclatura* machine closely linked to both Tashkent and Moscow (including many criminal, Mafia, and lumpen elements), and second, of the rural population of the poor and backward Kulab area, many of whom felt nostalgia for the old Soviet regime and regarded the Gharmis as outsiders, exploiters, and Mafia-style traders. The driving force of the Islamic-Democratic coalition was aptly described by Barnett Rubin as mostly Gharmis and Pamiris who "formed much of the Tajik cultural intelligentsia, which, unlike the party and administration, by definition excluded Uzbeks and Russian-speakers . . . these subethnic groups played disproportionate roles in the nationalist and religious opposition."[10] Thus, virtually all the genuine political parties, which had emerged in the aftermath of independence, spearheaded the Islamic-Democratic alliance that later became known as "the opposition" and lost the civil war. This "unholy alliance" was the result of two different trends which characterized the Tajik intelligentsia. One trend was mainly represented by the Democratic Party of Tajikistan modeled on the democratic movement in Russia and led by Shodmon Yussef, the other by the Islamic Renaissance Party and the *Rastakhiz* (Rebirth) movement. All of these groups drew their support mostly from the Gharmis and Pamiris. In spite of their ideological differences, which really were not unsurmountable since the Islamic leaders never called for an Islamic state or the imposition of Islamic laws (*shari'a*), both groupings managed to unite and put forward a joint candidate for presidential elections in November 1991. This candidate was Davlat Khudonazarov, a movie director born in Pamir, in the Ismaili community. He lost out to the former first secretary of the Communist Party of the Republic Rahmon Nabiev—naturally, a Khojenti.

In the spring of 1992, the opposition called for a mass anti-government meeting in one of the largest squares of the capital, Dushanbe. This meeting, attended largely by Pamiris, Gharmis, and many local dwellers, soon became a permanent event. In another square, mass pro-government meeting was then held in which thousands of Khojentis and Kulabis participated. Armed clashes inevitably began, and the confrontation ended in a victory of the opposition Islamic-Democratic forces which forced President Nabiev to agree to the formation of a coalition government. Soon Nabiev was deposed, but the alliance's victory was destined to be short-lived. Just as the struggle for power reached its climax in the capital, much bloodier events were reported from Kurgan Tyube where armed gangs of both sides started large-scale fighting. It was in Kurgan Tyube, called in a Moscow newspaper headline "a city of the dead," that some of the worst massacres of the Tajik civil war occurred. Most of the massacres were reportedly perpetrated by the infamous Kulabi militia, formed and led by a particularly vicious character named Sangak Safarov. A professional criminal, a convicted murderer who had spent twenty-three years in jail, Sangak was instrumental in creating a political organization embracing the bulk of the "pro-Communist" forces. Called "the People's Front of Tajikistan," it was financed by the Khojenti Mafia-cum-Party *nomenclatura*. The fighting arm of the Front, the Kulabi militia under the awesome Sangak, was reinforced by another gangster force composed of Kurgan Tyube Uzbeks and Tajiks and led by a young mafioso named Faizali Saidov. Yet another "pro-Communist" armed gang made up of both Uzbeks and Kulabi Tajiks was formed in Gissar, closer to the capital. As these militias got the backing of both the Uzbekistan leadership which provided them with weapons and air support, and the Russian 101st motorized division stationed in Tajikistan, the fate of the Islamic-Democratic regime in Dushanbe was sealed.

On December 6, 1992, forces from Gissar broke into Dushanbe and after several days of street fighting captured the capital just as the militias of Sangak and Faizali took control of Kurgan Tyube and, after slaughtering the Gharmis and Pamiris in that region, were sweeping south to Gharm, the hotbed of the Islamic-Democratic movement. Barnett Rubin describes what followed their advance:

They systematically destroyed and looted Gharmi villages. Signs of the ethnic character of the war were visible in June 1993; for example, several houses in Kolkhoz Turkmenistan . . . bore inscriptions such as, "this is an Uzbek house; do not touch." The UN High Commissioner for Refugees estimates that 5,000 houses were destroyed in the two *raions* of Shartuz and Qabadian alone, with a combined population of less than 200,000. As a result of these expulsions, areas already largely Uzbek lost a large portion of their Tajik population, aggravating Tajik nationalist fears of "pan-Turkic" aggression sponsored by Uzbekistan."[11]

Tens of thousands of refugees—Gharmis and Pamiris—fled into Badakhshan and even farther, into Afghanistan.

By that time, yet one more aspect of the civil war became noticeable, namely, the sinister influence of drug dealers selling heroine and marihuana. Afghanistan is now considered to be the second largest region in the world, after Burma, which produces drugs. Badakhshan is also a center of opium cultivation. The narcotics from both Afghanistan and Badakhshan are being transported to Russia. Warlords on both sides have been able to use the drug trade to finance arms purchases and create independent bases of power. There were also reports of fierce competition between drug gangs supporting opposing sides in the war.

The defeated Islamic-Democratic coalition became armed opposition to the new regime led by Imamali Rahmonov and representing an alliance between the two victorious factions, Khojentis and Kulabis. This alliance, however, soon began to crack; the Kulabis, who had been the main fighting force, soon took an upper hand and ended up by controlling the most important positions. Although the militia leaders Sangak (who for a few months had been a real strongman, the most powerful person in the country) and Faizali quarrelled and then killed each other in a typical Mafia shootout, the Kulabis retained control over the military establishment of Tajikistan. This establishment, however, exists only in name; the only real military forces in Tajikistan are Russian troops, including the frontier guards who are busy beating back the ongoing attacks of the opposition guerrillas entrenched in Afghanistan. These guerrillas are at present composed almost exclusively of Islamic *mujaheddin*, which is quite understandable. As soon as the grand opposition alliance was forced out of Tajikistan, the balance of forces inside it inevitably changed. The Democrats have retreated into the background as negotiations with the Rahmonov regime appear to be deadlocked and the idea of a military solution has gained ground. In this situation, armed men have emerged at the forefront, and it is the banner of Islam, not that of democracy, which is best suited to inspire the people calling for revenge.

Unfortunately, there can be no doubt that if the opposition wins the next round of the war, large-scale bloodshed is likely to follow, as the *mujaheddin* will attempt, vendetta-style, to settle the old scores. During the fighting, both sides committed horrible atrocities which, according to journalists, exceeded by far everything that has happened in all the other ethnic conflicts in the former Soviet Union. On the other hand, if the Rahmonov regime, inefficient and corrupt as it is, remains in control without some kind of accommodation with the opposition, the latter is certain to persist in its attempts to overthrow it by force. In these attempts, the opposition can reckon on the growing support from across the border as Afghani Tajik *mujaheddin* are likely to do their best to combat what they regard as the Russian-backed and Uzbek-controlled Communist "infidel" government in Dushanbe. A logical way out of the deadlock appears to be a coalition government; however, Rahmonov and his Kulabi clan currently in charge have every reason to be apprehensive about their fate in that case, and are certain to try to cling to power at any cost. In these circumstances, the future of Tajikistan seems bleak indeed.

One of the worst aspects of the civil war has been the steady worsening of relations between Tajiks and Uzbeks. From the conversations I have had with many Tajiks in Uzbekistan, it became clear that virtually all of them believe that it is Uzbekistan which has made possible the victory of the Rahmonov side, thus ensuring its grip on Tajikistan and trying to transform the republic into an Uzbek protectorate. It can be assumed, therefore, that an opposition victory will greatly increase anti-Uzbek feelings in Tajikistan as native Uzbeks will be declared traitors and stooges of the Tashkent government. Just how dangerous this turn of events could be in a country where ethnic Uzbeks make up almost a quarter of the population is not difficult to imagine.

The growth of anti-Uzbek feeling does not yet mean a deterioration of relations between Tajiks and Uzbeks in everyday life. As noted earlier, both people, belonging to the same ancient civilization, have been quite close throughout centuries. In the city of Namangan, in the Fergana valley, I was invited to a wedding party; an Uzbek boy was marrying a Tajik girl. Both of them, like their parents, were fluent in three languages: Uzbek, Tajiki Farsi, and Russian. The bridegroom told me: "What does it matter that I am Uzbek and she is Tajik? The important thing is that we both are Muslim." As I did not get an impression that the two young people were particularly religious or even knowledgeable about Islam, I believe that what the boy really meant was not so much religion as sense of belonging to a common shared civilization, tradition, and way of life.

So far, ethnic Tajiks residing in Uzbekistan have not been eager to leave for Tajikistan or to demand that Bukhara and Samarkand be made a part of the Tajik republic. They would rather live in a stable Uzbekistan than in their ruined motherland. It can even be questioned whether they regard Tajikistan as their motherland at all; Samarkandi or Bukhari Muslims—this has always been their identity. Ethnolinguistic issues have never been relevant. This feeling can change, though, as a result of a narrowminded nationalism of the Uzbek authorities, some symptoms of which are already visible. For example, on my recent visit to Samarkand I learned that a "linguistic Uzbekization" was in progress. Although I heard only Tajik or Russian in the streets, it appeared that Uzbek had been proclaimed de facto the only official language, and all the administrative paperwork from now on had to be not in Russian but in Uzbek. In practical terms it proved to be extremely embarrassing since officials, even in the case of ethnic Uzbeks, do not master literary Uzbek and have to employ translators from Russian to Uzbek. This is an issue of major irritation to Tajiks for whom Russian has been a neutral and quite acceptable idiom, while the "linguistic Uzbekization" emphasizes the Uzbek character of the state and makes ethnic Tajiks, a clear majority in both Samarkand and Bukhara, feel like aliens in Uzbekistan.

Thus, a potential conflict between the two brotherly ethnic communities cannot be ruled out, and this is the single most dangerous thing that can happen in Central Asia. Some people, sensing the danger, believe that only Islam can prevent the disaster; in their opinion, if religion, and not ethnicity, could become an essence of new identity of both Tajiks and Uzbeks, the menace of an inter-ethnic confrontation would be avoided. As noted in the beginning of this chapter, however, this option seems doubtful. Islam can strengthen the newly found ethnic and state identity vis-à-vis the former Soviet world—an alien, Slavic, Russian world—but it is hardly capable of overcoming the powerful appeal of State nationalism based on ethnicity and to forge a Central Asian community overriding the ethnic differences.

In this context, it is precisely Tajiks who seem the weakest and most vulnerable since, as the civil war has demonstrated, they lack true national self-consciousness on the scale of the republic as a whole. Nor do they even share a common religious affiliation: In Pamir, where the population is Ismaili, not Sunni, not a single mosque can be found. At present, the Pamiri administrative unit, Gorno-Badakhshan, can be regarded as a virtually independent entity not subject to the Dushanbe government control. A truly gigantic effort will be needed to forge a Tajik nation.

TURKMENISTAN AND KYRGYZSTAN

While events in Uzbekistan and Tajikistan have been more or less adequately reported in Western media, the other two Central Asian republics, Turkmenistan and Kyrgyzstan, have never attracted much interest. It is easy to see why: The latter republics are not as important in the geopolitical sense as the former, and developments there are not as dramatic. Turkmenistan is largely renowned for its fabulous reserves of natural gas and a "neo-Stalinist" regime; interest in Kyrgyz affairs is mostly explained by the unusual personality of the young republic's leader, an academic turned politician.

Turkmenia has always been regarded as one of the most backward, culturally underdeveloped areas of the Soviet Union. Having suddenly gained independence—with not a slightest hint of something like national liberation movement—the desert country on the Caspian Sea turned its back on the outside world and started on its own indigenous way of development. President Niyazov's course can by no means be called isolationist; the republic is quite active both on the international scene (in the regional dimension, of course) and in its relations with CIS states. The feeling is, however, that Turkmenistan is not particularly interested in Central Asian cooperation projects and generally does not care much about its neighbors. This attitude is reciprocated; while on a recent visit to Uzbekistan, I was surprised to learn just how little Uzbeks and Tajiks knew and cared about Turkmens, their coreligionists and ethnic cousins. They continue to regard Turkmens as little more than uncouth nomads. As if to compensate for this low stature in the Central Asian ethnic hierarchy, Turkmens can boast of two blessings denied to their neighbors: an amazing political stability and more than just bright economic prospects.

Turkmenistan is the least-populated country in Central Asia—approximately 3.6 million, with ethnic Turkmens estimated at about 2.5 million. The society has been traditionally built around a tribal system. Former nomads, Turkmens have been divided into nine major tribes, the two largest and politically most important being Tekins and Yomuds. It is from these two tribes, particularly from the former, that the Party and managerial elite has always been drawn. At present, President Saparmurad Niyazov, formerly first secretary of the Communist Party in Turkmenistan, is trying to forge a real full-blooded nation out of a tribal conglomerate with no overall national self-consciousness to speak of. Tribal affiliation is being played down. The regime is undoubtedly authoritarian to the extreme if not dictatorial, with Niyazov's personality cult quite grotesque in a typical Oriental way; he has been proclaimed Turkmenbashi, Father of Turkmens, and his pictures are everywhere to be seen; lots of streets and villages have been named after him. On a personal level, Niyazov is a quite genial, thoroughly Russian-educated man; he spent more than eleven years in Russia and has no traits of a cruel despot, which does not, however, make the fate of his political opponents any easier.

Whether or not Turkmenbashi can make good his promise to turn the country into a second Kuwait thanks to its natural gas resources, second only to Russia in the former Soviet space, is a matter of debate. Two things are certain: First, lack of political culture and democratic traditions coupled with the weakness of democratic forces and the toughness of the Niyazov regime ensures political stability in the foreseeable future. Second, there are no signs of ethnic conflicts in Turkmenistan and precious little prospects of Ashkhabad's meddling into the complicated and unpredictable political and interethnic affairs of its neighbors.

The same cannot be said, however, of Kyrgyzstan, where the situation is volatile if not fraught with dangers. This is a three-ethnoses country: 2.3 million Kyrgyz, one million Russians and other Slavs, 600,000 Uzbeks. This is what the American professor Eugene Huskey has to say:

The modern Kyrgyz formed as a people in the mountain ranges and foothills of inner Asia. Their ancestors were the Turkic tribes of the Altai and Irtysh, the Mongols, and the ancient peoples of the Tian-Shan, the mountain range that has been home to the Kyrgyz for at least five centuries. . . . It was only their subordination to Russian rule, beginning in the mid-nineteenth century, that planted the seeds of nationalism among the Kyrgyz. . . . Formed originally on October 14, 1924 as the Kara-Kirgiz autonomous region within the Turkestan republic of the USSR, Kyrgyzstan underwent several name changes and administration redesignations before emerging in 1936 as the Kirgiz Soviet Socialist Republic.[12]

Speaking of Russification in the Soviet era, Huskey notes that Kyrgyz was marginalized in its homeland. "Not a single new Kyrgyz-language school was opened in the capital of Frunze (Bishkek) after the 1930s. By the 1980s, only three of Frunze's sixty-nine schools used Kyrgyz as the primary language of instruction. . . . In 1959, less than 10 percent of Frunze's population was ethnic Kyrgyz, and even as late as 1989 the Kyrgyz represented less than 23 percent of the capital's population."[13]

While on a visit to the Kyrgyz capital a few years ago, I was given the following figures: The Russian-speakers (Slavs as well as the ethnic Germans who had been deported to Kyrgyzstan by Stalin during World War II) accounted for almost 30% of the country's population and for 45% of the urban population; Kyrgyz made up just 8% of skilled workers and 3% of engineers and technicians. I noticed a curious pattern of division of labor: in administrative and party offices, mostly Kyrgyz were to be seen; they also predominated among university students and faculty staff; skilled workers as well as truck drivers were mostly Russians and other Slavs but in textile factories largely Kyrgyz women were employed. In the countryside, Kyrgyz were herding cattle while Russian-speakers worked in the fields; it was noticeable, by the way, that the most affluent among the workers in collective and state farms were Germans (the second and third generation of those ethnic Germans who had been deported by Stalin from the European part of Russia during the war with Germany). Koreans were selling vegetables in market places. I was told that things were different in the second largest city of Osh, close to Uzbekistan, where ethnic Uzbeks were the overwhelming majority. Uzbeks were reported to control all the trade in the Osh area which, of course, provoked the resentment of the local Kyrgyz population. It was precisely there, in Osh, that bloody clashes between Uzbeks and Kyrgyz were to occur later, in 1990.

The point is that the Kyrgyz, traditionally nomadic cattle-breeding people, used to live in the mountains and in the foothills. In the last few decades, they have begun to move into towns where either Uzbeks or Slavs used to be in clear majority. This process has created tensions, especially in the areas around the old Uzbek trade cities Osh and Uzgen. There, Uzbeks were traditionally engaged in trade and agriculture, and Kyrgyz in cattle-breeding. Economically, Uzbeks were much better off, but in the administration Kyrgyz were predominant; they held as much as 70% of staff positions in the Osh administration, for example. Both sides were unhappy with the situation. The conflict in Osh was triggered by the decision of the Kyrgyz-dominated local authorities to allot plots of land for private housing construction to Kyrgyz newcomers in June 1990. As the land belonged to an Uzbek collective farm, conflict was inevitable. Once started, it grew into vicious fighting; 230 persons had been killed, some of them in a very brutal and sadistic way, before the army restored order.

Since then, the relations between the Kyrgyz and Uzbeks, although no more marked by violence, remain rather tense. As Huskey puts it, "While sharing a Turkic and Islamic heritage with the Uzbeks, the Kyrgyz have been suspicious of calls for pan-Turkic or pan-Islamic unity, fearing that such movements could lead to the hegemony in Central Asia of the larger and more historically prominent Uzbek nation. For the Kyrgyz, Uzbekization appears more insidious than Russification. The latter affects language and culture, the former ethnic identity itself."[14]

Says President Akaev: "A table can stand on four legs, even on three, but not on two legs. An exodus of one of the nations—Uzbeks or Russians—would break the fragile balance of interests."[15] He was referring to the fact that in

1993, more than 100,000 ethnic Russians left Kyrgyzstan. This exodus was not motivated by harassment; Russians just do not see any prospects for themselves in a state where ethnic nationalism is undisputably growing.

Interethnic tension is not the only issue bedeviling Kyrgyzstan's ethnic landscape. Inside the Kyrgyz ethnos itself, homogeneity has always been lacking. Huskey mentions long-simmering tensions between the northern and southern Kyrgyz elites. "Distressed by the erosion of their traditional dominance of key republican posts, some southern Kyrgyz began to agitate for structural changes that would ensure greater autonomy for their region. These proposals ranged from dividing the republic into two regions, with equal representation from each in republican bodies, to the formation of a Kyrgyz federation, with northern and southern republics."[16] While the majority of the population clearly rejects these projects, it is obvious that regionalism, parochialism, tribalism in a very uncertain and precarious economic situation pose a great challenge to the enlightened president's plans for turning his picturesque mountainous country into a "second Switzerland."

NOTES

1. Boris Z. Rumer, *Soviet Central Asia: A Tragic Experiment* (Boston: Unwin Hyman, 1989), 148.

2. Michael Mandelbaum, ed., *The Rise of Nations in the Soviet Union: American Foreign Policy and the Disintegration of the USSR* (New York: Council on Foreign Policy Press, 1991), 19.

3. Donald S. Carlisle, "Uzbekistan and the Uzbeks," *Problems of Communism* (September/October 1991), 24.

4. Gregory Gleason, "Uzbekistan: From Statehood to Nationhood," in *Nation and Politics in the Soviet Successor States*, ed. Ian Bremmer and Ray Taras (New York: Cambridge University Press, 1993), 337.

5. Barnett R. Rubin, "The Fragmentation of Tajikistan," *Survival* 35, no 4 (Winter 1993–94), 74.

6. Muriel Atkin, "Tajikistan: Ancient Heritage, New Politics," *Nation and Politics*, 372.

7. Olivier Roy, *The Civil War in Tajikistan: Causes and Implications* (Washington, D.C.: U.S. Institute of Peace, 1993), 14, 15.

8. Eden Naby, *The Emerging Central Asia: Ethnic and Religious Factions* (Boston: Harvard University Press, 1992), 12.

9. Rubin, "Fragmentation," 76.

10. Ibid.

11. Ibid., 81.

12. Eugene Huskey, "Kyrgyzstan: The Politics of Demographic and Economic Frustration," *Nation and Politics*, 398, 399, 400.

13. Ibid., 402, 404.

14. Ibid., 409.

15. *Izvestia*, October 5, 1994, 4.

16. Huskey, "Kyrgyzstan," 409.

6

Kazakhstan

Most people believe that Kazakhstan is a part of Central Asia, and from the point of view of geography, this is correct. The Kazakh authorities, however, do not agree; they call their state a Eurasian power, stressing that Kazakhstan belongs to both Asia and Europe and, moreover, should be regarded as a bridge between the two continents, a unique state.

Kazakhstan is really unique in the sense that it is the only one of all the former Soviet republics where the titular nationality—Kazakh—is a minority population. "According to the 1989 census, Kazakhs constituted 39.7 percent of the population, although Kazakhstan's officials maintain that they are now about 42% of the republic's residents. But regardless, Russians and Ukrainians (43.6% combined) still outnumber the Kazakhs."[1] According to the Russian press, ethnic Russians number 7 million out of 16 million of Kazakhstan's residents.[2]

The Kazakhs are a young nation but an ancient people. Like most Central Asians, they are of a mixed Turkic-Mongolian origin due to the countless invasions of various ethnic groups. After all the conquerors left or mixed with the indigenous population, Kazakhs, a thoroughly nomadic people, lived from the fifteenth century on in their own Khanate subdivided into three tribal agglomerations called *jooz*. (This ancient division into the Great, Middle, and Lesser *joozes* is very much relevant even now; more about it later.) Two of these *joozes* were incorporated into the Russian Empire in the eighteenth century and the remaining one in 1860s. The Kazakh ethnic identity was never acknowledged by the Tsarist authorities, and the lands inhabited by the Kazakhs were just divided among several Russian provinces. The very term "Kazakhs" was not used, and even after the Bolshevik Revolution the land of the Kazakhs, curiously enough, was officially called the Kirgiz Autonomous Republic within the Russian Federation while the country of the genuine Kyrgyz, the Kyrgyzstan of today, was called the Kara-Kirgiz Autonomous Republic. Obviously, by that time, Lenin's regime found it hard to differentiate between the two nations. It was not until 1925 that the term "the Kazakh Republic" was introduced, but again as an autonomous unit of Russia. The Kazakh Soviet Socialist Republic was proclaimed as late as 1936.

By that time, a horrible disaster had already struck Kazakhstan, namely, Stalin's inhuman forced collectivization of land which led to a sharp reduction in the country's population. Famine, slaughter of the cattle, flight of the people unwilling to abandon their nomadic lifestyle resulted in a virtual depopulation of whole regions. The foremost Kazakh expert on demography M. Tatimov told me in Alma-Ata that the number of ethnic Kazakhs had fallen by one-third from 1926 to 1939—from 3.4 million to 2.3 million. Altogether in the period from 1916 to 1945 the Kazakh population decreased by 45%, the largest peacetime population reduction of the century.

In the meantime, the number of Russian-speakers was steadily growing. The first wave of Russians and Ukrainians came into the country in the 1930s as industrialization was initiated and labor force was required in great numbers. Then, during the war against Germany, hundreds of thousands of Russians were evacuated from the western regions into Kazakhstan; most of them found jobs in the expanding industry and settled in the land. To these, hundreds of thousands of deported people must be added, ethnic Germans from the prewar German Autonomous Republic on the Volga River (abolished by Stalin after the beginning of the war), as well as Caucasians. This was the second wave. The third wave came in the 1950s as Khruschev launched his great campaign for the cultivation of the virgin lands in Kazakhstan in order to make the republic a new Soviet granary. As a result of these waves of immigration, the percentage of Kazakhs, according to the 1959 census, fell to 30% while the share of Russian-speakers reached 63%. In the following three decades, the Kazakh population increased due to a higher birthrate. Still, in 1989, on the eve of independence, the Slav population constituted more than 44% of the total while the share of Kazakhs was close to 40%.

By the beginning of the 1980s, Kazakhs accounted for little more than 20% of the urban population compared to about 70% of Russian-speakers. As regards even the rural population, in 1979 Kazakhs made up just 53.5% while Slavs and Germans were 36.6%[3]

Almost 40% of the whole population of the republic live in the six *oblasts* (provinces) where the Russian-speakers constitute around 60% of all residents or even more, urban and countryside dwellers alike. Some provinces, particularly in the North, bordering on Siberia, are predominantly Russian and, from the point of view of ethnic composition, can hardly be called Kazakh at all. The share of Kazakhs there varies from 18.6% in the North Kazakhstan *oblast* to 28.9% in Kokchetav *oblast*. Russian-speakers prevail even in the capital city,

Alma-Ata, where they account for 56% of the population against 26% for Kazakhs; on my recent visit there, I heard mostly Russian in the streets. By the
way, the streets have been renamed, mostly after some obscure Kazakh Khans,
but people seem to prefer the old Soviet names.

In independent Kazakhstan, a new process has begun—the return of diaspora
Kazakhs to the home country. More than 100,000 people have returned from
China and Mongolia, tens of thousands are coming from Russia. The demog-
rapher Makash Tatimov, noting that the natural growth of the Kazakhs is 23–
24 per thousand while that of the Russians—just 2–3 per thousand, estimates
that by the year 2015 the Kazakh population of the republic will be as high as
13 million, or 60% of the whole population. This fundamental change in the
demographic situation has been facilitated by the outflow of ethnic Slavs: in
1993 alone, 365,000 Russian-speakers left Kazakhstan for Russia.[4] They are
emigrating mostly from small towns because of the decline of the mining industry, and from the areas where they used to be employed in enterprises of the
military-industrial complex. According to a poll conducted by Yuri Startsev, a
well-known leader of the Russian community in Kazakhstan, about 35% of
Russians (except for the northern and eastern provinces) are already bent on
leaving, and another 30% are seriously considering this possibility. Also, it must
be noted that ethnic Germans have been leaving for Germany en masse.

This poses two grave problems: the fate of those Russians in the South (including the capital city), who prefer to stay, and options for Russians in the
northern and eastern regions where they are likely to remain a majority. The
first question is linked to the policy of Kazakhization allegedly being pursued
by the Nazarbayev regime. It is hard to determine whether a full-scale Kazakhization is really the ultimate aim of the somewhat enigmatic Kazakh leader,
who has managed so far to walk the tightrope in a very skillful way. It is on
Nazarbayev's initiative that the official rule was made to use the adjective "Kazakhstani" instead of "Kazakh": There is no Kazakh science, army, diplomacy,
and so on, only Kazakhstani, which reflects the notion of a nonethnic state and
a common cause. In a newspaper interview in November 1995, Nazarbayev said:

In the old Constitution it was postulated that Kazakhstan was the state of the Kazakh
nation that had achieved self-determination. For three days I was locked in battle against
the then parliament, resisting that formula, but I was unable to succeed. At that time,
Russian was given a status of the "language of transnational communication" that you
can find nowhere else in the world. As to the current Constitution, it starts with the words
"We, the people of Kazakhstan," there is no assertion any more that it is the state of
Kazakhs only. . . . Russian, as well as the state language, has been accorded an official
status. . . . In 70 percent of Kazakhstan's state schools, children get their education in
Russian.[5]

(It is, however, the same reportedly "pro-Russian" Nazarbayev, contemptuously
called by extreme Kazakh nationalists "our Russian President" who has firmly
stood out against any idea of a federal arrangement for Kazakhstan providing

for autonomous Cossack regions, and has claimed throughout that in his republic the rights of the individual have an unconditional priority over those of ethnic communities.) "I am the President of all Kazakhstanis irrespective of their nationality and religion," he claims.[6]

The point is that there is a major ambiguity in Kazakhstan's ethnocultural situation. On the one hand, virtually all the educated Kazakhs—which in practice means "Russian-educated"—are more fluent in Russian than in literary Kazakh, although they speak colloquial Kazakh at home and in everyday life. Russian culture is a part of their life. The men in their thirties who at present hold key jobs in the administration know very well that they will be the first to suffer if ultranationalists come to power. They are also aware of the colossal damage that would be done to the country's economy, technology, and science in the event of a mass exodus of Russians. Finally, they cannot help thinking about Kazakhstan's relationship with Russia, knowing as they do that there is no way their economy can stabilize without cooperation with Moscow; and they certainly realize what harm will be done to this relationship if Alma-Ata is seen in Moscow as pursuing an unfriendly policy toward ethnic Russians residing in Kazakhstan. All these considerations dictate a "soft approach" to the Russian community and prompt Kazakh politicians to try a model of genuine and equitable interethnic cooperation.

On the other hand, however, the very closeness to Russian culture and language, the obvious preponderance of the Russian cultural ingredient in the Kazakh mentality make Kazakh intellectuals apprehensive. Many of them seem to resent their own "excessive Russianness," not unlike, for example, the young Algerian nationalists of the 1960s who had to admit, sometimes with shame, that they spoke better French than Arabic, that their very mentality was essentially French. There is an underlying suspicion in the hearts of many young Kazakh intellectuals that, if things are allowed to go their natural course, Kazakhstan will eventually become Russianized and their indigenous culture will be submerged by the much more prominent and powerful Russian culture. Also, it has to be borne in mind that Russians and Kazakhs are quite compatible as regards mentality and way of life. Kazakhs have never been particularly religious, Islam came late to them, they have never known the *shari'a* laws. There is no strong mentality barrier between Kazakhs and Russians; they communicate very easily, there are a lot of mixed marriages. And precisely here, according to some Kazakh ideologues, lies the danger. They believe that their own cultural heritage will not be able to hold its own unless "Russianization" of the Kazakh life is resisted by some drastic means. This, of course, means forceful Kazakhization.

In the broadest sense of the term, the Law on Language, mentioned above, can also be called Kazakhization; anyway, this is exactly how it is regarded by the Russian community. Only one percent of the non-Kazakh population of the republic speak Kazakh. As to Kazakh ethnics, about 30% prefer to use Kazakh only and 15% would rather use Russian; for the rest it just does not matter.[7]

Practically all the urban dwellers understand Russian perfectly, although the less educated ones speak it with difficulty. Russians have never felt any need to learn Kazakh, and many of them are now outraged at the prospect of having to study the language of the state they live in. This feeling can hardly be justified, of course; after all, people who prefer to stay in a country rather than leave must acknowledge the necessity of learning its language. But the point is that it is not language as such that is causing anxiety to Russians; the language issue is seen in a larger context. Russian residents of the city of Petropavlovsk, for instance, point out that those school teachers who instruct in Kazakh have a salary that is 15–20% higher than that of their Russian-speaking colleagues. Russians also complain that more and more Kazakhs are being appointed to higher administrative positions; that 105 out of 170 deputies of the new parliament are ethnic Kazakhs, and so on.

Anyway, the fate of the Russians residing in the South seems more or less clear. If they do not leave, they are destined to live as a constantly shrinking minority due to the demographic pattern outlined earlier. But what about the Russians who live in the North and East—this is the second, and much more alarming, question.

I have had a chance to speak to some Russians from the northern and eastern provinces. Their stand is unanimous: "if we go, we go with the land"—in other words, secession. Many Russians living in this area, if not the majority, regard it as just a continuation of Siberia which is a part of Russia. The famous Russian writer Solzhenitsin believes that the incorporation of the area in point into Kazakhstan has been a historic error and that it must lawfully belong to Russia. For this, the Kazakh nationalist organization Alash has demanded the death penalty for the writer. Many of Kazakhstan's ethnic Russians, however, wholeheartedly support Solzhenitsin's proposal to "return" mostly Russian-populated regions of Kazakhstan to "the motherland." The most active and intransigent among them are the Cossacks.

In the era of the conquest of Kazakh lands, Cossack troops spearheaded Russian invasions. They came and did not leave; instead, they settled in fertile new lands. The Cossacks built their villages called *stanitsa* both in the west and the east of what was later to become Kazakhstan. Peasant warriors, they loyally served the Tsar, fiercely fought the Bolsheviks during the civil war, and were all but exterminated by the Soviet regime. The Cossack revival came about after the collapse of the Soviet Union, exactly at the time when Kazakhstan became independent. Suddenly, the Cossacks found themselves torn away from Russia, in an alien state.

A few years ago I attended a meeting in Moscow. At some point, a man in a strange, completely unfamiliar semimilitary uniform came up to the rostrum and introduced himself as *ataman* (headman) of the Cossacks residing in western Kazakhstan. He was very upset, he said, and felt betrayed because a few days before President Yeltsin had signed an agreement with Nazarbayev, recognizing Kazakhstan's border with Russia. It meant that the Cossacks were doomed to stay in a foreign state, and they were vigorously protesting against this "unjust and preposterous" decision.

In 1994, another *ataman*, Viktor Achkasov, the chief of the "Community of Siberian Cossacks," banned in Kazakhstan, said: "We do not put in doubt Kazakhstan's sovereignty but we do not intend to flee. Why, look at the Bosnian Serbs who constitute just 6 percent of the population; they have been able to assert their rights. We make up more than 70 percent; we'll tough it out!"[8]

What Achkasov meant was the Cossacks' autonomy within Kazakhstan's framework; though not as radical a solution as secession, this notion has been rejected outright by Nazarbayev and his government. Since then, Kazakhstan's Cossacks, who consider themselves to be a vanguard of all the Russians in Kazakhstan, have been vacillating between these two options. Obviously, secession can be ruled out at this point; neither Kazakhstan nor Russia could agree to such an outrageous violation of a guiding principle of the relations between the CIS states. A federal arrangement providing for the autonomy of the largely Russian-populated regions of Kazakhstan would seem to be one way out of the deadlock; there is practically no chance, however, that Nazarbayev could accede to this demand without a disastrous loss of face. Certainly, in this case he would be condemned and rejected by the Kazakhs. Thus, the regime appears to face a very serious challenge.

Speaking on this subject in November 1995, Nazarbayev said:

Some of the bloodiest pages of the pre-revolutionary history of the Kazakhs happened to be related to the Cossacks. It is the Cossacks who were robbing the Kazakhs of their best lands, they had the right to shoot Kazakhs who approached their settlements. In this way, thousands were killed. The Cossacks swept the Kazakh lands with fire and sword. . . . There can be no paramilitary formations in Kazakhstan. If the Cossacks want to serve in the army, let them serve in the army of Kazakhstan. We cannot afford and we will not permit any other military units, all the more so if they have to be subordinated to some Russian councils of *atamans*.[9]

The fate of the Russians is certainly the most worrisome and menacing political problem of today's Kazakhstan. Some aspects of relations between ethnic Kazakhs, however, also give ground for concern. The old-standing differences between the three *joozes*, traditional regional agglomerations, have been exacerbated lately by the competition and confrontation of new business elites and local mafiosi groups. Some of the people I talked to in Kazakhstan were even of the opinion that major disturbances were to be expected to occur between various parts of the Kazakh ethnos rather than between Kazakhs and Russians.

NOTES

1. Martha Brill Olcott, "Kazakhstan: A Republic of Minorities," in *Nations and Politics in the Soviet Successor* States, ed. Ian Bremmer and Ray Taras (New York: Cambridge University Press, 1993), 313.

2. *Nezavisimayia Gazeta*, April 20, 1993, 5.
3. *Materials of the 1979 Census*, vol. 4, part 2, book 2, 128–276.
4. *Moscow News*, May 15, 1994, 4.
5. *Nezavisimaia Gazeta*, November 15, 1995, 3.
6. Ibid.
7. *Mysl*, no. 5 (1993), 43.
8. *Moscow News*, May 15, 1994, 4.
9. *Nezavisimaia Gazeta*, November 15, 1995.

7

Ukraine

In the center of Kiev there is a monument to Bohdan Khmelnitsky, the famous seventeenth-century Cossack *ataman* (chieftain) who signed the treaty incorporating Ukraine into the Russian Tsardom, later to become Empire. About twenty years ago I happened to come near the monument and was greatly surprised to hear an old man, looking at the hero's statue, mutter sotto voce in Ukrainian: "Oh, Bohdan, Bohdan, what have you done, stupid? You sold Ukraine to the beastly Moskali!" Thank God, no "Soviet patriot" heard this blasphemy, those monstrous words blatantly contradicting the official line which, of course, always stressed the unshakable friendship between Russia and Ukraine. For me, it was a revelation; later I learned that those were the words of the greatest Ukrainian poet Taras Shevchenko. I doubt, though, that they were included in his "Complete Works" published under the Soviet regime.

Nowadays, when my Western colleagues ask me about the likelihood of the relations between Russians and Ukrainians deteriorating to the extent of those between Serbs and Croats (also "brotherly" Slavic nations), I answer in the negative, for reasons to be explained later. Still, I can never forget Shevchenko's verses repeated by an obscure old Ukrainian in front of Khmelnitsky's statue.

Few people in the West know how the Ukrainians were called under the Tsarist regime. The official term for them was "Malorossy" (Little Russians), since the Slavic part of the European Russia consisted of Great Russia (Russia proper), Little Russia (Ukraine), and White Russia (Belarus). To understand it, try to imagine, for instance, Scots or Welsh being officially termed "Little English"; hardly stimulating for national pride and self-esteem. And although most Ukrainians of the present generation, I believe, have never even heard the word

"Malorossy," the inferiority complex is still there. The Ukrainians—who are
they? Little Brothers? Slavic cousins? or victims of the conquerors who deprived
a great nation of independence for more than three hundred years?

One thing is undisputable—common origins. Both nations belong to the eastern branch of the Slavs. In the ninth century, a powerful state called Kievan
Rus was founded, and Christianity was adopted in 988. The famous and magnificent Kiev, the capital of Ukraine, had been the main city and center of that
mighty East Slavic state which later succumbed to the Mongol invaders. At that
time, the words "Russia" and "Ukraine" did not exist, and the language was
one and the same—"ancient Slavic." For centuries, Kiev has been hailed in
Russia as "Mother of Russian cities." It is probably because of this that it
seems just outlandish, if not weird, for the ordinary Russian to realize that
Ukraine is no more a part of Russia. For this is how it really was: For most
people in the Soviet Union, the terms USSR and Russia were practically interchangeable, especially when dealing with the European part of the huge empire.
Kiev in everybody's eyes was simply a Russian city, just like Rostov or Gorky,
and people there were speaking Russian; by the way, each time I happened to
come to Kiev I heard practically only Russian; Ukrainian was used mostly by
peasants coming to town for shopping.

Speaking of language, it must be noted that after the collapse of the Kievan
Rus the land which later came to be known as Ukraine had been virtually
separated from Rus (Russia proper) and eventually came under Polish rule. The
Ukrainian language was developing as separate from Russian and under strong
influence of Polish. Later, when Ukraine got incorporated into Russia, the local
idiom came to be regarded as just a vernacular, a kind of vulgar deviation from
the "pure" Russian. In the eighteenth century Ukrainian was practically banned,
and in the nineteenth century it was officially considered a dialect spoiled by
Polish influence. It was not proper for educated people to speak this language,
and the very word "Ukraine" was not officially used, although, paradoxically,
the Kievan origins of Russia were always acknowledged and Kiev remained a
revered, almost a holy, city.

At present, Ukrainian nationalists are trying to present a somewhat different
story of the Kievan Rus. The newspaper *Batkivshehina* (Fatherland) wrote in an
article entitled "The Messianism of the Russian Leaders": "The mystical image
of Russia adopted by the European world is a product of the persistent propaganda conducted by Moscow governments. Russian historians have adapted the
history of the Kievan Rus to needs of the history of Muscovy and Russia. . . .
Western European historians regard the Kievan Rus as the beginnings of Muscovy and the Russian state. . . . But (the Ukrainian historian) Grushevsky has
proved that the Kievan state was a creation of the Ukrainian people."[1]

Historically speaking, this thesis does not hold water if only because in the
era of the Kievan state there was no people that could be called Ukrainian. The
word "Ukraine," meaning "some place at the extremes" or "at the edges,"
was used as early as the twelfth century to designate southern and southwestern

"outskirts" of the realm but had no ethnic connotation. Later, by the eighteenth century, "Ukraine" acquired an additional meaning—"the country" ("kraina" is a common Slavic word, for instance Srpska Kraina in former Yugoslavia). As to the language, the so-called old Ukrainian came into existence only as late as the sixteenth century; the "New Ukrainian" (a literary idiom) was shaping up during the eighteenth century, and its development could be considered complete only in the beginning of the nineteenth century.

This is not to deny the fact of a gradual process of the formation of the Ukrainian nation (as distinct from the Russian nation) that was going on for centuries and culminated probably about two hundred years ago. This was a nation without statehood. Only for a brief period during the Civil War in 1917–1920 did a sovereign Ukrainian republic exist; then, the country again became a part of the Empire ruled from Moscow, albeit under the name of the Ukrainian Soviet Socialist Republic. And it is really not necessary to try to prove the existence of a distinct Ukrainian nation centuries ago, at the time of the Kievan Rus; suffice it to acknowledge the undisputed existence of this nation today, a numerous, full-blooded nation. Ethnic Ukrainians in the republic number 37.4 million, 72.7% of the population; Russians 11.4 million, 22.1%. About 68% of the whole population are urban dwellers. The population of Ukraine is 18% of that of the former Soviet Union, although the territory of the republic is less than 3% of the defunct empire.[2]

Independence came to Ukraine in 1991, almost overnight. The referendum of December 1 marked the birth of the new state. But, unlike some of the other republics, Ukraine's emergence as an independent state was not a total surprise. The nationalist movement there was in existence before Gorbachev's *perestroika* and the chain of events culminating in the collapse of the Soviet Union.

While on my yearly trips to Ukraine as a lecturer on behalf of a Soviet lecturing society, I became familiar with two distinct kinds of Ukrainian nationalism. The first can be called *career nationalism;* it was represented by many (although not all) Party and state apparatchiks anxious to hold their positions and privileges in the face of rivals from Moscow, and to achieve more economic and financial autonomy vis-à-vis the Center. Those local elites, composed of people speaking virtually only Russian regardless of their ethnic origins, did not know much and cared even less about Ukrainian culture, language, or literature. This brand of nationalism was nothing less than a typical struggle for the place in the sun.

The second type of nationalism was that of *humanitarian intelligentsia*, professors and university students bent on resurrection and revival of the Ukrainian cultural identity. Those were the people who were passionately striving to assert Ukrainian self-consciousness as a distinct nation with a glorious past and rich culture. Frustrated by the relentless unification and Russification, afraid of a gradual fading away of their language, folklore, and way of life, they felt it their duty and sacred mission to restore all things Ukrainian in the face of Russian domination. The poet Taras Shevchenko was their idol but many of them sym-

pathized as well with anti-Bolshevik independence leaders of the civil war period. Their ultimate goal was independence.

It is precisely this second, "genuine" kind of nationalism which gave birth
to the most powerful and influential nationalist organization on the eve of independence, namely, "Rukh" (Movement). A virtual alliance of both nationalisms after the August 1991 events assured the emergence of the present
Ukrainian regime.

Rukh was spearheaded by writers and professors. It started an energetic cam-
paign in 1989 during several months preceding the elections to the new Congress
of People's Deputies of the USSR. In this election, Communists were beaten in
Kiev, Lviv, and a number of other cities, especially in western Ukraine (formerly
Polish territory, rapidly turning into a stronghold of Ukrainian nationalism). In
September 1989, Rukh was formally inaugurated at a congress, and two months
later, as a campaign was launched for the elections to the Ukrainian Supreme
Soviet, a coalition called the Democratic Bloc was formed, with Rukh as its
leading component. The elections, held in March 1990, resulted in the Demo-
cratic Bloc winning 110 out of 450 seats in the new national parliament. The
Democrats captured the most important cities in western Ukraine, including
Lviv, as well as half of the seats in Kiev. Finally, on July 16, 1990, the Supreme
Soviet overwhelmingly adopted a declaration on the state sovereignty of
Ukraine—a truly striking event, considering that the Democrats were still only
a minority. It showed the strength of nationalist feeling which by that time
clearly spread to all sectors of public opinion, including Communists. An atmosphere was gradually created in which it was impossible to reject calls for sovereignty, if not yet for outright independence.

True, in the all-Union referendum on the future of the USSR, initiated by
Gorbachev and held in March 1991, more than 70% of the Ukrainian voters
supported the preservation of the Union. But, as Bohdan Nahaylo rightly points
out, "this result was offset by the voters' more enthusiastic endorsement (80.2%
of those who voted) of the supplementary proposal which specified that Ukraine
would only join a new 'Union of sovereign states' on the basis of the principles
of the republic's declaration of sovereignty."[3]

The final step on the road to independence was taken on December 1, 1991,
following such momentous events as the failed Moscow coup and the banning
of the Communist Party. In the December referendum, voters endorsed the declaration of independence and elected the new president, Leonid Kravchuk, the
last leader of the Communist Party of Ukraine. After December 1, it was clear
that the Soviet Union was doomed, and it was finally dissolved eight days later,
with Kravchuk as one of the three actors instrumental in breaking up the once
powerful Empire.

As Professor Roman Szporluk puts it, "Ukrainian independence—contrary to
virtually all scenarios advanced by its supporters in the past—was achieved in
a most paradoxical manner. . . . Ukraine was able to proclaim independence and
gain Russia's approval of it owing to the support of Communists who switched

to a national, pro-independence position. Without any doubt, this outcome owed very much to the leadership of President Leonid M. Kravchuk, who was able to build an alliance between the opposition and those elements of the party willing to opt for Ukrainian independence."[4]

How could it happen that people like Kravchuk became Ukraine's top nationalist leaders? It would be naive to suppose that they were "closet nationalists" all along, just masquerading as Communists for career reasons. On the other hand, it is just as difficult to see them as convinced Communists forced to don their nationalist cloak by the force of events. To understand this phenomenon, two preliminary remarks must be made. First, the West always tended to overestimate the degree of "socialist committment" of leading Soviet Party members of the post-Stalin generation. Qualities were ascribed to them that they already lacked—devotion to the ideal of Communism, genuine belief in truths and virtues of Marxism. Actually, it can be said of the majority of Party cadres that their ideological committment was skin-deep. They were just playing according to rules of the game without giving much thought to theory and high ideals. I know more than one former Party boss of regional level who has happily turned to private business after the fall of the Communist regime. They seem to have quietly forgotten their Marx and Lenin. Bosses of a higher level, while not going in for business, have become leaders and members of ruling elites of new sovereign entities. The point is that the former Communists have managed to switch over to nationalism rather painlessly. It is in this category that new Ukrainian leaders belong. It has clearly not taken an agonizing effort for them to discard their Party membership as well as their former convictions.

Ukraine's potential is impressive. Although it has only 2.7% of the territory of the former USSR, its share of the total Soviet Net Material Product was 16.5%. Ukraine produced about 20% of the Union's agricultural output, over 40% of its iron ore. In Europe, Ukraine held the first place in steel and coal production, the second place in the production of grain and milk, the third place in meat production. The republic produced more than half of the Union's uranium ore, about half of the tanks and missiles, more than half of sugar.[5]

The fatal weakness of Ukraine's economy is its meager oil production—less than 5 million tons of crude annually while the country needs about 60 million tons. Ukraine has been the largest importer of Russian oil as well as of natural gas; it has to import about 78% of the latter. Both oil and gas were always bought at prices below world levels. If oil and natural gas are to be paid for at world prices, the country, as the new President Kuchma admitted, will need $13 billion.[6]

Russia has always been Ukraine's main trade partner: three-fourths of Ukraine's imports and two-thirds of its exports. Ukraine is dependent on Russia in such commodities as oil, oil products, and gas, metal, timber, trucks, buses, while it covers 20–25% of Russia's need in black metal, 30–40% in iron pipes, 13% in oil, and so on.

The Ukrainian military-industrial complex is truly powerful—in the Union it was second only to Russia's. It comprised 1,300 factories with the number of employed exceeding 2 million; it accounted for 18% of all the enterprises of its kind in the Soviet Union. It is, however, also dependent on Russia and the rest of the CIS states. For instance, Kharkiv tank plant had to import equipment, details, and parts of vehicles from as many as 973 factories located outside Ukraine.[7]

This impressive economic potential, however, has not so far been used to create even a viable, if not prosperous, state. Szporluk noted that

Ukraine was lagging behind the developments in Russia. Even though economic reform in Russia was accompanied by a number of very painful phenomena, there was a general sense that things were changing and a new class of entrepreneurs and businessmen became a visible element of the Russian urban scene. Many people in Russia felt that there was now room for individual initiative, private enterprise, for getting things done without government direction. In Ukraine this sense of change was lacking.[8]

Everything has been falling drastically—GNP, industrial output, national income, food production, living standards. Kuchma, at that time head of government, said on assuming office: "Ukraine does not have an economic crisis. It has a catastrophe." One of the Rukh's leaders summed up the situation: "Ukraine's economy is quite simply broke. . . . Stagnation encompasses heavy industry, agriculture, transport, the construction industry, and foreign trade. The financial system is totally destroyed. . . . The economic situation in Ukraine. . . . is much worse than not only in Russia, but in any other European ex-Soviet state."[9]

How could it happen in a country blessed with fertile land, excellent climate, rich natural resources, impressive industry, a country which has not experienced bloody ethnic conflicts and violent internal strife? Valeriy Vyzhutovich, a *Moscow News* correspondent, gives the explanation:

The so-called special Ukrainian road to capitalism means government decrees perpetuating departmental management of the economy. It is the Kiev bosses who are ordering everybody about, including people in faraway villages. It is abolition of the meagre management rights that the laws gave to factories and mines. It is a plethora of words uttered by self-righteous and pompous ignoramuses with parliamentary deputies' badges dictating emission policy to the state bank. . . . It is a breakdown of economic ties with neighbors, abundance of customs dues and regulations that have sharply raised prices for all goods. It is Ukraine leaving the ruble zone, introduction of "coupons" with the simultaneous underground dollarization of the economy that has brought about hyperinflation and thrown more than two thirds of the population beyond the poverty line.[10]

The unholy alliance of former apparatchiks and anti-Communist intellectuals has proved unable to shape up an imaginative and coherent policy. While the former are too narrowminded, selfish, and incapable of shedding their Socialist mentality, the latter are totally inexperienced in economic matters, lacking any concept of development and bitterly divided by group and personal rivalries.

Unlike Russia, Ukraine has made no bold, radical steps aimed at genuine economic reform opening the way to market economy. For a while, at the beginning of 1992, this was considered by some as an advantage for Ukraine, allowing it to avoid hardship and misery which accompanied Gaidar's reform in Russia. Very soon it became clear that a total lack of vision and will, absence of any comprehensive program, and unwillingness to infringe upon the elite's vested interests were preventing any real movement. The Kravchuk leadership has made a monumental mess of things. Timid, half-hearted attempts at reform have turned the Ukrainian economy into a basket case.

As the British weekly *The Economist* put it, "Since independence in 1991, Ukraine has been a disaster waiting to happen. The disaster is now upon it. . . . Rarely can misguided policies and mismanagement have led so quickly to a country's collapse. . . . The predicament of Ukraine points up a bankrupcy of economic gradualism in revolutionary times."[11]

"Ukrainian society today is dispersed, atomized, and unstructured," says the Ukrainian journalist Mykola Riabchouk.[12] Some of his fellow countrymen, speaking at a roundtable in Kiev, were equally pessimistic. Gorelov, a political scientist, stressed Ukrainian mentality:

The ordinary Ukrainian is an apolitical person. . . . Such has been the fate of the Ukrainian people that they could not but develop a national inferiority complex, which they have learned to overcome in the shells of their private life. Add to this the seventy years of the Soviet "education" during which tens of millions of the most active members of society were physically liquidated and the rest had a virus of blind obedience to any authority, even the most inept one, force-fed into their genetic code—and you will understand that it was only the old nomenclatura, a leftover from the previous regime, that could become, and actually became, a "popular choice" in Ukraine.

The editor-in-chief of the journal *Political Thought,* Polokhalo, deplored "the poor articulation of interests and the weakness of political will of social actors," "the low intellectual and cultural level of all the echelons of the Ukrainian post-Communist nomenclatura, the lack of professionalism and competence."[13]

The Ukrainian politicians and managers seem to lack any clear ideas about economic reforms; they believe in gradual movement and in preserving a high degree of state dirigism. The new Ukrainian "capitalists" are mostly of a rentier variety; they derive their income from a highly regulated economy based mainly on state property, and show no real interest in building a genuine market with private enterprises and competition.

Even when Kuchma was elected president and embarked on a program of serious reforms, it appeared that the economy was in such a disastrous shape that it was a really uphill struggle trying to revive it. In 1994, industrial production fell by 28% and agricultural production by 17%. It has been reported that 40% of the money in circulation belonged to the "shadow economy" sector.

On the eve of my last visit to Ukraine I called an old friend in Kiev and asked him: "How are things? Is it as bad as here, in Moscow?" "Twice as bad" was his answer. Upon my arrival in Kiev, I found this to be an understatement. There were money-changers galore in the streets, offering to exchange coupons for roubles, roubles for dollars, and so on, but except for this, there seemed to be no sort of private entrepreneurial activity whatsoever. People were gloomy and depressed. Nobody seemed to have any trust in the government, parliament, political parties (which were engaged in interminable quarrels and bickering, constantly splitting and reuniting, making and unmaking blocs and coalitions). When I asked cab drivers, street vendors, barmen, or chambermaids in the hotel about independence, they were just furious. I found not the slightest trace of nationalist euphoria. By the way, everybody was speaking Russian. Ukrainian was almost as hard to hear on the streets as several years ago.

One of the polls in 1994 provided some telling results. Answering the question: "How would you have voted today in a referendum on Ukraine's independence?", twice as many citizens of Ukraine said that they would have voted against independence than those willing to vote for it (47% and 24%); 23% of those polled expressed doubts as to the probability of Ukraine overcoming the crisis in the near future, while 21% were of the opinion that the country would *never* overcome it. Answering another question—about the country's urgent needs and priorities—32% favored a restoration of the USSR while just 15% opted for the strengthening of the Ukrainian statehood. At the same time, however, only 32% of those polled voiced their readiness to personally take part in strikes with political or economic demands; this phenomenon can be regarded as fairly typical of the Ukrainian mentality at the present stage of the nation's history.[14]

The relations between Russians and Ukrainians at the time of my trip there seemed to be pretty good and generally quite friendly. Actually, people did not even bother to differentiate between the two nations, it just was not a point of reference. Living side by side, with a lot of mixed marriages and with everybody speaking Russian, it was hard to imagine people beginning to regard each other as belonging to a particular ethnic group. All were Kievans, ethnicity was not an issue. Still, for the first time I heard some of my friends—ethnic Russians— voice vague fears about the eventuality of pogroms "in the worst-case scenario." The point is, how can this worst-case scenario come about? It is time to turn to the issue of the relations between the two nations in general. They are not as simple and clear as it would appear if I based my opinions just on talks with my friends and colleagues—intellectuals and university professors who were brought up in a mixed if not cosmopolitan society and never bothered about their ethnic identity.

First of all, it must be noted that Ukraine is huge and diverse. The Kiev mentality is that of capital city dwellers, mostly educated ones. Even if they are ethnically Ukrainian, they have always felt at least as much Russian as Ukrainian. However, people in small towns and villages of central Ukraine, let alone the fiercely nationalistic western Ukrainians, have a different type of mentality.

Among big city dwellers, only a small number of people, mainly nationalistic-minded writers and professors, really felt their Ukrainian identity and were unhappy because they had to live in a "subjugated," "dependent" country. The overwhelming majority of the population never gave this issue a thought. However, for small town and country people who actually conversed in Ukrainian, ethnic Russians were outsiders, "the others"; all things Russian were felt as rather alien. The derogative word "moskali" (those from Moscow) has always been used to designate not the ethnic Russians but the Russians from Russia.

As to western Ukraine, it is a special case: Under Polish domination for centuries, incorporated into the Soviet Ukraine only as late as 1939, the western provinces have an identity of their own. It was shaped up in stubborn resistance against Warsaw's policy of Polonization, against Polish culture and the Catholic church. Since the end of the sixteenth century the western Ukrainians have had a unique, mixed brand of religion called Uniate, or Greek-Catholic, acknowledging the Pope and combining Catholic dogmas with Orthodox rituals. Bitterly hostile to the Poles, western Ukrainians turned against the Red Army when the latter, in pursuit of the defeated Germans in 1944, restored the Soviet control and destroyed the westerners' short-lived dream of independence.

While visiting a truly impressive military cemetery in Lviv, the main city of western Ukraine, I noted the dates of death of the Red Army officers and men buried there. Almost without exception, they were killed after March 1944, the month of the area's liberation from the Germans. They died at the hands of the UPA (the Ukrainian Insurrection Army), a nationalist military formation set up during the war under the German occupation. Fiercely anti-Russian and anti-Polish, the UPA at first hoped to create an independent Ukraine under the aegis of Nazi Germany. Since Hitler would not even hear of it, the nationalists turned against the Germans. As the latter were driven out by the Red Army, the UPA mounted a large-scale guerrilla campaign against the "liberators" which went on for years. Large segments of the local population regarded the UPA men, called "fascist bandits" by the Soviets, as freedom fighters. Their leader, Stepan Bandera, became a legendary figure. Shortly before he was assassinated by a Soviet intelligence agent in Germany in 1959, I remember walking along the main boulevard in Lviv where I was having my training as a reserve officer in the Soviet army. A drunk suddenly stood up from a bank he had been lying on, and exclaimed in a shrill voice: "Long live Stepan Bandera and his wife Paraska!" The word "banderovtsy" (Bandera's men) was widely used throughout the Soviet Union as a derogatory term; it referred not only to actual guerrilla fighters but to western Ukrainians in general; once in Odessa at a soccer match, as a team from Lviv scored a goal against the home side, I remember Odessa fans groaning in dismay: "Oh God, the bloody banderovtsy are winning!"

Nowadays, Bandera's statues have been erected in western Ukraine, and his sympathizers have been elected city mayors. On the whole, western Ukraine (Halitchina) has, according to many an observer, entered a period of decay. "Corruption is typical of Lvov. Nationalism is just a ringing slogan camouflaging new forms of social and economic exploitation of 'old' Soviet-style workers by 'new Ukrainians.'' The mentality of the small Halitchina has remained the same. People still believe that business in Lvov is in the hands of Jews and 'moskali.' The motto is—national consciousness first, competence and professionalism afterwards. . . . Today Lvov is a Ukrainian city taken over by non-socialized and non-urbanized Halitchian peasants who only wish to live a quiet life.''[15] On the other end of the spectrum are eastern and southern Ukraine. I used to travel fairly often to the second largest Ukrainian city, Kharkov, and the center of the mining industry, Donetsk. Each time, I felt just as if I were in Rostov, Kursk, Saratov, or any other big Russian city. Ukrainian was hardly to be heard. The vast majority of the urban population are Russians or "Russianized" Ukrainians. The same applies to the giant industrial city Dnepropetrovsk, where intercontinental missiles used to be produced. As to the lovely and inimitable Odessa, the jewel on the Black Sea, it was a Russian, Jewish, and Ukrainian city with a charming and unique atmosphere of its own. Now, of course, most Jews have left. Odessa is being Ukrainized.

Between these two extremes lies the middle Ukraine with its rural and small town population, mostly indifferent to Russia and Russians. It is hard to tell exactly what they feel about Russians. They probably do not mind living in an independent state, they enjoy hearing Ukrainian all around them and not having to write all kinds of necessary bureaucratic papers in Russian, but they do not care about such things as state politics, history, national glory. If they lack sympathy for the Russian, it is not due to ethnic feelings; they are probably just as unfriendly to Kiev intellectuals of their own blood. It is provincialism and parochialism versus big city culture and mentality.

Things were like this before the October Revolution and even during the civil war. General Denikin, who had been the commander in chief of the White Army, wrote later in his memoirs that chauvinism and anti-Russian sentiments had not been at issue. "If the word " 'moskal' " became odious, it was not because of ethnic factors but only inasmuch as it was associated with the people from the outside—the Commissars, members of military-revolutionary committees and so on.''[16]

Historically, political relationships between Russia and Ukraine (as distinct from interhuman relations) have been tense ever since their "unequal marriage" three and a half centuries ago. At first, the Ukrainian Cossack elite led by Bohdan Khmelnitsky and his successors regarded the merger of the two nations as a kind of vassalage relationship while the Russian tsars believed in a total subordination of Kiev to Moscow. Soon the office of the Cossack *hetman* was abolished altogether. The Moscow authorities, however, continued to regard the Ukrainians as potential traitors. The Empress Catherine the Great, in one of her letters, wrote that what she noticed in the Little Russians was an "inherent hatred" for Great Russia. Even now, talk about "three hundred years of slavery" can be heard in Ukraine, although this relates mostly to the Moscow authorities rather than to the ethnic Russians residing in Ukraine.

How do Russians feel about Ukrainians? Any two nations living side by side are bound to develop ethnic stereotypes, some of them rather nasty. Many Russians would say this about the "khokhly" (plural from "khokhol"—a mildly derogative term for Ukrainians): "Oh, they are really sly and crafty, they are just kulaks." The Ukrainians have the reputation of being thrifty and meticulous, prudent and calculating, hard-working, stubborn, and incredulous. It is worth noting that the majority of the non-commissioned officers in the Soviet army appeared to be of Ukrainian origin. At any rate, whenever I met a sergeant, he would have a Ukrainian name. Ukrainians are reputed to be strong disciplinarians, sticklers for order and punctuality, generally conservative in their outlook, not eager for any innovations or rapid changes.

There have been no attempts at Ukrainization on the part of the present authorities. The Russian language is widespread. By the end of the 1980s more than 50% of all students in Ukraine were attending Russian-language schools; in Kiev, only 70,000 out of 300,000 pupils were studying Ukrainian.[17] A Kiev magazine told in 1992 about a local beauty contest; when the reporter asked the contest manager why there had been no test for intellect, the answer was: "You see, in this kind of test the girls would have to talk, and not a single one of them can speak Ukrainian."[18] I was told in Kiev that even in those schools where teaching is being conducted in Ukrainian, children speak Ukrainian in class and Russian between classes.

The ethnic Russians residing in Ukraine make up about 22% of the population—almost 12 million. Most of them live in the *oblasts* of Donetsk (44% of the population), Crimea (67%), Lugansk (44%), Kharkiv (33%), Zaporizhie (32%), Odessa (27%).[19] About 40% of the population of Ukraine claim Russian as their mother tongue, including eleven out of twelve cities with the population of more than half a million people.[20] A research done in Zaporizhie area has shown some very illustrative figures: While ethnic Ukrainians make up more than 67% of the population, the overall share of those inhabitants of the area who speak Russian at home is 82.9%, and at workplace 81%.

By the time Ukraine became independent, only 40.3% of the personnel of the military forces deployed on its territory were ethnic Ukrainians, while 44% were Russians. There were 75,000 ethnic Russians serving as military officers.[21] On the other hand, right after independence, officers and generals began to arrive in Ukraine from the other CIS republics, by no means all of them ethnic Ukrainians. At that time Ukraine, a rich country with a good climate, politically stable, clearly presented a better option than a poverty-stricken, politically insecure Russia. It is not surprising, therefore, that in Kharkiv, for instance, with its huge Russian population, there was an 80% vote for the independence of Ukraine in the 1991 referendum. Disillusionment came later.

Since there has been no anti-Russian campaign in Ukraine and no Ukrainization was in sight, ethnic Russians felt no reason to be unhappy about becoming citizens of a republic which seemed destined to become the wealthiest and most stable state in the CIS. The tension which began to rise in the Russian-Ukrainian relations in 1992 was by no means caused by some interethnic conflicts within Ukraine, contrary to what occurred, for example, in Estonia or Moldova. It was solely the result of interstate differences, of worsening relations between Moscow and Kiev. However, it was not so much actual rivalry as mutual suspicions that led to strains in the relations between the two states.

Geopolitical rivalry was predicted and feared at the time of the Union's breakup, but in reality it failed to materialize. Rivalry usually develops when two strong and dynamic states aspire to be power centers in a certain area and display regional hegemonic tendencies. Thus, Germany and France waged wars not so much over Alsace and Lorraine as for mastery and hegemony in Western Europe; Japan and Russia clashed in 1903 because only one of those two powers could be overlord in a specific geopolitical area—the Far East. Iran and Iraq fought the recent Gulf war primarily (although not exclusively) for one overwhelming reason: Each of them strove to assert itself as a regional superpower in the Gulf area. Seen in this light, rivalry between Russia and Ukraine in a strictly geopolitical sense lacks any reason, since there is no neighboring territory to dispute nor a sphere of interests from which to drive the opponent. The only commonly shared neighbor—Belarus—is hardly a prize for either Russia or Ukraine; domination in the Black Sea area is largely an abstraction, and the Crimean conflict is by no means about "ruling the waves."

Thus, the very term "geopolitics" can be used here only in the broadest sense, if at all. The real issue is: *Can only Russia be regarded as a legitimate successor state to the Soviet Union or can Ukraine claim to be one as well?* Can Russia, reentering Europe in a new historic setting, have the right to negotiate on behalf of the CIS as a whole? Should Russia have the right to unilaterally settle conflicts in the Caucasus and in other areas of the former USSR, or should Kiev's voice be heard as well?

The point is that of all the successor states in the CIS, *only Russia and Ukraine can claim a great power status*, and Ukraine is desperately trying to prove that it is on an equal footing with its former lord. Ukraine's dream is *to be acknowledged by the world community as a power equal to Russia*, and it cannot get rid of the suspicion that neither Russia nor the outside world is willing to accord Kiev the coveted status.

This gives rise to an inferiority complex the background of which has never been far away, considering centuries of humiliation caused by Ukraine's dependent status. This complex has been reinforced by Ukraine's failures in the domestic field as well as by its inept and lackluster foreign policy. The more disappointing Ukraine's performance, for the whole world to see, the more vulnerable its leadership feels, the more frustrated and touchy it grows. And, of course, Moscow, with its rather heavy-handed policy and its sometimes overbearing attitude, is always at hand as a scapegoat for all of Ukraine's misfortunes.

The problem is largely psychological. *Ukraine feels that Moscow does not really take its independence seriously, that it stubbornly refuses to treat Kiev as an equal partner.* At the same time, many Russian politicians seem to regard

Ukraine as an insolent upstart and as a not-too-reliable neighbor, quite capable of going back on its promises if not of outright double-crossing.

The American scholar Eugene Rumer wrote:

For Ukraine's first post-Soviet leaders, the need to protect independence and the effort to maintain equality with Moscow may have seemed the only ideological and political platforms available. The alternative of internal transformation was fraught with even greater challenges. Hence, Russia, Ukraine's independence from it, and Ukraine's relationship with it have become the crucial elements of Kiev's domestic policy and politics. Ukraine's independence was achieved *from* Russia. Presumably, it also had to be maintained *against* Russia.[22]

A Russian writer is of the opinion that what dominates Ukraine's foreign policy is "symbol diplomacy": ostensibly visible features of national independence such as "inviolable borders," red carpet at the exit from the plane, setting up frontier posts at the Russian border count more than really important issues. "There is a danger that the number of political conflict points with Russia and the intensity of differences will soon become main criteria for evaluating the degree of Ukraine's independence."[23] This opinion is shared by a prominent Moscow journalist: "There are quite a few politicians in Kiev who keep thinking that the harder they push off from the Kremlin, the sooner they will arrive at Washington's shore."[24]

A very serious aggravating factor has been Crimea, especially Sebastopol. Until the end of the eighteenth century Crimea had been a Tatar khanate. It was incorporated into the Russian Empire in 1783 and became a province of the Russian Federation after the Bolshevik Revolution. In 1944, as the peninsula was liberated from the German occupation, ethnic Tatars who had made up the bulk of the population were deported by Stalin to distant Asian lands because of their alleged treason and collaboration with the Germans during the war. The remaining population was largely Russian, although many Ukrainians were settled there as well. In 1954, in commemoration of the 200th anniversary of Ukraine's unity with Russia, Khrushchev made a generous gift to Kiev, transferring Crimea to Ukraine's jurisdiction. At that time, nobody cared because such purely administrative changes did not really matter in a de facto unitary state ruled by the Kremlin. Little did anybody think at that fateful moment that less than forty years later the issue would acquire such grave proportions.

At present, Russians make up about 70% of the peninsula's population while Ukrainians' share is probably not much more than 10%. In the meantime, the Crimean Tatars, who had been rehabilitated and given the right to return to their historic homeland, have been steadily streaming into the peninsula. Juridically, Crimea is a legitimate part of Ukraine, including the seaport Sebastopol. However, a lot of Russians both in Russia and in Crimea—probably even the majority—are not happy about it, and many are those who adamantly refuse to acknowledge Ukraine's rights over Crimea, particularly Sebastopol.

There is no need here to tell the story of the dispute between Russia and

Ukraine over Sebastopol and the Black Sea Fleet based in this port; all the details have been amply reported in the press. What is probably not very well-known in the West are psychological attitudes of both Russians and Ukrainians toward this sensitive issue.

I have had a chance to discuss the Crimean problem with many of my fellow countrymen, including my academic colleagues. Most of them were clearly less than happy with the prospect of Sebastopol remaining under the Ukrainian rule. Even persons with impeccable democratic credentials bitterly blamed Khrushchev for having ceded Crimea to Ukraine. For Sebastopol, Russians have a cliché: "The city of Russian glory." Every schoolchild knows about the heroic defense of Sebastopol both in the Crimean War in the nineteenth century and during the war against Nazi Germany. In the city itself, all relics of the two glorious sieges are carefully and lovingly preserved; children would recite memorable war episodes, their eyes shining with pride. Probably nowhere else in the country, be it Moscow, St. Petersburg, or Volgograd, are local people so proud of the city they live in and so knowledgeable about its history. If there is a really legendary city for Russians, it is Sebastopol; it does not, however, belong to Russia anymore.

The issue of the fleet is closely linked to the whole problem of Sebastopol. Not that the average Russian cares much about his country's naval power at this point. Nobody really needs that fleet. The issue, however, is deeply rooted in the Russian psyche. It is not the current political or military situation that counts, it is Russian history, memory of the heroic past, legend, national pride. Seeing their country rapidly losing all the vestiges of a great power, Russians feel bitter and humiliated, and this feeling of hurt national pride and dignity requires taking a stand, drawing a line somewhere. Yesterday it was the Kuril Islands issue, tomorrow it may be Sebastopol.

Naturally, the Ukrainians see it all quite differently. While not denying Sebastopol's role in Russian history, they point out that ethnic Ukrainians had their share in it. The journal *Ranok* made it clear: "The Black Sea Fleet was built in 1783. It is hardly possible to figure out today who exactly made a bigger contribution to building battleships and fortresses, seaports and shore batteries— Russians or Ukrainians, who shed more blood in battles. . . . This land was won for the Slavs with the bayonets of Russian soldiers as well as with the swords of Ukrainian Cossacks."[25] The newspaper *Literary Ukraine*, commenting on the Russian parliament's decision to reconsider Sebastopol's status, wrote that "the so-called city of Russian sailors has become a trump card for Moscow."[26] Another newspaper wrote: "As the Zaporizhye Cossacks were navigating the Black Sea, Peter the First was not yet born. Ukrainians at all times made up the bulk of the Black Sea personnel. Ukrainians were predominant in the whole Russian navy. Sebastopol has always been a city of Ukrainian glory."[27]

The Ukrainian nationalistic mass media are blaming the country's leadership for being too timid in stressing the Ukrainian national character of the republic. Said a provincial paper in an article entitled "Civil, not national Ukraine?":

"government members constantly say: people of Ukraine, government of Ukraine, state of Ukraine, but it is very seldom that they use the word Ukrainian as though they were afraid of offending ethnic minorities."[28] The leader of the Congress of Ukrainian Nationalists, Slava Stetsko, said in a public speech: "We have a nation, although the Constitution-drafters lacked the courage to call it the Ukrainian nation. We have a territory, although reduced for the benefit of our neighbors, but we hope that the government of Ukraine will be able to take care of our brothers and sisters outside Ukraine."[29]

It should be noted, however, that these are minority views. Rabid nationalists are rather few in Ukraine, although the number of those who would welcome a tougher line in the relations with Moscow was until recently quite considerable. A distinction must be made between fervent nationalists exalted over all things Ukrainian and full of contempt for the "moskali," on the one hand, and ordinary people who have no particular grievances against Russians, on the other. If this second category (undoubtedly, a vast majority of the Ukrainians) feels, or is persuaded to think, that it is Moscow which is the main obstacle on Ukraine's road to prosperity, that Russia is actually sabotaging all Ukrainian efforts to achieve equitable and honorable status with the former Big Brother—then the relations between the two states will turn sour indeed.

So far, no particular patriotic fervor is noticeable. Drafts into the Ukrainian army have largely proved to be failures. A great patriotic appeal was made to the ethnic Ukrainians who served in the armed forces in various CIS republics, to come home and join the newly born Ukrainian army. The result, however, has so far been negligible. By the summer of 1994, just 20,000 officers and men came home to serve their country, out of the total of 150,000. About 60% of the junior officers appeared willing to leave the army; mass desertion of privates and NCOs has led to to the depletion of some units by 30%. The number of those willing to study in military academies has fallen by two-thirds.[30] Young men are not eager to serve. As in Russia, they are in for business. The slowly growing business community is by and large indifferent to nationalistic slogans. In the mentality of the new businessmen—a lot of them former apparatchiks— there is no room for dreams of Ukraine's grandeur. Some people in Kiev told me that if they could trust a political party that would promise real prosperity, even at the expense of independence, they would have voted for it. The euphoria of the first post-independence days (if ever there was one) is largely gone.

While in Kiev, I visited the headquarters of the Rukh (Popular Movement of Ukraine), and talked to Party officials. What struck me was the spirit of ethnic tolerance and total absence of extremist and chauvinistic tendencies. There were no signs of either anti-Russian xenophobia or anti-Semitism. Indeed, the person in charge of the department dealing with relations between nationalities in the Kiev office of Rukh was Jewish. By the way, contrary to some predictions, independence has not brought about any upsurge in anti-Semitism, which can only partly be explained by the fact that, due to the increasing emigration, the number of Jews still staying in Ukraine has been steadily dwindling. Obviously,

positive changes have been taking place in the mentality of the Ukrainian population, which had traditionally been blamed (not always justly) for widespread
anti-Jewish feelings.

I was shown Rukh documents which said: "The Ukrainian people has, in
many millions of the citizens of Ukraine belonging to other ethnic groups, loyal
friends just as eager to build an independent and free Ukrainian state. This fact,
as well as the tolerance proper to the Ukrainian people, has made it possible to
avoid interethnic conflicts in the country during the Ukrainian revolution.'' Nationalist extremism was sharply criticized, in particular the decisions taken at
the Lviv regional conference of Rukh where "integral nationalism" had been
manifested and, in fact, the slogan "Ukraine for Ukrainians" had been put
forward.[31]

At the same time, it was probably inevitable that after independence, worrisome symptoms of Ukrainian ethnonationalism began to emerge. Actual facts
of discrimination on ethnic grounds are rare, but there are many ways to give
preferential treatment to one ethnic group at the expense of others, especially
in the area of civil service when it comes to employment. The field of education
is very important, too, as an indicator of the state of interethnic relationships.
A recent poll conducted by Chernovitsy sociological center in Northern Bukovina (southwestern part of Ukraine) provides some insights into this issue. When
questioned: "Have you ever had any difficulties or encountered embarrassing
situations at your workplace on account of your ethnic origin?'', 93% of Ukrainians but only 48.6% of Russians answered "Never.'' When the same question
was asked in regard to applying to state offices with some requests, 90.0% of
Ukrainians and just 51.5% of Russians said they had nothing to complain about.
Of the ethnic Russians polled 47% said that they felt they were being treated
with more disregard and arrogance than before independence. More than one-
third of the respondents believed that ethnic Ukrainians should be given privileged treatment in matters of appointment to Civil Service jobs.[32]

What about the prospects of relations between Russia and Ukraine? Except
for the painful, but by no means insoluble, conflict over Crimea, Sebastopol,
and the Black Sea Fleet, the two nations have no real territorial disputes. The
situation, however, can change drastically if the current economic and political
crisis in Ukraine deepens and its leadership proves totally unable to put forward
a realistic and comprehensive program of reform focusing on market economy.
In this case, millions of Russians and Russian-speakers in the East may demand
a degree of regional autonomy bordering on separation. Voices calling for this
kind of solution were already heard during miners' strikes in Donbass. This
trend is certain to provoke a violent reaction in the other areas, since it is clear
that the Ukrainian economy cannot function without heavy industry. Kharkiv
and Donbass are indispensable for the country's successful development.

But the problem may be even bigger. Some separatist ideologues have already
hinted at the desirability of setting up "Novorossia" (New Russia), stretching
from Kharkiv and Donetsk to Dnepropetrovsk, Zaporizhye, and Krivoy Rig to

Nikolaev and Odessa, thus cutting off from Ukraine the whole Southeast and South. It is true that what most of the advocates of this idea have in mind is not a completely independent state but an autonomous area. And this is not all. During the 1991 referendum on independence, Transcarpathia and Bukovina in the West held their own separate polls on the question of greater autonomy, and in both regions majorities were in favor of this proposition. The government in Kiev took a hard stand, categorically rejecting any idea of federalism; so far, federalization seems a remote possibility, but if the internal crisis deepens, more and more voices will be heard in the "unreliable" areas calling for autonomy and maybe even for secession.

As *The Economist* puts it,

worsening economic conditions are likely to deepen the divisions between the Russian-speaking, industrialized eastern Ukraine and the more progressive, intensely Ukrainian western regions. When hyperinflation erodes the spending power of the government's handout to the miners of eastern Ukraine, they could easily strike again . . . they are likely to demand that Ukraine, or at least the eastern part, should rejoin Russia. This possibility would become greater if, as is just possible, the Russian economy were to stabilize as Ukraine's began to gurgle down the drain.

The government in Kiev tolerates separatist movements in practice, though they are formally outlawed. But if they were to become a real threat, the government could try to crack down. If it did, and if the easterners fought back, nationalists in the Kremlin would be under pressure to intervene on the side of their Russian-speaking brethren. For this reason a Ukrainian version of the civil wars embroiling other former Soviet republics—Georgia and Azerbaijan, for example—would be much more dangerous.[33]

This "nightmare scenario" seems far from plausible right now but it cannot be completely ruled out in the future. Of course, a Russian-Ukrainian conflict would be a colossal absurdity, considering that, unlike Serbs, Croats, and Bosnian Muslims, Russians and Ukrainians have no historic feuds, no blood legacy, no irreconcilable differences, no reasons to hate each other. Indeed, it would take an incredible lot of blundering and political stupidity to drive the two nations to the point of a full-scale conflict; unfortunately, exactly these qualities are not in short supply at present both in Kiev and in Moscow.

A more likely scenario seems to be just muddling through in the relations between Russia and Ukraine, a kind of long, drawn-out cold war, periodically taking ugly forms and fraught with danger of a real conflict but not actually reaching a point of no return.

Much will depend, of course, on Russia's behavior. So far, official Ukrainian arrogance and unwillingness to cooperate has only too often been matched by Russia's contradictory and contemptuous attitude. Even some of the Russian Democrats are reluctant to acknowledge that Ukraine is not Russia any more but a completely independent state. It was one of the leaders of the short-lived Ukrainian republic, proclaimed during the Russian civil war in 1918, who said that Russian democracy ended as soon as it came to the Ukrainian issue. The

Canadian professor Zenon Kohut believes that ''the Russian unity has been and continues to be so embedded in the Russian psyche, that it is very difficult for Russians—from conservative nationalists to liberal democrats—to acknowledge the right of Ukrainians to their own history and national identity.''[34] Obviously, reciprocity is needed in adapting to new realities. While Moscow has to part with illusions about Ukrainian independence being just a short-lived phenomenon, Kiev must admit that Ukraine is hardly likely to be recognized by the world as a power absolutely on the same level as Russia.

In the aftermath of independence, it was felt in Ukraine that the country really was a ''second France.'' Leaving aside this comparison that everybody knew was just a hyperbole, people actually had in mind such nations as Spain, or Poland, or Turkey: Were Ukrainians in any way inferior?

A major flaw in this ''comparative reasoning'' was that it overlooked the main issue: The economies of Spain, Poland, or Turkey were developing for centuries as national economies. But there never was such a thing as Ukrainian economy. Industry, agriculture, finances, trade, services, transport—everything was just part of a gigantic machine the main component of which was the Russian economy. Interdependence of the former Union's republics was actually greater than in any federal or multinational state in the world. Even the vaunted military might of Ukraine does not look so terribly impressive if we realize that it cannot on its own ensure the maintenance of its strategic missiles or build a battleship, for lack of technology and experts.

Ukraine's case is the best illustration of a tremendous historic error that was committed when the collapse of Communism was followed by the breakup of the enormous and complicated socioeconomic mechanism the Union had been.

NOTES

1. *Batkivshchina*, nos. 7–8 (July-August 1992).

2. *Ukrainskii Vestnik*, Agency Postfactum, no. 42 (1992), 20.

3. Bohdan Nahaylo, *The New Ukraine* (London: Royal Institute of International Affairs, 1992), 11.

4. Roman Szporluk, *Independent Ukraine* (The Aspen Institute, ''Russia, Ukraine and the U.S. Response,'' Twelfth Conference, January 1993, vol. 8, no. 1. Queenstown, Md., 1993), 23.

5. Nahaylo, *The Ukraine*, 21; *Rossiya* (Moscow), April 14, 1993, 2.

6. Nahaylo, *The New Ukraine*, 22, 29; *Izvestiya* (Moscow), May 4, 1993.

7. Vladimir Kolinko, ''Voenno-polevoi roman po ukrainski'' (War love story, Ukrainian way), *Rossiia*, no. 24, June 9, 1993; Vladimir Malinkovich, ''Razoitis nie rasstavayas'' (To separate without saying good-bye), *Nezavisimaya Gazeta*, April 9, 1993.

8. Szporluk, *Independent Ukraine*, 27; Serhiy Holowaty, *Ukraine: One Year of Independence*, in The Aspen Institute, ''Russia, Ukraine and the U.S. Response,'' 57.

9. Holowaty, *Ukraine*, 57; Viktor Timoshenko, ''The Military Doctrine and Reality,'' *Nezavisimaia Gazeta*, November 18, 1995.

10. *Moskovskie Novosti*, no. 30, July 25, 1993.

11. "Warnings from Massandra," *The Economist*, September 4, 1993, 52.

12. Meeting Report, Kennan Institute for Advanced Russian Studies, The Woodrow Wilson Center, 1995, vol. XII, no. 11.

13. *Politicheskaia Mysl* (Political Thought), Kiev, no. 2 (1994), 20–27.

14. *Nezavisimaia Gazeta*, July 15, 1994.

15. Viktor Linko, "The Eclipse of the Political Capital of Ukraine," *Nezavisimaia Gazeta*, November 10, 1995.

16. A. Denikin, *Essays on Russian Turmoil* (in Russian), vol. 5 (Berlin: n.p., 1926), 133.

17. Celestine Bohlen, "A Borderland Whose History Reflects That Troubled Role," *New York Times*, December 1, 1991.

18. *Ranok* (Kiev) (July 1992), 29.

19. *Ukrainskii Vestnik*, 20.

20. *Nezavisimaia Gazeta*, April 9, 1993.

21. Nahaylo, *The New Ukraine*, 34.

22. Eugene B. Rumer, "Eurasia Letter: Will Ukraine Return to Russia?", *Foreign Policy*, no. 96 (Fall 1994), 135–136.

23. Vladimir Razuvaev, "The Future of Russian-Ukrainian Relations Will Be Determined by Businessmen, Bankers, and TV-Viewers," *Segodnia*, November 3, 1995.

24. Viktor Loshak, "No Changes on the Ukrainian Front," *Moscow News*, November 5–12, 1995.

25. *Ranok* (Kiev) (July 1992), 3.

26. *Literaturna Ukraina*, December 24, 1992, 1.

27. *Batkivshchina*, nos. 7–8 (July-August 1992).

28. *Holos Lemkivshchiny*, November 1992.

29. Ibid.

30. Yuri Selivanov, "V armii izbytok generalov, a soldat i ofitserov nekhvataet" (In the Army: A Surplus of Generals, a Shortage of Men and Officers), *Segodnia*, July 1, 1994.

31. Zvernennie Rady Natsionalnostei Narodnoho Rukhu Ukrainy . . . Appeal of the Council of Nationalities, Popular Movement of Ukraine "Rukh," to Ukrainian national minorities, November 23, 1992, no. 771; Zaiava 7 sessii Rady Natsionalnostey NRU . . . Statement of the Council of Nationalities, Popular Movement of Ukraine "Rukh," regarding the events in Lviv in October-November 1992, November 23, 1992, no. 776.

32. D. Turchenkov and D. Nemirovskü. "Interethnic Relations in Northern Bukovina," *Polis* (Moscow), no. 2 (1994), 184.

33. "Ukraine: Galloping towards the Brink," *The Economist*, July 3, 1993, 43.

34. Zenon E. Kohut, *History as a Battleground: Russian-Ukrainian Relations and Historical Consciousness in Contemporary Ukraine*, Russian Littoral Project, University of Maryland at College Park and The Johns Hopkins University, SAIS, no. 9, May 1993.

8

Inside the Russian Federation: Russia and Tatarstan

The Russian Federation is not only the most populous of the new post-Soviet states (around 150 million people); it also contains more ethnic groups. Here are some figures. There are 126 different peoples, or ethnic groups, in the Russian Federation. Ethnic non-Russians make up about 27 million, or 18.5%. The bulk of the Federation's territory—areas with a predominantly Russian population: 56 *oblasts* and 6 *krays* (bigger provinces). Besides, there are 19 autonomous republics formed on ethnic grounds; theoretically, it would seem that non-Russian ethnic groups must constitute the majority of the population in the autonomous republics; however, this is not the case. Out of 26 million people living in these administrative units, which is about 15% of the whole population of the Federation, the titular nations number only 10 million, or less than 40% of the population of the autonomous republics. The other 60% are not necessarily ethnic Russians; there are also other peoples or ethnic groups, nontitular but non-Russian.

To make the situation clear, let us look at Tatarstan. According to the 1989 census, the population of the republic numbered 3,642,000 people. The ethnic breakdown was as follows: Tatars, 1,765,000 (48.5%), Russians, 1,575,000 (43.2%), Chuvash, 134,000 (3.7%), and so on. But the number of the ethnic Tatars in the Russian Federation as a whole was 5,520,000. Thus, it appears that less than a third of the Tatar nation live in Tatarstan and more than two-thirds in Russia proper, in Bashkortostan, and other autonomous republics while the share of Tatars in their nominal homeland, Tatarstan, is less than half.

As regards other autonomous republics, Table 8.1 illustrates the ethnic situation.[1]

Table 8.1
Percentage of Titular Ethnoses and Russians in the Russian Federation

Republic	Population (in 1,000s)	Titular ethnos (%)	Russians (%)
Bashkortostan	4,077	Bashkirs—21.9	39.3
Chuvashia	1,361	Chuvash—68.0	26.8
Mordovia	959	Mordva—32.5	40.0
Udmurtia	1,641	Udmurts—30.9	58.8
Mari-El	767	Mari—43.3	47.5
Komi	1,203	Komi—23.3	57.7
Karelia	789	Karels—10	74.0
Yakutia (Sakha)	1,035	Yakuts—33	50.0
Khakassia	583	Khakass—11	79.0
Buryatia	1,052	Buryats—24	70.0
Daghestan	2,009	Avars—27.5, Dargins—15.6 Kumyks—12.9, Lezgins—11.3	9.2
North Ossetia (Alania)	664	Ossetians (Alans)—53.0	29.9
Adygeia	450	Adygei—22.1	68.0
Checheno-Ingushetia (now divided)	1,232	Chechens—57.8 Ingush—12.9	23.1
Kabardino-Balkaria	787	Kabardins—48.2 Balkars—9.4	32.0
Karachaevo-Cherkessia	435	Karachai—31.2 Cherkess—9.7	42.4
Kalmykia	320	na	37.7
Tuva	308	na	32.0
Altai	200	na	60.4

Source: 1989 RSFSR census, *The Economist,* January 14, 1995, p. 23.

The figures show the situation in some of the republics to be truly paradoxical. Thus, in Bashkortostan (the Bashkir republic) the titular nation, Bashkirs, are in the third place, constituting just under 22% of the population, while Russians make up almost 40% and Tatars 28%. There are more Tatars than Bashkirs in Bashkortostan. As to ethnic Russians, they constitute an overwhelming majority in Khakassia, Karelia, Buryatia, Adygeya, Mordovia, Komi, and Yakutia—between 79 and 50%—and almost equal the titular nation in Tatarstan; in Bashkortostan and Udmurtia they also outnumber the titular nation. Even in Chuvashia, North Ossetia, and Kabardino-Balkaria Russians make up almost one-third of the population; it is only in Daghestan that Russians are a small minority.

Altogether, according to the 1989 census, ethnic Russians numbered 120 million, or 81.5% of the whole population of the Russian Federation. The other most numerous nationalities were: Tatars, 5,520,000 (3.8%), Ukrainians, 4,364,000 (3.0%), Chuvash, 1,771,000 (1.2%), Bashkirs, 1,345,000 (0.9%).[2]

What are the implications of this extraordinary setup in the Russian Federation? First, what is striking is an artificial character of most of the autonomous republics. How can Tatarstan be regarded as a "Tatar state," a home for Tatars, if less than a third of all the ethnic Tatars in Russia live there, and inside the republic non-Tatars outnumber Tatars? How can Bashkortostan consider itself a state of the Bashkir nation while ethnic Bashkirs make up just one-fifth of its population? How can the Komi republic claim to be a "sovereign Komi state" while the number of ethnic Komis in the republic is less than one-fourth?

Wherever I went in the republics, I heard practically only Russian. Even in Daghestan, where just 9% of the population are Russians, everybody in the cities speaks Russian; otherwise, the people who speak twenty-nine languages simply could not understand each other. Russian is everywhere an official idiom, a language of instruction, of administrative paperwork, and so on. As to the economy, all the republics are integral parts of Russia, none can be viable as an independent entity. Practically everybody, including die-hard nationalists, acknowledge this total dependence on Russia. Still, local nationalism is a fact of life.

One of the reasons for this is a bizarre and unprecedented character of the Russian Federation's ethnic composition. An inherent ambiguity of this federal entity is reflected in its very name: According to the new Constitution, the terms "Russia" and "The Russian Federation" are interchangeable. Still, the question remains: Is it Russia or a federation headed by Russia? In the first case, non-Russians must regard themselves as Russians first and Tatars, Yakuts, Komi afterwards, something they will never agree to. In the second case, if this is a union of equals, why this stress on "Russianness?"

To avoid this trap, a new word has been coined—*Rossiyanie,* meaning not ethnic Russians but rather citizens of Russia, regardless of ethnic background. It is not easy to convey the meaning of this nuance. The point is that in English the word "Russian" means both ethnicity and state belonging, or citizenship. In Russian, there are two separate terms: one is *Russkiy,* with an ethnic connotation, and the other *Rossiyskiy,* belonging to the Russian state, history, culture, but devoid of an ethnolinguistic meaning. It is the second term that is used in the term "Russian Federation," and it is precisely from this nonethnic term that the word *Rossiyanie* has been shaped. The Russian Federation, therefore, is Russian not in the sense *Russkiy* but in the sense *Rossiyskiy,* just as an ethnic Bashkir, Karel, or Yakut residing in the Federation is not Russian-*Russkiy* but Russian-*Rossiyskiy*; that is, *Rossiyanin,* citizen of Russia which is defined in this case as not an ethnic state but as a federal entity just deriving its name from the biggest of its constituent parts.

Do the Tatars, Bashkirs, Yakuts, et al. live in a *Russian* state as minority citizens, or are they equal with ethnic Russians within the framework of a federal entity called Russian simply because this happens to be the name of the largest ethnos in this entity? This question arose for the first time after the collapse of the USSR. The more nationalist-minded representatives of non-Russians have, of course, chosen the second option. Some of the more extremist among them stretched the notion of equality to the point of sovereignty if not outright independence. Thus, the "battle of the autonomous republics" for sovereignty was launched right after the Soviet Union was pronounced dead in December 1991, and it was Tatarstan which became a focus of this battle, because Tatars were the most numerous among the Federation's non-Russians as well as more politically and culturally advanced than any other "autonomous" nation. Also, Tatarstan is economically quite important, located as it is between the Moscow area and the industrial Urals region; it is also oil-rich. If Tatarstan had been successful in breaking out of the Russian Federation and asserting its independence, other major autonomous republics such as Bashkortostan and Komi could have been expected to follow. Moreover, this development might have triggered an implosion of the Federation as a whole, a disintegration of Russia not only along the ethnic lines. Ominous calls for the creation of a Far East or a Siberian or a Urals republic already began to ring. So, it would not be an exaggeration to say that in 1992 and 1993 all of Russia was following the confrontation between Moscow and Kazan with a deep anxiety and apprehension.

As I arrived in Tatarstan in the summer of 1993, I noticed at once two parallel patterns: first, the intensity and ferociousness of the extreme nationalist movement, and second, the apparent lack of a genuine mass support for the idea of independence. The tone of the extremist press was unambiguous; here are some excerpts from newspapers.

Tatarstan will be an independent state in spite of all the obstacles erected by the official Moscow. . . . Can we, Tatars, not lacking in national pride, honour, and dignity, be citizens of Russia, an empire that has arisen as a result of the colonial wars which had destroyed the Tatar state along with the majority of its population?[3]

The introduction of two state languages in Tatarstan [Tatar and Russian] is a death verdict against the Tatar language and the Tatar nation. . . . To make us citizens of the Russian Federation means supporting Russia's imperial policy.[4]

The All-Tatar Community Center, inspired by the experience of the Jewish people in the field of national consolidation, is convinced that the survival and spiritual consolidation of the Tatar nation is impossible without the existence of a sovereign Tatar state.[5]

Tatarstan will never be a state within the framework of a wretched and famished Russian Federation; the independent state of Tatarstan has broken away from the neighboring Russian Federation like a spaceship reaching out to far-away worlds and planets. . . . Whoever comes to power in neighboring Russia, in the case of their attempts to claim the territory of the state of Tatarstan the peoples of Tatarstan will do their utmost to defend their Motherland and resist the foreigners.[6]

Tatarstan can live without its neighbour, Russia, but Russia can hardly survive without Tatarstan. . . . The people of Tatarstan will build a flourishing state not subordinated to any foreign power, Tatarstan will become a member of UN.[7]

I met with one of the top officials of the All-Tatar Community Center, the main body of Tatar nationalists. Suddenly, he told me: "Of course, we are ready to sign a peace treaty with Russia." I was dumbfounded. "How come?" I asked him, "Do you consider Tatarstan to be in a state of war with Russia?" Rather embarrassed, he answered: "Well, you know, technically we may be said to be in war since the time of Ivan the Terrible who captured Kazan, our capital." It became clear to me that this kind of person just could not be taken seriously; the Community Center, however, was not the most extreme of Tatar nationalist organizations. A political party was founded by a woman, Fauziya Bayramova, which has been engaged in a fierce anti-Russian campaign.

The nationalists speaking through such pro-independence newspapers as *Souverenitet* and *Nezavisimost* (Independence), both printed in Russian, by the way, as well as in Tatar, were proudly boasting of the fact that the all-Russian referendum of April 1993, conducted during the standoff between Yeltsin and the Russian parliament, had failed to attract the majority of voters in Tatarstan. "People have shown that they do not care about referenda of a neighboring state." By that time, it had been already stipulated in the Tatarstans' constitution that the republic was a "sovereign state," a "subject of international law" (though nobody seemed to know what this term exactly meant), associated with the Russian Federation by a treaty which did not even exist at the time. Still, there seemed to be a fine shade between two key terms; "sovereignty" was on everybody's lips but "independence" was officially avoided. President Shaimiev was clearly reluctant to cross the final line and to burn his bridges. An extremely skillful politician, he was walking the tightrope for two years before finally arriving at a compromise solution which has proved satisfactory not only to the authorities in both Kazan and Moscow but also—most importantly—to the bulk of the Tatar population as well.

The road to this solution was difficult indeed. As early as 1989, when the Soviet Union still existed, the newly founded All-Tatar Community Center came forth with an idea of upgrading the autonomous republic's status by proclaiming it a Union Republic. On August 30, 1990, a declaration of sovereignty was adopted by the local Supreme Soviet, and the Republic of Tatarstan was proclaimed, the word "autonomous" being dropped. In July 1991, presidential elections were held and Mintimer Shaimiev, the Communist Party first secretary, defeated the other three candidates. The nationalists immediately demanded full independence; in October 1991, on the anniversary of the fall of Kazan in the seventeenth century, an attempt was made to storm the parliament building. Shaimiev managed to control the situation. Skillfully maneuvering, he proposed a referendum. It was held in March 1992; about 63% of the voters supported the ambiguous status of the republic, sovereign but not fully independent, "associated'' with Moscow but stopping short of actually seceding from the Russian Federation.

By that time, the correlation of political forces became more or less clear. The results of the polls conducted in 1992 showed that the Communal Center enjoyed the support of just 4.1% of the population, most of this support coming from the countryside; in the capital city, Kazan, the number of those who backed the independence option was more than twice lower than in the republic as a whole.[8] According to Leonid Tolchinsky, one of the leaders of Tatarstan's Russian community, nationalist organizations combined have never enjoyed the support of more than 20% of the Tatar population. The lowest rate of the nationalists' support happened to be in Kazan where Russians outnumbered Tatars by about 20%. It might have been expected that precisely in the capital city this disproportion would have caused an upsurge of Tatar nationalist feeling; however, this was not the case. The point is that the ethnic Tatars residing in Kazan have been quite close to Russians for centuries; many of them have become thoroughly Russianized. There are a number of Christian Tatars in Kazan, and even Muslims are by no means religious fanatics. Tatars, by the way, have never known *shari'a* laws. The Islamic factor has not played a major role in the Tatar nationalist movement.

Tatars in general are quite compatible with Russians as regards mentality and way of life. Both nations respect each other, there are neither superiority nor inferiority complexes in the relationships between them. The urban dwellers speak fluent Russian; there are a lot of mixed marriages. Speaking to Tatars in Kazan, I never noticed even a trace of anti-Russian feeling or a genuine desire to break away from Russia. Meetings of extreme nationalists in Kazan and most other cities have never attracted large crowds. For this reason, nationalists have been contemptuously calling the Kazan Tatars "mankurts," a word from an ancient legend depicting persons taken prisoner by enemies and subjected to a surgical operation which made them forget their origins and loyally serve the invaders. I also heard this word in Kazakhstan where it has been applied to those ethnic Kazakhs who had become "Russianized."

It is the great industrial city of Naberezhnye Chelny, the center of the auto industry, which has grown into a hotbed of Tatar nationalism. There, too, the number of ethnic Russians is large; they constitute the bulk of the skilled labor force; unlike in Kazan, however, the Tatar residents are mostly newcomers from the countryside. They lack the experience of having lived with Russians side by side. The poorly educated peasant boys have proved more susceptible to nationalist slogans than the relatively well-to-do and long-established Tatar community in Kazan.

On the other hand, in some regions where ethnic Russians predominate, signs of a possible Russian backlash began to emerge. For instance, Russian activists in the city of Bugulma let it be known that in the case of Tatarstan withdrawing from the Russian Federation they would demand the city with the adjoining areas be made part of the neighboring Ulyanovsk *oblast* of Russia.

In this precarious situation, it has taken a real masterpiece of a balancing act on the part of President Shaimiev to come to terms with Yeltsin. After months of tough bargaining, a treaty was signed in February 1994; claims of sovereignty based on "association" with Russia were dropped. Tatarstan remains a part of the Russian Federation. A repetition of the Chechen version has been avoided, and the menace of a breakup of Russia can be considered nonexistent at this point.

Logically speaking, it could not be otherwise. Even such a highly industrialized country as Tatarstan cannot exist on its own. I remember talking to Marat Mulukov, the leader of the All-Tatar Community Center. He told me that the issue at hand was not the creation of an independent Tatar state but the restoration of one. Mulukov referred to a well-known historic fact: in the Middle Ages, Tatars, or rather Tataro-Mongols, coming all the way from the Asian steppes, invaded and conquered Russia and ruled it for a few centuries. After Russia had succeeded in throwing off the Tatar yoke, there was a standoff for awhile between the Tsar and the ruler of the Kazan Khanate. A war broke out in the mid-sixteenth century, and Ivan the Terrible defeated and destroyed the last Tatar state. Now, Mulukov claimed, the time has come to restore independent Tatarstan. He spoke in favor of creating a confederation of nations of the Middle Volga and the Urals area, a notion that suggested merging in a single entity not only peoples of non-Russian origin, such as Tatars, Bashkirs, Chuvash, and others, but also ethnic Russian population farther east, close to the Urals mountains. The idea was dubious in the first place since there was no proof that all those peoples, irrespective of their ethnic background, were willing to join a confederation which would clearly be dominated by Tatarstan. Also, Mulukov was ill at ease when I asked him: "How could Tatarstan exist as an independent state, surrounded as it is by Russian territories? What would you do with all your oil when the first Tatar truck or petrol tank crossing the border is stopped by a Russian traffic policeman?" President Shaimiev certainly took all of this into consideration when he opted for a treaty with Russia which allowed him to ensure Tatarstan's sovereignty in the political and judicial sphere while maintaining close cooperation with Russia as regards such vital issues as economy and environment. Dealing with economic and ecologic problems is certainly impossible except by common efforts. This is not the case, however, with political and administrative issues, and it is in this field that threats of an ethnic conflict can emerge.

The point is that even if the supreme republican authorities fully realize the danger of anti-Russian nationalism, their capacity to control lower-level officials is limited. The best example would probably be the police. Every republican leader's dream is to place local forces of law and order under his control and out of Moscow's jurisdiction. Once this is achieved, it could be tempting for a "native" town police chief to surreptitiously, albeit gradually, start a "Tatarization" or a "Bashkirization" of his force. This is certain to trigger a nasty response among ethnic Russians ("See, now it's happening! We are being squeezed out!''). The relations between the titular nation and ethnic Russians will immediately begin to sour, particularly because there is almost no republic where the titular nation constitutes a majority of the population. Thus, any kind of ''nationalization'' or ''nativization'' of the apparatus is bound to be regarded by Russians and other nontitular ethnoses as totally unfair, actually as a minority rule.

Tatarization reportedly is already proceeding in Tatarstan. According to the figures published in 1993, out of sixty-one chiefs of local administrative bodies, forty-nine were ethnic Tatars and twelve Russians and Russian-speakers. In fifteen districts where Tatars account for less than 50% (in some of them as little as 29%), Tatar officials are in charge.[9] This does not remain unnoticed by Russian ethnics. It is precisely over the Tatarization issue that President Shaimiev probably faces his biggest challenge.

So far, there is every indication that he has been able to deal with it. No interethnic conflicts have been reported. Speaking on the eve of the fifth anniversary of the declaration of Tatarstan's state sovereignty, Shaimiev said: ''Tatarstan has never yet had the kind of independence, both political and economic, as we enjoy today.''[10] Currently, the president is riding high, and Tatarstan's model of relationship with Russia—sovereignty within the Federation—is being universally regarded as an example to be followed by all the other former ''autonomous republics.''

NOTES

1. 1989 RSFSR census, *The Economist*, January 14, 1995, 23.
2. *Svobodnaia Mysl*, no. 2 (1993), 67.
3. *Nezavisimost*, no. 3 (5) (1993), 3.
4. *Suverenitet*, no. 2 (23) (1993), 4.
5. *Izvestia TOTS*, no. 1 (13) (March 1993), 4.
6. *Nezavisimost*, no. 4 (6) (1993), 2.
7. *Suverenitet*, no. 6 (26) (1993), 1.
8. *Tatarstan*, no. 4 (1993), 3–8.
9. *Sovetskaia Tataria*, April 3, 1993, 7.
10. *Segodnia*, August 25, 1995.

9

Russians in the Near Abroad and the Problem of "Neoimperialism"

The term "Near Abroad" was coined some time after the disintegration of the Soviet Union; it refers to the former Soviet republics as opposed to the "far abroad," that is, the foreign countries which were never parts of the USSR. The new term is being used largely in the context of the "fate of Russians," meaning the ethnic Russians residing outside the Russian Federation—25.3 million at the time of the 1989 census. Three-quarters of this number lived in Ukraine, Belarus, and Kazakhstan. A sizeable Russian population was in Central Asia (Kazakhstan excluded)–3.3 million (see Table 9.1).

At the same time, it must be noted that the number of people who call Russian their mother tongue is bigger than that of ethnic Russians. For instance, in Ukraine, Russians account for 22.1% of the population while 32.8% consider Russian their native language; the corresponding figures for Belarus are 13.2% and 31.9%, in Kazakhstan 37.8% and 47.4%, in Moldova 13.0% and 23.1%, in Kyrgyzstan 21.5% and 25.6%, in Azerbaijan 5.6% and 7.5%, in Uzbekistan 8.3% and 10.9%, and so on.[1] These figures reflect the high degree of spontaneous "Russianization."

Persons of non-Russian ethnic origin regarding Russian as native language are quite numerous: in Ukraine, for instance, they counted 5,700,000; in Kazakhstan 1,600,000, in Uzbekistan 500,000, in Georgia 142,000, in Azerbaijan 137,000, in Latvia 228,000, in Moldova 446,000, in Kyrgyzstan 174,000, and so on, totaling 11.2 million.

Especially high is the proportion of those of the titular nationality who have adopted Russian as their native language in urban areas, particularly in the capitals of the republics: in Ukraine, where 12.2% of ethnic Ukrainians speak Rus-

Table 9.1
Numbers of Ethnic Russians in the Soviet Union

Republic	Number	Percentage of the Republic's Population
Estonia	474,000	30.3
Latvia	905,000	34.0
Lithuania	344,000	9.4
Belarus	1,342,000	13.2
Ukraine	11,355,000	22.1
Moldova	562,000	13.0
Kazakhstan	6,227,000	37.8
Kyrgyzstan	916,000	21.5
Uzbekistan	1,653,000	8.3
Tajikistan	388,000	7.6
Turkmenistan	333,000	9.5
Azerbaijan	391,000	5.6
Georgia	341,000	6.3
Armenia	51,000	1.6

Note: All the figures are for 1989.
Source: Naselenie Rossii, A yearly demographic report issued by the Center for Human Demography and Ecology (Moscow, 1993).

sian as their native language, this proportion reaches 19.0% in urban areas and 21.3% in the capital, Kiev. In Kazakhstan the corresponding figures are 1.4, 2.5, and 4.3%, in Kyrgyzstan 0.3, 1.0, and 2.0, in Uzbekistan 0.4, 1.2, and 1.9.[2] It can be said, therefore, that the sphere of use of Russian is much wider in the Near Abroad than could be suggested judging by the figure of ethnic Russians alone which is quite natural, of course, in any empire. This does not mean that people of the titular nationality who are fluent in Russian must necessarily be less nationalistic-minded and even less anti-Russian than those who do not.

Most Russians in the NIS (New Independent States) are urban dwellers: from 95 to 97% in Turkmenistan, Azerbaijan, and Uzbekistan, to 85 to 86% in Georgia, Moldova, and Latvia. In Kazakhstan the Russians constitute 51% of the total urban population, in Latvia 41%, Kyrgyzstan 40%, Estonia 39%, Ukraine 29%, Moldova 24%.[3] Especially high is the percentage of Russians in the capital cities: in Kiev in 1989 the percent of Russians in the whole city population was 20.9, in Minsk 20.0, in Vilnius 20.2, in Riga 36.5, in Tallinn 41.2, in Kishinev 26.4, in Baku 18.0, in Tbilisi 12.1, in Alma-Ata 59.1, in Bishkek 55.8, in Dushanbe 32.8, in Ashkhabad 32.4, in Tashkent 34.0; in Yerevan, the capital of Armenia, ethnic Russians constituted just 1.9%.[4]

Table 9.2 illustrates the occupation of Russians in the Union republics. It

Table 9.2
Occupation of Russian-Speakers in the Republics of the Soviet Union

Republic	Industry	Agriculture	Construction	Health	Education	Science, Art	Management
Ukraine	+24	-65	+11	+16	+8	+55	+40
Belarus	+11	-78	+3	+22	+30	+99	+195
Lithuania	+30	-76	-3	-31	-20	+6	+195
Latvia	+47	-70	+5	-19	-16	-24	+105
Estonia	+78	-84	-13	-13	-28	-49	+98
Moldova	+108	+79	+28	-3	+2	+136	+133
Georgia	+22	-78	+32	+26	-28	+34	+121
Armenia	-2	-68	-14	+8	-3	+43	+98
Azerbaijan	+90	-90	+15	+22	-23	+105	+169
Kazakhstan	+109	-70	+76	-8	-24	+38	+28
Kyrgyzstan	+171	-72	+119	0	+4	+98	+87
Uzbekistan	+126	-94	+108	+9	-12	+328	+217
Tajikistan	+122	-95	+90	+36	+1	+161	+144

Notes: The figures with "+" or "−" show the difference (in percents) between the number of Russian-speakers and persons of titular nationality in a given field. For example, the figure "144" in the last line of the last column means that in Turkmenistan, the number of Russian-speakers in management surpassed that of Turkmens by 144%.[5]

Russian-speakers include all persons of nontitular nationality, for instance in Central Asia—Ukrainians, Belorussians, Jews, Germans, etc.
Source: Rossiyskaia Gazeta, June 26, 1993.

gives a fairly accurate picture of fields of occupation of ethnic Russians and Russian-speakers on the eve of the breakup of the Soviet Union.

The two largest fields in which the Russians appear to have had a clear numerical edge on the natives seem to be industry and management. Next come sciences, art, and medicine. Much less was the proportion of Russians in education and in agriculture, they were in clear minority.

While on a visit to the Kirgiz Union Republic in 1985, I noticed that skilled factory workers and engineers were mostly Russians and other Slavs; so were most managers and middle-level state employees. High-level bureaucrats, university professors, school teachers, and students were largely Kirgiz. In agriculture, among farmers in state and collective farms there appeared to be a substantial number of ethnic Russians and Germans, the latter being descendants of Germans who had been deported by Stalin from Russia and the Caucasus during the war, while cattle-breeding was exclusively in the hands of natives. In trade, Uzbeks, Koreans, and people from the Caucasus seemed to be predominant. Police was mainly native.

The Russian expert Nikolai Rudensky gives this description:

Relatively most Russians are employed in industry, typically holding blue-collar or middle management jobs. The proportion of industrial workers among Russians in Estonia, for example, is 44 percent versus 25 percent among ethnic Estonians. The respective figures for Ukraine are 39 percent and 31 percent, Latvia 37 percent and 25 percent, Lithuania 36 percent and 28 percent, Moldova 35 percent and 17 percent, Azerbaijan 34 percent and 18 percent, etc.

Mentioning also construction, transportation, and communications where from 10 to 16% of Russians were employed, Rudensky notes that the importance of farming for Russians is comparatively low (2 to 5%, except for Kazakhstan and Kyrgyzstan, 10 and 8.5% respectively), and concludes: "This general pattern of employment goes back to the period of the 1930s to the 1950s, when Soviet authorities promoted the large-scale migration of workers, predominantly Russians."[6]

Those Russian newcomers had a mentality of their own. As Rudensky puts it,

many Russians outside Russia never perceived themselves as minority groups: just the opposite, they considered themselves to be representatives of the dominant nation in the multinational state. . . . Because of this basic attitude, most Russians felt no need whatsoever to master local languages and traditions. Many of them, in fact, showed contempt for the cultural patterns of their ethnic environment, which could hardly improve their relations with native ethnic groups.[7]

Indeed, in Kazakhstan less than 1% of the Russian population had good command of the Kazakh language; in Kirgizia the corresponding figure was 1.2%, in Turkmenistan 2.5%, in Tajikistan 3.5%, in Uzbekistan 4.6%. Worst of all was the situation in the capital cities where ethnic Russians felt no need at all to learn the titular language since all the natives knew Russian: in Alma-Ata, just 0.6% of Russians knew the local idiom, in Bishkek 0.6%, in Dushanbe 2.3%, in Tashkent 3.5%, in Ashkhabad 1.7%, in Kishinev 11.1%, in Tallinn 15.4%.[8] I recall speaking to some Party officials in Lithuania and Uzbekistan, persons who were in charge of propaganda work and thus had to have constant verbal contact with natives; when I expressed surprise at their lack of command of the native language, they just laughed at me: "Why bother to learn this damned barbaric language?", they said, "Everybody here understands Russian."

There was a difference, however, in the Russians' attitude toward Central Asians and Baltics. While for the former, many (by no means all) of the Russians felt contempt and regarded them as backward and uncultured, thus displaying a distinct superiority complex, in regard to the Baltic peoples their feelings were not so simple. Ethnic Russians residing in Estonia, Latvia, and Lithuania, most of them workers, middle-level state employees, and military men, being not highly cultured themselves, instinctively felt that they were confronted not with some "Asian barbarians" but with people of European civilization. While it would be an exaggeration to suggest that Russians in the Baltic republics possessed an inferiority complex, they had some respect, if not sympathy, for the natives, which is more than could be said of the Russians' feelings for Kazakhs or Turkmens. The net result, however, appears to be the same: segregation and high-handed attitude.

This situation abruptly came to an end with the breakup of the Soviet Union. Overnight, ethnic Russians became just a minority in independent states. To quote Rudensky,

all of them now have to rethink their social status, to assimilate new patterns of social behavior, characteristic of minority groups. . . . Russians in non-Russian republics were much more disapproving of the dissolution of the USSR than Russians living in Russia. . . . Many of them (57 percent in Moldova, 50 percent in Kyrgyzstan and Tajikistan, 43 percent in Latvia, and 34 percent in Uzbekistan) believed that responsibility for protecting the rights and interests of Russian minorities should lie with the government of the Russian Federation. . . . Assessing their prospects for the future, about two-thirds of those polled (average for different republics) expressed the view that Russians in the NIS would exist as second-class citizens, while one-third believed that Russian groups would be dissolved in the majority populations.[9]

"Patriots"—really extreme Russian nationalists—are seemingly outraged by the alleged persecution of ethnic Russians in the newly independent republics. From time to time, there is even wild talk of genocide. This is pure nonsense. No Russian civilians are known to have been deliberately killed on ethnic grounds anywhere in the republics. Yet, most Russians in the Near Abroad are not happy with their situation. During my recent trips to Uzbekistan, for instance, I got an impression that the bulk of the Russian residents would prefer to leave the country for good, not because they are being harassed or maltreated in any way but simply out of the hopelessness caused by the lack of prospects. A feebly camouflaged Uzbekization is in progress, and for those not speaking Uzbek the future is bleak. From Kazakhstan, it has been reported that a program had been adopted requiring all the official documentation to be written in Kazakh; towns built by Russians are being renamed. Russians in Central Asia and elsewhere are now paying the price for having arrogantly refused to study the native language. The issue, however, is not just language. Thanks to their higher skills, both the standard of life and social position of Russians and other Slavs in the USSR's southern republics had always been better than those of titular nations. The Russians felt a certain superiority as representatives of a "higher civilization" and were used to treating the locals in a condescending way. Now, they have found themselves in a foreign state where all the prestigious jobs are being gradually taken over by people belonging to the titular nation; their situation has been made worse by the deteriorating economic conditions, in particular the steady growth of unemployment. At least 15% of the able-bodied population in Central Asia are unemployed, and no resources are available for creating new workplaces. All the best jobs are being naturally given over to relatives or just to well-connected and "useful" people.

While in Uzbekistan, I had a chance to meet some Russians who were on the verge of leaving. Not a single one of them complained of harassment, although some admitted that they had heard yells of the sort: "If you cannot speak our language, go sweep the streets or get the hell out!" A movie director told me that she was generally treated quite nicely but because of the ongoing Uzbekization saw no prospects for herself as she did not speak Uzbek fluently enough.

The main brake on the emigration is the lack of financial means necessary for moving over to Russia and settling there. The gap between the price of apartments in Central Asia and Russia is huge, and finding a new job is a tremendous problem. It must be added that the refugees are largely being directed to villages and small towns in central Russia where they are poorly suited to live. In towns, unemployment is rising due to the closure of factories engaged in military production and to the general decline of industry. In the countryside, industrial workers, engineers, and state employees who constitute the bulk of the refugees could hardly be expected to adapt to unfamiliar conditions and agricultural work. Besides, nowhere in Russia are they welcomed. There have been numerous reports of harassment of newcomers, of utter dislike felt for them by local Russian peasantry; even the mentality of the new Russian settlers appears to be different from that of the central Russian people. The newcomers are more laborious and diligent, not so lazy, indifferent, and hard-drinking as the ordinary Russian persons working in state and collective farms.

Overall, it is estimated that, in order to provide housing and a job for just one emigrant, 80 million roubles are needed, in 1995 prices. In the last few years, from 500,000 to 700,000 people have been arriving yearly. Thus, hundreds of billions of roubles will be necessary to settle the newcomers. The budget of the Federal Migration Service is about twenty times less than is needed.[10]

The correspondent of a Russian weekly wrote as early as 1992: "The former Soviet Union was unable to protect its citizens. It was unable not only to guarantee the safety of the future forced emigrants in their permanent place of residence but even to compensate for the material losses suffered by the refugees after their resettlement. I found out that in Kaluga, for instance, not a single refugee who had come to this oblast (many Russians and Armenians from Baku) had received any compensation for the housing and property he had left behind or abandoned."[11] It is not easy to get the residential permit, either. "All that is being offered is rooms in hostels for single people. Furthermore, there is the ban on issuing residential permits for the large cities, the absence of a normal housing market, and a poorly functioning 'placement service.' Millions of people experienced the charm of the internal passport system, under which they could not be hired without a residential permit, while a residential permit could not be issued to people who had no jobs."[12]

Yet, people are leaving. According to official estimates, around one-quarter of Uzbekistan's ethnic Russians have emigrated; the corresponding figure for Kyrgyzstan is more than 20%—almost 200,000 people. The share of the Russians in Kyrgyzstan's population has shrunk from 21.5% to 17%. In Tajikistan, devastated by the civil war, out of 388,000 Russians about 300,000 have already fled. Altogether, almost one-third of the Russians who lived in Central Asia and the Caucasus have left for Russia.[13] As regards Kazakhstan, about 350,000 people emigrated to Russia in 1994. Of course, it is not only Russians who have been emigrating but also Armenians, Azerbaijanis, Ossetians, Meskhetian Turks, and others; however, the share of Russians among the migrants and refugees exceeds 60%.

In the Duma (the lower house of the Russian parliament) a special committee has been set up dealing with the issues of the CIS and the relations with fellow countrymen. Its head, Konstantin Zatulin, said in October 1995, that 600,000 ethnic Russians had been emigrating to Russia each year. Every one of them is being given by the state a lump sum of just 2 billion roubles (at that time a little more than $400) to start a new life.[14]

Figures about the overall number of emigrants who have arrived in Russia vary considerably, from one to four million. Just as varied are the forecasts—from one to six million. The last figure seems vastly exaggerated; after all, the majority of Russians in the Near Abroad live in Ukraine and Belarus where the ethnic situation is fairly calm. Yet, the Russian public appears to be genuinely concerned about the fate of those people; about 80 million Russians inside the Russian Federation are reported to have relatives in the newly independent republics. Of course, the plight of Russians in the Near Abroad, especially in Estonia and Latvia, has been exaggerated and overdramatized in Moscow media; however, there is no denying the fact that hundreds of thousands of ethnic Russians have become second-rate citizens in the new states. This is perceived by the Russian public opinion as humiliating, as a direct insult to the nation's dignity, and what matters in this kind of situation is perception, not reality. The average Russian, largely ignorant of details and prone to mix together the situations in the Baltic states, Central Asia, the Caucasus, or Moldova, has been increasingly outraged by what he regards as intolerable national humiliation at the hands of former Soviet vassals.

Two distinct types of psychological frustration are manifest here. The source of one of them is bitterness over the alleged ingratitude of non-Russians. "We have done everything for them, we have built factories and roads, they live at our expense" and so on. The second kind of frustration is more general and can be traced to the perception of Russia, a great power, having been relegated to a third-rate status in world affairs. It is precisely this sort of feeling that has generated a clearly visible anti-Western, anti-American backlash among large sections of the Russian population. By no means universal, it is, however, this very feeling that accounts for the millions of votes given to Zhirinovsky in the 1993 elections.

Hence Yeltsin's problem: He cannot afford to ignore the widespread sentiment of national humiliation and popular frustration. He must be seen as a leader who really cares about the fate of 25 million Russians in the "near abroad" and is prepared to act tough if necessary. Yeltsin has been on record as the author of a special decree demanding active defense of Russian citizens and their interests outside of the Russian Federation; this decree also instructs Russian authorities to consider the issue of economic relations with the republics of the former USSR according to the degree of their respect for human rights. What has been clearly meant is the attitude of the republics toward the Russian minorities.

In July 1995, a body called The Council of Fellow Countrymen was formed in Moscow following a Congress of Fellow Countrymen which had been attended by Prime Minister Chernomyrdin. The head of government promised to allocate 125 billion roubles for the assistance to ethnic Russians abroad. Instead, a new decree was published, signed by Yeltsin and entitled "On Russia's strategic course in respect to the CIS countries." The decree calls on state officials to "actively contribute to the adaptation of Russians abroad to new sociopolitical conditions."[15] It is not hard to imagine the disappointment of many Russian nationalists offered just "adaptation" instead of the active and militant defense of rights of Russians in the Near Abroad they have been calling for.

At this point, however, a question is bound be asked: What precisely can this "defense" be; what form can it take? Logically, it would seem that, first of all, attention should be paid to the views of the most interested party, namely the diaspora Russians themselves. This, however, does not appear to be the case. Much lip service is being paid in Moscow and elsewhere in Russia to the plight of the unlucky brethren but very little genuine interest is shown in their grievances, and few people seem to listen to what they have to say. It can partly be explained by the fact that the Russians in the Near Abroad are badly split and have no single strategy or concept.

Some extremist and secessionist views, expressed by ethnic Russians in parts of Kazakhstan, particularly by the Cossacks, have already been mentioned. They are not typical because nowhere else, with the possible exception of Crimea and parts of eastern Ukraine, can even a remote possibility of secession be contemplated. The bulk of those who have preferred to stay and tough it out rather than to emigrate appear to have reconciled themselves to the existence of the new independent states and to the necessity of getting by as best one can. As mentioned above, it was exactly the Russians in the newly independent republics who disapproved most severely of the breakup of the USSR. Things, however, have changed since that fateful moment, and the mainstream opinion in the diaspora seems to be that what is done cannot be undone, that the hopes of Moscow coming to the aid of the "fellow countrymen" have proved futile and that the Russians in the Near Abroad have to try to cut their losses and adapt to the new situation.

Some activists tried at first to create "popular fronts," the idea being that if multinational democratic movements could be promoted in the new republics, this would become a sort of counterbalance to nationalist forces and would even allow democratically minded representatives of the Russian population to dominate the political scene due to their higher level of education and political maturity. The champions of the concept of "popular fronts" believed in unity, first, with native democratic parties, and, second, with the Democrats in Russia proper who seemed to be in ascendancy at the time. Later, however, this idea proved illusory both because of the weakness of "native" democratic movements and as a result of the gradual decline of Democrats in the Russian Federation.

Opponents of the "popular fronts" set out to form "international fronts," or interfronts, intent on restoring somehow the Soviet Union and the Communist ideology. These attempts also ended in fiasco. While in Kazakhstan, I had meetings with some leaders of the Russian community, including former champions of the idea of interfront. They told me that the whole idea of uniting all the nonnatives with the aim of resisting the "titularization," or Kazakhization of the republic, had proved counterproductive and had played into the hand of Kazakh chauvinists who had used it as a means of frightening the Kazakh population by the spectre of a renewed Russian domination. Moreover, some average Russians told me: "Please try to explain to people in Russia that, the louder they yell about genocide of Russians in Kazakhstan, the worse our situation here becomes. All this fuss and outcry about persecutions of Russians will yield no practical results; on the contrary, Kazakh nationalists will immediately capitalize on this in order to boost anti-Russian feelings among the Kazakh population." I heard similar opinions in Uzbekistan as well.

On the other hand, the Russian emigrants who have already settled down in Russia and do not have to care about popular opinion in their former Central Asian homeland tend to exaggerate the plight of their fellow countrymen; some of them, possibly trying to arouse pity and bring forth sympathy for themselves, have been spreading totally false rumors of genocide, massacre, and so on. Of course, the Russian "patriots" are all too happy to catch up and wildly exaggerate those rumors. In all fairness, it must be admitted that this kind of agitation feeds on undisputable facts of "Kazakhization," "Uzbekization," and similar campaigns in the CIS states which are, of course, something other than genocide or ethnic cleansing, but still strike a chord in Russian ears. And, in the current political atmosphere in Russia, the issue of the alleged persecutions and discrimination of the Russians in the Near Abroad can acquire major proportions.

There is no doubt that the desire to look tough and to be regarded as a staunch champion of Russian interests has been a major motivation in Yeltsin's decision to invade Chechnya. This issue is closely linked to what is sometimes described in Western media as the resurgence of Russian imperialism. There is no denying that Russia has been vigorously reasserting itself in the Near Abroad and that the CIS seems to be given a new lease of life.

With the initial post-independence euphoria gone, it is the republican leadership itself which seems to be anxious to ensure political and, in some cases, military cooperation with Russia. It has become abundantly clear that the economy of the republics just does not work without genuine cooperation with Russia. As two American authors put it, "you can take the republics away from Russia, but you can't get Russia out of the republics. . . . In the late Soviet period, most republics exported approximately 50 percent of their net material product to other republics and imported around 40 percent; the comparable Russian figures were approximately 18 percent both for imports and for exports. The reality of intense economic interdependence could not be eliminated simply by declarations of independence and economic sovereignty."[16]

To sum it up, it would be wrong to see Russia's political and military reappearance in the Near Abroad as a vicious design to resurrect the Soviet Empire or to reimpose Moscow's rule in its former dependencies. Nobody is able, and few are willing, to restore the defunct Union.

NOTES

1. *Naselenie Rossii. Ezhegodnyi demograficheskii doklad. Tsentr demografii i ekologii cheloveka* (Russia's population. A yearly demographic report issued by the Center for Human Demography and Ecology, Moscow, 1993), 15. All the figures are for 1989.

2. Mikhail Guboglo, "Demography and Language in the Capitals of the Union Republics," *Journal of Soviet Nationalities* 1, no. 4 (Winter 1990–1991), 4. Of course, much higher would be the percentage of citizens of titular nationality who do not consider Russian as their native language, yet speak it fluently (from 22.3% in Uzbekistan to 59.5% in Ukraine); ibid., 5.

3. Nikolai Rudensky, *Russian Minorities in the Newly Independent States: An International Problem in the Domestic Context of Russia Today*, Russian Littoral Project, University of Maryland at College Park and The Johns Hopkins University, SAIS, no. 15, May 1993, 4.

4. Guboglo, *Demography and Language*, 11, 13, 15, 18, 19, 21, 23, 25, 26, 29, 30, 31, 32, 33.

5. Aleksandra Dokuchaeva, Dmitrii Pisarenko, Lyudmila Falekstova, Yuri Stroganov, and Anatolii Strogov, "Kak starshii brat stal natsmenshinstvom" (How the Big Brother became an ethnic minority), *Rossiyskaia Gazeta*, June 26, 1993. The Russian-speakers include all persons of nontitular nationality (in Central Asia, for instance, Ukrainians, Belorussians, Jews, Germans, etc.).

6. Rudensky, *Russian Minorities*, 7, 8.

7. Ibid., 10.

8. Ibid., 6; Guboglo, *Democracy and Language*, 40.

9. Rudensky, *Russian Minorities*, 13.

10. Valerii Galenko, "Nuzhny novye formy pokrovitelstva etnicheskim rossiyanam" (Needed: New ways to protect ethnic Russians), *Nezavisimaia Gazeta*, November 11, 1995.

11. Viktor Perevedentsev, "Repatriatsiia" (Repatriation), *Nedelia* (January 1992), 5.

12. *Social and Cultural Affairs*, FBIS-USR-92-024, March 5, 1992, 116.

13. Valerii Tishkov and Igor Rotar, "Slavianie novogo zarubezhia" (Slavs of the Near Abroad), *Nezavisimaia Gazeta*, January 20, 1994, 5; Evgenii Denisenko, "Russkie v preddverii chasa pik" (Russians in anticipation of a showdown), *Nezavisimaia Gazeta*, June 16, 1994, 3.

14. Viktor Timoshenko, "V poiskakh istoricheskoi rodiny" (In search of a historical motherland), *Nezavisimaia Gazeta*, October 7, 1995, 3.

15. Ibid.

16. Bruce D. Porter and Carol R. Saivetz, "The Once and Future Empire: Russia and the 'Near Abroad,' " *The Washington Quarterly* (Summer 1994), 76, 78.

10

On Russian Nationalism

It would be a commonplace to say that, after the collapse of the Soviet Union, ethnonationalism became a dominant, if not the only political ideology and mass-inspiring idea in the successor states. Marxism-Leninism having been dispatched to the dustbin of history, nothing has emerged to take its place. What we are witnessing at this point is an ideological vacuum; no real committment to ideas and beliefs, no political culture, no respect for law and state authority, no trust in politicians and parties with all their slogans and programs, no class solidarity, no civil society.

People need to identify with some group, to belong to a community. Ethnonational community is just one of many, but now, in the post-Soviet states, there is virtually nothing people can identify with except for this one. State, Party, class, profession—everything has deteriorated to such an extent, everything looks so ugly and worthless that the only firm ground, the only basis for self-assertion can be found in belonging to a stable, long-established community, traditionally respected or even sacred. It is ethnicity and religion, rather than unstable, fragile, ever-changing and rapidly deteriorating political and economic dimensions of life, that provide inner security and ensure belonging to a group, a community, thus making it possible to escape from total emptiness and lack of any meaningful identity.

These general observations can apply to all the post-Soviet nations. However, to understand the nature of Russian nationalism, it is necessary to have a clear picture of just where the Russians stood within the Soviet Empire and what their identity was. Some historical remarks, therefore, would be helpful.

HISTORIC ROOTS

The history and background of the Russian nation, from the point of view of ethnicity and anthropology, are well-known. For centuries, Russians have had a consciousness of belonging to a single community around which an empire had been created.

The notorious nostalgia that some older people feel at this point in Russia, remembering Stalin's and Brezhnev's eras, is nothing compared to the powerful sentiment of loss felt by much broader segments of population, including many young people. It is the loss of "derzhava," a term difficult to translate, something between "the mighty state," "the great power," and just Motherland. It is the feeling of national humiliation, at least partially explaining Zhirinovsky's success in the last year's elections.

The cases of the Kuril Islands and Zhirinovsky's success, put together, are revealing: it is impossible to comprehend today's nationalism outside the historic context.

The "nascent" Russian nationalism so much talked about nowadays can better be called "reborn" nationalism. It is actually very old and deep-rooted, reflecting a deeply entrenched identity and pride of a long-existing and stable community with a very distinct and pronounced national consciousness, and also, with a sense of mission. Here we come to another important aspect of the problem, namely: the Russians' attitude to the outside world. After all, "us" and "they" is what nationalism is all about.

The idea of Russia's historic mission is of a long duration. Its origins can be found in the semireligious idea that it is Moscow that was destined to become Christianity's bulwark. This was the famous notion of Moscow as the Third Rome, and it emerged even before Russia as a state began to shape. The idea was put forward by Ivan the Terrible's predecessors and this was how it sounded: "Two Romes have fallen (Rome and Byzantium), the third one stands (Moscow), and a fourth one will never exist."

Later, the religious connotation somehow faded away as the Russian Orthodox Church lost its autonomous position and gradually became just a spiritual arm of the powerful state. But the idea of a historic mission has never been totally separated from its religious and mystical origins although with the passage of time it was increasingly growing into a statist and geopolitical notion. The mystic part of the idea was being reinforced by Russian mentality.

The Russians have always had a dual kind of complex vis-à-vis the West (and it is precisely the West, not the East, that has always been a reference point for Russia in regard to the outside world). Both inferiority and superiority complexes somehow managed to coexist in the Russian collective psyche. On the one hand, Russians always knew, although often would not admit it, that Western peoples were much more prosperous, better fed, educated, and better governed than they were. The reluctance to admit this, however, has usually been limited to contacts with foreigners. Among themselves, Russians have always been only too willing to indulge in self-criticism. The Russian writer Shchedrin wrote more than a century ago about Russians saying to each other: "Isn't it a wonderful country, ours? Everybody is stealing and everybody is saying with laughter: Well, well, where else in the world can you find such mess and havoc?" Actually, Russians could never look at their past with pride, except for military victories, science, art, and literature.

On the other hand, this recognition of Russia's inferiority in comparison to the West oddly existed side by side with a peculiar kind of superiority complex. It has always been vaguely felt that, the Westerners' higher standard in the material sphere notwithstanding, Russians had an edge on them as regards things spiritual. Europeans were regarded as too materialistic, totally preoccupied with such less-than-dignified matters as money and property. They were conceived as lacking high spirituality, concern for global, transcendental issues such as a sense of existence, man's ultimate destiny, universal brotherhood of peoples, and so on. Spirituality, indeed, was a key word in this thinking, probably rooted in the notion of a religious mission (the Third Rome) but also in the idea of the "broad and generous Russian soul." (It seemed obvious that Western bourgeoisie were simply not capable of spending whole nights in discussions on global and philosophical matters. This was felt to be a legitimate realm of that unique breed, the famous Russian intelligentsia.)

Even now, many a Russian emigré would tell you that, apart from the enormous wealth, material and technical superiority, Western society is rather dull, uninspiring; people are too practical, narrowminded and down-to-earth; their concerns are too shallow; human contacts are far less warm, more formal than in Russia; and so on.

Feelings of this kind could not but be greatly reinforced by the Soviet propaganda which spared no efforts to depict the Western capitalist society as completely greedy and selfish. "*Homo homini lupus est*" was the favorite formula for describing human relations under capitalism. Everybody knew Stalin's words: "The lowest-ranking Soviet citizen is head and shoulders above any highest-placed bourgeois official bent down by the yoke of Capitalist slavery."

THE SOVIET LEGACY

A question is asked from time to time: Have the Soviets succeeded in creating what they called "a new historic community, the Soviet people?" Does such a person as *Homo Soveticus* actually exist or is it just an intellectual cliché?

The answer would seem to be yes and no. Of course, a better human being was never born under the Soviet regime, and the hideous, demoralized society which exists in Russia today is a living proof of the dismal failure. The worst features that used to be attributed to the Western person by Soviet propaganda— greed and selfishness, unwillingness to help fellow citizens, contempt for both law and morals, widespread criminal tendencies—are all too noticeable at present in the "homo post-Soveticus"; the gruesome seeds, however, were sown during the Soviet era.

Thus, the great experiment failed. Still, one of the results of the Soviet rule was the creation of a certain atmosphere in which the populace felt it was unique, totally separated from the rest of the world. "Capitalist encirclement" was the name of the game: The first country of the victorious proletariat was surrounded by capitalist enemies just waiting for an opportunity to crush it. Of course, this idea was extremely useful for the regime, which was thus able to constantly keep alive an atmosphere of the besieged fortress and to incessantly call for vigilance and for the mobilization of the people in defense of "socialist gains." In this way, a powerful sentiment of solidarity was fostered among the population. Even those who disliked or, deep in their hearts, totally rejected the Soviet system (and there were millions of them) felt that somehow, against their will, they found themselves in the same boat with the Communist regime, since the outside capitalist world would sooner or later certainly unleash the war. In this case, it was felt, it would be Mother Russia, not the Kremlin bosses, that would have to be defended—which is exactly what happened when Hitler attacked the Soviet Union. While hundreds of thousands of soldiers surrendered to Germans and many of them chose to fight on the enemy's side, the majority of Russians courageously defended their country.

The feeling of being surrounded and besieged by enemies could not but foster that monstrous corollary of "vigilance"—widespread suspicion inevitably breeding belief in foreign-sponsored plots, conspiracies, and subversive activities. All of this was firmly engrained in the Soviet mentality.

I happened to talk to some well-known Russian left-wing intellectuals, scholars of genuinely democratic convictions, and I was surprised to hear them voice suspicions about America's real intentions vis-à-vis Russia. Most of them are inclined to believe that the Americans are not all that sincere when they profess their support for new Russia. Dark hints at some hidden agenda, some deep American games and less than laudable motives are rather widespread. It can only partially be explained by a lack of knowledge as to the workings of Western political systems. Of course, average Russian citizens are totally ignorant of American politics and some of them still believe in sinister plots cooked up by the CIA, Wall Street, and the Pentagon. However, academics and journalists should know better, and yet distrust of America and the West in general is typical for quite a few of them, too. Those, by the way, are the people who genuinely like America and Americans, who never miss a chance to make a trip to the United States or get their children to study at American schools.

Throughout modern history, Americans have easily been favorites with Russians. No amount of anti-American propaganda could erode sympathy for Americans as people, as distinct from such bogeys as the Pentagon or the CIA. People of the older generation recall the war years when it was America that saved dozens of millions of Soviet people from starvation. Why, then, this apprehension about the United States in the post-Soviet Russia?

It can largely be explained by the cumulative effect of the two old complexes: the pre-revolutionary one—of inferiority vis-à-vis the West, and the post-revolutionary one—of suspicion and conspiracies. It is an organic part of the contemporary Russians' collective psyche; it is deep-rooted and will take time to die. Compared to the Soviet era, the difference now is that nobody regards the external threat as something motivated by class hatred. The idea at present seems to be that Russia, old and eternal Mother Russia, is being menaced by outside forces which can hardly believe their fabulous good luck: the powerful Communist regime gone, Russia is lying open before them, open for grabs. This notion, crude and primitive as it is, should not be contemptuously brushed aside; after all, it obviously prompted millions to vote for Zhirinovsky or neo-Communists in December 1993. Many people would argue this way: The West hated Russia all along but had been afraid of its might ever since the times of Ivan the Terrible and Peter the Great; now at last the West sees its chance and will not let it slip away. What is this chance? To fatally weaken Russia, to deliver a knock-out blow, to put an end to the Slavic-Asian peril that was over-shadowing Europe for centuries. And the result, they would say, is clearly visible: Russia is being pillaged and sold out.

According to some recent polls, 72% of Russians believe that Russia follows a special and unique historic road; 75% are of the opinion that Russia can survive without Western economic aid; 52% regard Western cultural influence as harmful. More than 70% of those polled regret the disintegration of the Soviet Union, although 53% admit that it is impossible to bring it back to life; 81% want to restore Russia's place in the world as a great power.[1]

It is amazing how many people in Russia, when you talk to them about the dissolution of the Soviet Union, decided in Minsk in 1991 by Yeltsin and two other leaders, would wink knowingly and say: "Don't be so naive; the decision to destroy the USSR—do you really think it was made in Moscow?" This thinking is perfectly in tune with the old Soviet pattern: Whatever bad occurs, somebody must be behind it. Back in the 1930s, when your plumbing broke down or electricity went off or trains collided, you invariably said: "it's the work of those damned wreckers, saboteurs, they are everywhere." All the evil came from the outside world and its agents. Now, to many people such figures as Gorbachev and Yeltsin seem too small and insignificant to have been able to destroy one of the most powerful states in history all on their own. Some mastermind must surely stand behind it all; for some, it is World Zionism, for others—the United States. The word "imperialism" is not in use any more but the essence remains: greedy bankers out to grab Russia's resources, and the Pentagon happy to smash to pieces the old enemy.

It would seem that for many people the Soviet Union still exists, it is still alive. Devoid of its power over the republics, free from Marxist ideology, horribly weakened and crippled, but still somehow unique and special, totally distinct from the rest of the world if not confronting it. Now, what is the correlation between this subconscious feeling and Russian nationalism?

In fact, there never was such a thing as the Soviet nation. One could ask a Soviet person who he or she was, and the answer would be: "I am a Soviet citizen," the latter being the operative word, or else: "I am Russian (or Armenian, Tatar etc)." Self-identification was possible either in a purely formal or strictly ethnic sense. However, there was another category—"*sovetskie ludi*" (Soviet people), the new politico-ideological community the Soviet leadership was always so proud of. It was related to state citizenship but not to ethnicity; and it also meant that loyalty was enforced to the paramount state; loyalty superceding both citizenship and ethnicity. Millions of people were conscious of the invisible border which separated them from the rest of mankind. No substitute for nationhood, this kind of pseudonational consciousness existed for decades and the strength of its legacy is undeniable. Ethnic nationalisms as such were definitely not encouraged inasmuch as they detracted from the paramount Soviet loyalty and could undermine class ideology. But in practice things were not as simple as that.

Basically, Marxism is thoroughly internationalist. One of the principal characters in Maxim Gorky's novel *The Mother* (a must-read for children and adults alike in the Soviet era) shouts at a meeting: "It is all a bloody lie that various nations exist in the world like Russians, Ukrainians, Germans! There are just two nations, two irreconcilable enemies—the rich and the poor!" World revolution was coming and nationality did not matter. Of course, "bourgeois leftovers and prejudices" (such as religion and nationalism) still persisted, and anti-Semitism, for instance, was never eradicated, but all this old stuff was declared to be fading away. Proletarian internationalism was the name of the game.

Practical policy considerations, however, dictated the need to acknowledge, and come to terms with, national sentiment. As Walker Connor puts it in his recent book *Ethnonationalism: The Quest for Understanding*, "Marxists-Leninists have discovered that, when forced to choose between national and class loyalty, people are most apt to opt for the former.[2]

No matter what Bolshevik leaders thought about the nationalities issue at the outset, they were quick to grasp the advantages they could get by encouraging ethnic identity of the numerous nations and ethnic groups under their rule. Local ethnic elites (of course, thoroughly Bolshevized) were co-opted into the all-Union establishment and given a substantial degree of autonomy. A stable and viable party-state structure was created, thus greatly facilitating the task of governing the enormous country. Theoretically, it easily fits into Marxist teachings which, alongside internationalism, envisaged the right of national self-determination; prior to merger in some distant future, nations first were to be given ample opportunities for self-fulfillment.

National identities were promoted and in some cases (Central Asia) almost artificially created. In order to forestall any suspicions of continuing Tsarist Russia's imperial and colonialist policy, stress was made on the advancement of "native" cadres who were put at the helm in the national republics (of course, under strict control from Moscow). National culture was fostered as well. The nations within the framework of the USSR were declared to be completely free, for the first time in their history, and voluntarily united in a brotherly alliance consolidated forever by "Great Russia" (the words of the Soviet state anthem). The culture of each of those nations was "national in form, socialist in substance." There was some truth in this formula if we substitute the Leninist-Stalinist Party system for "Socialism."

The Russian nation played a rather ambiguous role in this unique setup. On the one hand, Russia clearly was the big brother, *primus inter pares*, its preeminence was obvious. On the other hand, official efforts to promote Russian national consciousness were quite feeble compared to the other republics. Somehow it seems that the Kremlin, ever hostile to any manifestations of genuine nationalism, as opposed to the pocket "socialist" variety, was particularly afraid of Russian nationalism. It can partly be explained by the fact that the Bolsheviks seized power in a merciless war against the Russian nationalist White Army, which stood for the restoration of a "united and indivisible Russia." The legacy of this civil war, its mentality, the need to combat Russian nationalism as a main weapon of their enemies, predetermined for many years the Bolshevik leaders' aversion to all that smacked of revivalist nationalist tendencies in Soviet Russia. Besides, nationalism as a potentially alternative political force was, of course, especially dangerous precisely in Russia, the center of power of the whole huge country. Nationalism raising its ugly head somewhere in Tbilisi or Tashkent was nothing compared to the possible effect of a nationalist upsurge in Moscow.

Typical of this pattern, nationalist "deviations" in the republics were dubbed "bourgeois nationalism" (Ukrainian, Tatar, Georgian, etc.) while for the Russian variety a different term was used—"great power chauvinism." Now, there was nothing casual or accidental in the choice of words under the Soviet regime, and chauvinism is a much stronger and more negative term than nationalism. It must be assumed, therefore, that it was Russian nationalist revival that was regarded by the Kremlin rulers as the greater manace.

It was only during the war against Germany that Stalin decided it was useful to appeal to purely Russian national sentiment, openly evoking memories of great ancestors and allowing a renaissance of old Russian myths and legends as well as focusing on real victories of Russian armies in the glorious past. The manifestations of Russian national sentiment during the war can better be called patriotism than nationalism in the strict sense of the term. It was rooted, however, in the Russian national consciousness and thus inevitably acquired ethnic overtones.

RUSSIAN NATIONALISM REBORN

Of all the nationalisms in the territories of the former Soviet Union, Russian nationalism has proved to be one of the weakest so far. Several reasons can be suggested for explanation. First, as noted earlier, during the Soviet era Russian nationalist trends were regarded as being more malignant and dangerous than those of any other nation. Russian national consciousness was deliberately downplayed; to compensate the Russians for this, it was implied that anyway they were big brothers or senior partners. Conscious of their dominant role in the state as a whole, Russians had no reasons to be unhappy about the weak promotion of their ethnic "Russianness."

Second, and for the same reason, Russians, as a great and dominant nation under both Tsarist and Communist regimes, could afford to be generous, or at least condescending, in regard to "lesser nations" under Moscow's rule. No other nation ever challenged Russia's dominance in the Empire. The army was largely Russian-staffed and totally Russian-led. Russia was quite secure within its Empire. Russian was understood and spoken everywhere; ethnic Russians residing in the republics felt no need to learn the native idiom. Certainly, not everything was smooth in the relationships between Russians and other nations, bad feelings on both sides surfaced from time to time but what was lacking was hatred. And nationalism, of course, thrives on hatred. Nationalists in all the newly independent republics believe they have reasons to hate the Russians— the colonizers, occupiers, the root cause of all the misfortunes of their nations— As to the Russians, they can find nobody to blame for their predicament but themselves. What is absent is a visible enemy as an object of hatred, a catalyst of nationalism.

Third, some reflections on Russian mentality are in order at this point. Historically, the Russian Empire was not quite usual in the sense that there was no clear-cut border, no serious gap between leaders and led, the chief nation and the periphery. By nature, Russians are no colonizers, although they were by and large not the worst of colonial administrators, at least in the Tsarist era. They never regarded the peoples they conquered as a 'lower race," very rarely expressed overt dislike or contempt for "natives" at the level of human, personal relations, except for some cases in Central Asia. In the Russian psyche there is no room for genuinely racist ideas, for theories of "higher" and "lower" nations, for self-aggrandizement on ethnic ground. Russians, civil and military alike, were always tolerant to alien ethnoses and religions. A quite sizeable part of Russian aristocracy was known to be of Tatar, or Lithuanian, or Caucasian descent, to say nothing of ethnic German; some of the best army generals were Georgians and Armenians. What mattered was religion in the Tsarist era, Party loyalty under the Soviet regime. Ethnicity per se was never high on the agenda, at least until recently. This is not to say that there has been no racism in Russia; it is lurking somewhere, very deep.

Fourth, as Gorbachev's *perestroika* was on the march, to be followed by a period of troubles and upheavals, Russians were too busy taking part in political battles or just watching them, to care about nationalities and ethnic issues. New, unprecedented opportunities were opened in the realm of politics. Newly won freedoms of speech and press were absolutely exciting. Ethnic conflicts on the fringes of the empire, in Karabakh and Central Asia, were regarded as something disgusting; it could only happen "out there," but not here, in a civilized Russia. There was just no room nor time for nationalism and ethnic problems.

Now, the situation has changed. Russian nationalism, if not actually on the march, can be said to be raising its head. Several factors are at work here. First, as noted earlier, ethonational community remains the only one people can identify with, all the others having been shattered or discredited. The secession of Ukraine, Belarus, and Caucasian and Central Asian nations—for this is exactly how the dissolution of the USSR has been regarded by Russian public: secession—suddenly and abruptly put the ethnic issue, largely irrelevant until that moment, into focus. The point was that this "secession" was accomplished along purely ethnonationalist lines, all the arguments of economic, social, environmental nature contradicting that arbitrary decision. It would not be an exaggeration to say that it was at that juncture that Russians, for the first time in decades, became really conscious of their national identity. Now, it suddenly appeared that they belonged not to a great multinational empire transcending ethnicity but to a smaller Russian state. *The fact of being an ethnic Russian, formerly just taken for granted, became salient overnight.* Prior to that turning point, the "us and they" dichotomy was relevant only as determining relations between the "Soviet people" as a whole and the outside world. Now, all the other Soviet nations suddenly became the outside world; a part of "us" disappeared; even worse, it became "they." Russia as such was left alone, evoking feelings of pride and bitterness at the same time.

Russians became aware of their identity; "Russianness" emerged as a focus of attention and a center of gravity. However, at first the ethnic component of the term was overshadowed by a larger one—a feeling that all the nations of the Russian Federation, regardless of their ethnic background, belonged to Russia; were an integral part of that great and eternal entity which, although severely reduced in size and without Ukraine, still stayed as a whole. An old term, "Rossiyanie," was revived, meaning all citizens of Russia, including ethnic Russians, Tatars, Chuvash, Mordva, Komi, and so on. But with the passage of time, as Chechnya declared its independence, Tatarstan started to claim sovereignty, and ominous signs emerged of the birth of Komi and Yakutian nationalism, things began to change within the Russian Federation as well. It appeared that the non-Russian ethnoses inside the Federation were not so loyal after all. From now on, ethnic Russians not only had to reconcile themselves to the loss of Ukraine and the other republics but also had to confront a potential enemy within the very state they were destined to live in after the breakup of the Empire, within a narrower Russia. *And it was at this juncture that ethnic Russian nationalism came to the fore.* Russians began to feel that they were left all alone, that they were not *Rossiyanie* but *Russkie*, a purely ethnic community.

It coincided in time with a general weariness of politics and a disillusionment with all the politicians, particularly the Democrats, who were held responsible for the drastic deterioration of the economic situation. Time for excitement over politics, for manifestations and debates over Party programs was past. As always throughout history, ethnicity became a sanctuary for people lacking other outlets for self-fulfillment. This is the first, and major, cause of the rise of Russian nationalism.

Second is the fate of the ethnic Russians residing in the "near abroad," of those 25 million people whose predicament has been grotesquely exaggerated by "Russian patriots." Zhirinovsky and the likes of him talk incessantly of "genocide" without providing any proof of it, for the simple reason that it is nonexistent. Some Russians believe this demagoguery. Everything is confused in their minds: the underprivileged position of ethnic Russians in Estonia and Latvia; Russians fleeing from a war-torn Tajikistan; Russians being squeezed out of jobs and discriminated against in Kazakhstan; the plight of Russians caught in crossfire in the Caucasian wars; Russians being shot at in the self-styled Dniester republic by Moldavian nationalists, and so on.

Third is the disillusionment with Western aid and suspicion of Western intentions coupled with the belief that Russia is being pillaged and sold out. To this may be added widespread resentment at the alleged invasion of the American culture in its worst, indecent form—crime and sex movies, pornography, and so on. A lot of people are unhappy about what they perceive as "MacDonaldization" of Mother Russia. In accordance with the Russian proclivity to look for an alien source of every evil, they tend to see the sharp increase of drug abuse, street criminality, Mafia activity, and arrogance as direct results of the "Americanization" of Russia.

Fourth is a drastic worsening of relations between ethnic Russians and peoples of Caucasian background—native Chechens, Armenians, Azerbaijanis, Georgians, and so on. Actually, anti-Caucasian feelings have been in evidence for a long time. It all began many years ago, when first Georgians and then Azerbaijanis virtually monopolized the trade in open-air markets where urban people buy foodstuffs produced in collective and private farms. Russians do not differentiate between nations of Caucasus, they all look alike. The image of all those dark, swarthy, mustachioed types has always been that of profiteers and shameless bloodsuckers in view of the usually high prices they asked for their fruits and vegetables. They also had lots of money, drove fancy cars, and were fond of blond Russian girls, all of which greatly added to their negative image. At present, most Muscovites will tell you that the Caucasians are responsible for the rising crime wave more than anybody else. The fact is that the proportion of the crimes committed by Caucasians in the big cities exceeds by far their percentage in the population as a whole. Particularly notorious, as noted elsewhere, has been the Chechen mob. The hatred of the southerners is so intense and widespread that Zhirinovsky probably received a quite significant share of the votes he got in the parliamentary elections by addressing this issue. A part of the "born-again" nationalists, at least, have found the enemy: it is in the South.

NATIONALISM AND RUSSIA'S POLICY IN THE NEAR ABROAD

We have seen that Russian nationalism passed three stages in a remarkably short time: from a rather subdued feeling overshadowed by overall Soviet loyalty, to a *Rossiyanie* period characterized by a nonethnic loyalty to the Russian Federation, to genuine Russian ethnic nationalism with chauvinistic overtones in regard to southerners, particularly people from the Caucasus.

Russian feeling for the Caucasus has always been rather special. The area is dear to the Russian heart because it is engraved in the historic memory. It is the memory of that great nineteenth-century Caucasian saga when Russian troops battled with highlanders for decades to gain possession of the mountainous country. Pushkin, Lermontov, and Tolstoy all wrote about it; Russian blood was shed there. In later times, the best Soviet sea resorts were located there. Some Russian nationalist extremists probably would like to have the Caucasus for Russians, without Caucasians.

In a larger sense, of course, the Caucasus is a symbol. A rising nationalism has to make a stand somewhere, to prove and assert itself. It is only in this light, incidentally, that one can make sense of Russia's adamant stand on the Kuril Islands; quite a few Russians probably have a rather vague idea of exactly where these islands are located, not to mention their history. It does not matter; tomorrow it may be Sebastopol if Ukraine tries force to crush the Crimean autonomy, or Kaliningrad if by any chance the Germans were to claim it back.

There is yet another angle to the problem of Russia's involvement in the Caucasus and elsewhere in the South. *Russian nationalists are frustrated as they feel that the West does not acknowledge Russia as an equal and that Europe does not accept it as an organic part.* Age-old suspicions and complexes persist. What is missing is geopolitical legitimacy. Russia is regarded as having been pushed out of the world picture altogether. For many, the rebirth of Russia as a great power must begin at home, with a reassertion of its authority within the CIS.

In the western part of the post-Soviet space, however, Russia will find it hard to throw its weight around. Ukraine stays demonstrably aloof and, if anything, tries to become a part of Europe. Belarus is hardly a compensation for seeing the European door close before the imperial planners' noses. The *Lebensraum*, of course, is in the south and the east. And, in fact, Russia has been vigorously reasserting itself in the last years precisely in the Caucasus and Central Asia.

Is this the beginning of the restoration of the empire? Or is Russia, feeling snubbed by the West, trying a return to Asia?

In general, Asia for Russians was always a synonym of economic backwardness and social stagnation; even the Bolsheviks, including Lenin, with all their internationalist ideas, used to speak about a "modern Europe" and a "backward Asia." It would be hard to find a Russian who would willingly identify with

Asians, in spite of some intellectuals' attempts to appeal to the "eternal Asian" in the Russian soul. Probably this is why the so-called Eurasian idea has not made much of a headway, focused as it has been on the concept of a Slavic-Asian civilization based on a shared history, cultural interpenetration, and community of fate. Eurasianism seems to be progressively linked to, if not diluted in, the notorious "Russian idea" that has been gaining in strength as a result of the resurgence of Russian ethnic nationalism in the aftermath of the USSR's disintegration. Publications calling for a sort of hybrid concept, a mixture of both ideas, have been emerging lately in the Russian press. Thus, in an article entitled "A New Civilization in Russia? A Preview of a Eurasian Culture," Sergei Agadjanov suggested that Russia, located as it was on the borderline between Europe and Asia, lacked an ethnicity-focused mentality, and this made possible "the empire's transformation into a multiethnic commonwealth. . . . Ethnic diversity helped create a unique economic, social, spiritual and confessional image of the country-empire. Objectively, a new and original civilization has been shaping, which some scholars call a Euroasian culture."[3]

Sergei Kortunov, one of the outspoken champions of the "Russian idea" in its imperial variety, maintained that

as regards ethnicity, culture and civilization, the Russians, carrying a great empire on their shoulders, were always more *"Rossiiskie"* than *"Russkie"* and thus never constituted a nation in the western sense. As opposed to western European countries, Russia has never been guided by the idea of a nation-state and never equated the nation and state. For this reason, the Russian national idea has nothing to do with Russian nationalism; it has always been much higher than that. . . . The mutual openness of the Russians and of those ethnic aliens who were drifting to Russia, has led to the formation of a single ethnic community, a *Rossiiskii* super-ethnos.[4]

In a later article Kortunov wrote that "Russia, as an embodiment of the Eurasian civilization and a focus of a multinational community, is simply doomed to be an empire lest it disappears from the face of the earth and breaks up into many diminutuve states . . ."[5]

Vladimir Titorenko, a diplomat and political scientist, is quite outspoken:

Western civilizational values, including the democratic model, can hardly be expected to take root in Russia due to its unique character as regards culture, religion, socio-economic patterns and national-federalist structure. Russia has been growing throughout history as a symbiosis of two ethnoses and religions, Slavic-Orthodox and Turkic-speaking Muslims . . . a totally new type of civilization has admittedly been shaped in our country, a unique world of the worlds unlike any other classic model, be it European or Oriental; its name is Russia.[6]

This kind of idea, however, is by no means universally shared by Russian thinkers. Sergei Panarin, reflecting on Russian messianic traditions, believes that for Russians "the natives" used to be not so much people of different cultural roots as people not mature enough, not really grown up. "Even the best of Russians used to treat Orientals in a way that hurt the latters' dignity." At present, Panarin writes, "politically active Russians believe that the Oriental peoples of the former USSR are uncapable of acquiring democratic values and institutions. Even more widespread in the masses is the opinion that they are just an economic ballast for the Slav republics. In both cases, the conclusion is the same: they should be left to their fortunes." According to the author, there is, however, another point of view, namely that Russia should steer clear of its former fellow-countrymen because a union with them would mean a strengthening of traditional institutions that tend to suppress the autonomy of individual, to say nothing of a possible rise of the militant Islamic fundamentalism. "In general, Islamophobia that seems to have been born among ethnic Russians in the North Caucasus and Central Asia, threatens to grow into a deeply entrenched feature of the Russian ethnos as a whole."[7]

The "Russian idea," presented with such vigor by "patriotic" (virtually plain nationalist) writers such as Kortunov and Titorenko, is really quite vague, and therefore can be used by political forces of all colors. It can figure either as an expression of Russian national interest (*raison d'etat*) or a quietessence of the mystical concept of Russia's grand mission. As nobody seems to know just where Russian national interest lies at present and what Russia's historic mission can be in the modern world, the "Russian idea" proves quite useful as a general manifestation of one's patriotic credentials. Talking about the "Russian idea" in some intellectual quarters conveys a spirit of patriotic committment coupled with scientific profundity. Actual roots of the idea, however, are quite real and can easily be traced back to the first manifestations of Russian messianism of an imperial sort.

Aleksandr Lebedev, a contemporary Russian writer, puts it this way: "All along, a vague memory of the 'Russian idea' was being kept and sustained in some inaudible and inarticulate form. It was asleep yet sensitive. Dreams of a 'Third Rome' were ever present in the hearts and feelings of ideologues of the Soviet state. . . . Today the 'Russian idea' has emerged on the banners of champions of the statist ideology." This is how the leader of the nationalist Russian party, Nikolia Bondarik, presents it: "It is Russians who must rule Russia; we must have a Russian government, a Russian parliament made up of ethnic Russians who belong to the Great Nation in blood and spirit. 'All for the nation, nothing against the nation'—this slogan must be in the head, soul and blood of every Russian because all of us are just cells of one vital organism called Nation."[8]

Probably just a tiny minority of Russian nationalists would subscribe to Bondarik's chauvinistic slogans. The point is that he constantly uses the word *Russkii* (Russian in the ethnic sense) when talking about parliament and government; the majority of the "patriots," while also using this term in reference to the idea, never say *Russkii* when referring, for example, to the composition of governing bodies or the army. *Rossiiskii* is preferable as devoid of an ethnic content and meant to relate to all citizens of the Russian Federation regardless of their ethnicity.

This is, of course, much more than a linguistic difference. The bulk of Russian nationalists are perfectly aware that a narrow ethnic *Russkii* nationalism will lead them nowhere as regards their overall design, the resurrection of the Russian empire in some new form. In the non-Russian republics of the Russian Federation it is the titular ethnos, not ethnic Russians, that is in control. Even in Yakutia, now renamed Sakha republic, where Yakuts make up just 34% of the population, they hold 69% of jobs in local government, and even in Adygeia the natives (30% of the population) totally control the administration.[9] It can hardly be assumed that local "ethnonationalist" bosses could be meek partners in a purely Russian ethnic (*Russkii*) state, and they could always mobilize large masses of the native population to back them up in any conflict with Moscow.

On the other hand, the concept of a nonethnic Russian Federation (*Rossiiskaia Federatsia*) seems to be acceptable to the non-Russian republics provided they are free to exercise "home rule" and get a big share of the pie as regards taxes and income from the export of raw materials; suffice it to look at Tatarstan and Yakutia. Also, it must be noted that, so far, the majority of the population of Greater Russia are not particularly ethnically-minded. A poll in Tatarstan showed that just 24.4% of the population regard themselves as "Tatarstanians only," 12.8% as "more Tatarstanians than *Rossiianie*," 35.8% as being both, 12.3% as "more *Rossiianie* than Tatarstanians," and 10.4% as "*Rossiianie* only." Another poll, conducted in ten districts of the Russian Federation, shows that 47.9% of those polled consider themselves to be citizens of Russia while 14.2% refer to themselves as representatives of their nationality; 31.4% do not know who they are.[10]

This means, first, that the "Russian idea," to be viable at all, must make allowances for the feelings of non-Russians in the Federation, and second, that the scope of Russian nationalism has probably been exaggerated by many analysts both in Russia and abroad. Nationalism in Russia is not to be underestimated, yet for the time being it has not proved powerful enough to be regarded as a cardinal issue for the Russian people, preoccupied mainly with domestic problems such as poverty, inadequate wages and pensions, crime wave, corruption and so on.

A sharp upsurge of nationalism might follow real or perceived genocide of ethnic Russians in the "near abroad." So far, nothing of the kind has been in evidence anywhere in the post-Soviet space, and Russian public is generally intelligent enough to realize it. The failure of general Lebed's election bloc to reach the 5% barrier in the 1995 parliamentary elections is quite revealing as the bloc had made the plight of ethnic Russians abroad the main plank in its platform.

Of course, after Zhirinovsky's victory in 1993 elections, the "patriotic" theme became quite prominent in the ideas put forward by various Russian political forces including the government camp. President Yeltsin, too, has found it expedient to pay at least lip service to Russian nationalism. The Communist leader Gennadii Zyuganov appeals to nationalism and imperial traditions rather than to socialist ideas. A *New York Times* correspondent reported in April 1996:

Resentment and suspicion of the West, particularly the United States, have never been higher since the cold war ended. . . . Zyuganov . . . is seeking to reach beyond orthodox party members and capture the nationalist vote by reviving a common enemy. Mr. Zyuganov calls it "a planetary regime of political, economic and military dictatorship of the West, headed by the U.S.A." . . . The West is now an obsessive topic in Russian politics, much in the way American candidates were once defined by their attitude toward Communism. Politicians of all stripes talk about the "specialness" of Russia, of its intrinsic incompatibility with Western models of democracy. Figures as disparate as Mr. Zyuganov and Aleksandr Solzhenitsyn use "sobornost" to describe the Russian condition. The word loosely translates as "spiritual unity" and connotes a collectivist mentality far removed from the individualism that drives people in the West. It is a loaded phrase, conjuring the centuries-old battle between Westernizers and Slavophiles.[11]

The "Russian idea" continues to be the linchpin of ideological programs of a sizable segment of the Russian political class from ultra-chauvinists and Jew-haters to moderate nationalists and ex-democrats turned "patriots." Yet, it can hardly be called a winning card. The majority of the Russian population are not all that excited about the ideas of imperial grandeur. Certainly, Russian policy in the "near abroad" cannot be assumed to be motivated by the "Russian idea" and dreams of the resurrection of the empire. Reasons for the new Russian assertiveness lie elsewhere. First and foremost, they are to be evaluated in the context of the reintegration process in the CIS.

It is almost universally acknowledged throughout the former Soviet republics that the dissolution of the USSR without an arrangement for keeping alive the economic organism of the giant state was a colossal blunder. The erstwhile euphoria of the first years of independence is gone. As people in the newly independent states say, "at first, we were happy to be free though barefoot. Now, we are just barefoot." Economic reintegration is the name of the game at this point, and it is Russia that is destined to play a leading role in this process. It also has to pay the largest bill. Sacrifices will be needed that are unlikely to be welcomed by Russian public unless compensated for by a visible strengthening of Russia's positions in the CIS. It would be naive to expect economic integration to proceed without a substantial increase of Russia's political influence and military presence in the southern CIS republics.

Moscow is also concerned about internal stability in the southern republics not for any altruistic or humanitarian reasons but simply in order to prevent any upheavals that could necessitate Russia's intervention on a large scale, which is certain to be unacceptable to Russian public, obsessed as it is with the "Chechnya syndrome." For instance, apprehension of the vaguely defined "wave of Islamic fundamentalism" rolling north in the case of the Islamists taking control in Tajikistan can largely account for the decision to send Russian forces to protect Tajikistan's border with Afghanistan. This may rightly be called a Moscow domino theory.

It is a safe assumption that the current Kremlin leadership has no far-reaching designs or long-term plans as regards the restoration of the empire in any form or shape. The situation can change, however, if "national-patriotic forces" take control. The "Russian idea" could become quite dangerous. Again, Aleksandr Lebedev deserves to be quoted: "Of course, there is no automatic linkage between the "Russian idea" and war. Yet smell of blood can always be sensed when you are faced with the ideas of exclusiveness, imperial ambitions, Heavenly mission . . . The 'Russian idea' is always somewhere in the vicinity of blood." Lebedev also notes that Russian nationalism "is opposed to the project of civic nation: its key concept is that of a Russian ethnonation."[12]

Herein lies the danger. Some basic patterns of Russia's historical development—such as (1) the immense power of the state and its arbitrary rule; (2) the hasty and ill-conceived Westernization, the result of which was an ever widening gulf between the higher and lower classes (almost "two nations"); and (3) the lack of a strong middle class—combined to preclude the formation of civil society and *civic nation*, or *state nation*, as opposed to *ethnonation*. A true nation in the Western sense has yet to be formed in Russia. The explosion of Russian ethnic consciousness, suppressed after the Bolshevik revolution, is probably natural and inevitable. If, however, it results in the triumph of ethnonationalism, and the whole process of nation-forming gets frozen at that level, this will seriously hamper the formation of civic nation, and, as a consequence, of that civil society without which Russia can hardly hope to overcome its present malaise.

NOTES

1. Stanislav Kondrashov, "Kem bolshe nedovolen rossiiskii izbiratel—Klintonom ili Yeltsinym?" (Who is more to blame in the Russian elector's eyes, Clinton or Yeltsin?), *Izvestia*, October 13, 1995.

2. Walker Connor, *Ethnonationalism: The Quest for Understanding* (Princeton, N.J.: Princeton University Press, 1994), 161.

3. Sergei Agadjanov, "Novaia tsivilizatsia v Rossii?" (A new civilization in Russia?), *Nezavisimaia Gazeta*, April 20, 1993.

4. Sergei Kortunov, "Natsionalnaia sverkhzadacha" (The ultimate national goal), *Nezavisimaia Gazeta*, October 7, 1995.

5. Sergei Kortunov, "Kaiatsia Rossii ne v chem" (Russia has nothing to be ashamed of), *Nezavisimaia Gazeta*, January 31, 1996.

6. Vladimir Titorenko, "Zapadnye tsennosti i islamskii mir" (Western values and the Islamic world), *Svobodnaia Mysl*, no. 3 (1996), 72.

7. Sergei Panarin, "Aziia glazami russkikh" (Asia through Russian eyes), *Nezavisimaia Gazeta*, April 20, 1993.

8. Aleksandr Lebedev, "Russkaia Ideia: v okrestnostiakh voiny" (The Russian idea: in the vicinity of war), *Polis*, no. 2 (1995), 119, 120, 123, 124.

9. Valerii Tishkov, "Chto est Rossiia" (What is Russia), *Voprosy Filisofii*, no. 2 (1995), 6.

10. Ibid., 11.

11. Alessandra Stanley, "Stripped of Themes, Yeltsin Wraps Himself in Flag," *New York Times*, April 19, 1996.

12. Lebedev, "Russkaia Ideia," 123, 124.

Selected Bibliography

Akiner, Shirin. *Cultural Change and Continuity in Central Asia.* London and New York: Kegan Paul, 1991.

―――. *Islamic Peoples of the Soviet Union.* London: Kegan Paul, 1983.

Akzin, Benjamin. *State and Nation.* London: Hutchinson, 1964.

Alba, Victor. *Nationalities without Nations.* New York: n.p., 1968.

Allworth, Edward. *The Modern Uzbeks: From the Fourteenth Century to the Present.* Stanford, Calif.: Hoover Institution Press, 1990.

Amin, Samir. *Class and Nation.* New York: n.p., 1980.

Anderson, Benedict. *Imagined Communities: Reflections on the Origin and Spread of Nationalism.* London: n.p., 1980.

Armstrong, John A. *Nations before Nationalism.* Chapel Hill: University of North Carolina Press, 1982.

Azrael, Jeremy R. (ed.). *Soviet Nationality: Policies and Practices.* New York: n.p., 1978.

Bendix, Reinhard. *Nation Building and Citizenship.* New York: John Wiley, 1964.

Bennigsen, Alexandre and Marie Broxup. *The Islamic Threat to the Soviet State.* New York: St. Martin's Press, 1983.

Birch, Anthony H. *Nationalism and National Integration.* London and Boston: Unwin Hyman, 1989.

Bossenbrook, William J. (ed.). *Mid-Twentieth Century Nationalism.* Detroit: Wayne State University Press, 1965.

Brass, Paul R. *Ethnicity and Nationalism.* New Delhi and Newbury Park, Calif.: Sage Publications, 1991.

Bremmer, Ian and Ray Taras. *Nations and Politics in the Soviet Successor States.* New York: Cambridge University Press, 1993.

Breuilly, John. *Nationalism and the State.* New York: St. Martin's Press, 1982.

Carr, Edward H. *Nationalism and After.* New York: The Macmillan Co., 1945.

Cobban, Alfred. *The Nation-State and National Self-Determination.* New York: n.p., 1970.

Connor, Walker. *Ethnonationalism: The Quest for Understanding.* Princeton N.J.: Princeton University Press, 1994.

Critchlow, James. *Nationalism in Uzbekistan: A Soviet Republic's Road to Sovereignty.* Boulder, Colo.: Westview Press, 1992.

Dawa, Norbu. *Culture and the Politics of Third World Nationalism.* London and New York: Routledge, 1992.

Dawisha, Adeed and Karen Dawisha (eds.). *The Making of Foreign Policy in Russia and the New States of Eurasia.* New York: M. E. Sharpe, 1995.

Dawisha, Karen and Bruce Parrot (eds.). *Russia and the New States of Eurasia: The Politics of Upheaval.* Cambridge: Cambridge University Press, 1994.

Denber, Rachel (ed.). *The Soviet Nationality Reader.* Boulder, Colo.: Westview Press, 1992.

Deutsch, Karl W. *Nationalism and Social Communication: An Inquiry into the Foundations of Nationality.* Cambridge, Mass.: MIT Press, 1966.

———. *Tides among Nations.* New York: n.p., 1979.

Deutsch, Karl W. and W. J. Foltz (eds.). *Nation-building.* New York: Atherton, 1963.

Doob, Leonard W. *Patriotism and Nationalism: Their Psychological Foundations.* New Haven, Conn.: Yale University Press, 1964.

Dunlop, John B. *The Rise of Russia and the Fall of the Soviet Empire.* Cambridge, Mass.: Harvard University Press, 1995.

Emerson, Rupert. *From Empire to Nation.* n.p., 1962.

Epstein, A. L. *Ethnos and Identity.* London: n.p., 1978.

Ferdinand, Peter (ed.). *The New States of Central Asia and Their Neighbors.* New York: Council on Foreign Relations Press, 1995.

Fierman, William (ed.). *Soviet Central Asia: The Failed Transformation.* Boulder, Colo.: Westview Press, 1991.

Gellner, Ernest. *Nations and Nationalism.* Ithaca, N.Y.: Cornell University Press, 1983.

Gleason, Gregory. *Federalism and Nationalism: The Struggle for Republican Rights in the USSR.* Boulder, Colo.: Westview Press, 1990.

Hajda, Lubomir and Mark Bessinger (eds.). *The Nationalities Factor in Soviet Politics and Society.* Boulder, Colo.: Westview Press, 1990.

Hayes, Carlton J. H. *The Historical Evolution of Modern Nationalism.* New York: Smith, 1931.

Hertz, Friedrich O. *Nationalism in History and Politics.* London: Routledge and Kegan Paul, 1944.

Hobsbawm, E. J. *Nations and Nationalism since 1780.* Cambridge: n.p., 1990.

Kaiser, Robert J. *The Geography of Nationalism in Russia and the USSR.* Princeton, N.J.: Princeton University Press, 1994.

Kamenka, Eugene (ed.). *Nationalism: The Nature and Evolution of an Idea.* London: Edward Arnold, 1976.

Kedourie, Elie. *Nationalism.* Cambridge, Mass.: Hutchinson University Library, 1960.

Kohn, Hans. *The Age of Nationalism.* New York: n.p., 1962.

———. *The Idea of Nationalism: A Study of Its Origin and Background.* New York: MacMillan, 1958.

———. *Nationalism: Its Meaning and History.* Princeton, N.J.: Princeton University Press, 1955.

Kozlov, Viktor. *The Peoples of the Soviet Union*. Bloomington: n.p., 1988.

Krejci, Jaroslav and Vitezslav Velimsky. *Ethnic and Political Nations in Europe*. New York: St. Martin's Press, 1981.

Liebkind, Karmela. *Minority Identity and Identification Processes: A Social Psychological Study*. Helsinki: Societas Scientarum Fennica, 1984.

Lubin, Nancy. *Labor and Nationality in Soviet Central Asia*. Princeton, N.J.: Princeton University Press, 1984.

MacLean, Colin. *The Crown and the Thistle: The Nature of Nationhood*. Edinburgh: Scottish Academic Press, 1988.

Mandelbaum, Michael. *Central Asia and the World*. New York: Council on Foreign Relations Press, 1994.

Manz, Beatrice (ed.). *Soviet Central Asia in Historical Perspective*. Boulder, Colo.: Westview Press, 1992.

Mesbahi, Mohiaddin (ed.). *Russia and the Third World in the Post-Soviet Era*. Gainesville: University Press of Florida, 1994.

Minogue, K. R. *Nationalism*. London: B. T. Batsford, 1967.

Motyl, Alexander J. *Dilemmas of Independence: Ukraine after Totalitarianism*. New York: Council on Foreign Relations Press, 1993.

——— (ed.). *Thinking Theoretically about Soviet Nationalities*. New York: Columbia University Press, 1992.

Nahaylo, Bohdan. *The New Ukraine*. London: Royal Institute of International Affairs, 1992.

Nahaylo, Bohdan and Victor Swoboda. *Soviet Disunion: A History of the Nationalities Problem in the USSR*. New York: n.p., 1990.

Olcott, Martha Brill. *The Kazakhs*. Stanford, Calif.: Hoover Institution Press, 1987.

——— (ed.). *The Soviet Multinational State: Readings and Documents*. Armonk, N.Y.: M. E. Sharpe, 1990.

Olson, Mancur. *The Rise and Decline of Nations*. New Haven, Conn.: Yale University Press, 1982.

Palumbo, Michael and William O. Shanahan (ed.). *Nationalism: Essays in Honor of Louis L. Snyder*. Westport, Conn.: Greenwood Press, 1981.

Powell, Wendall and Walter Freeman. *Ethnicity and Nationbuilding*. Beverly Hills, Calif.: Sage, 1974.

Roy, Olivier. *The Civil War in Tajikistan: Causes and Implications*. Washington, D.C.: U.S. Institute of Peace, 1993.

Rumer, Boris Z. *Soviet Central Asia: A Tragic Experiment*. Boston: Unwin Hyman, 1989.

Seton-Watson, Hugh. *Nationalism, Old and New*. Sydney: Sydney University Press, 1965.

———. *Nations and States*. London: Methuen and Co., 1977.

Silvert, Kalman H. (ed.). *Expectant Peoples: Nationalism and Development*. New York: n.p., 1963.

Smith, Anthony D. *Theories of Nationalism*. New York: Harper and Row, 1971.

———. *The Ethnic Origins of Nations*. Oxford: Basil Blackwell, 1986.

Smith, Graham. *The Nationalities Question in the Post-Soviet States*. London and New York: Longman, 1996.

Snyder, Louis L. *The New Nationalism*. Ithaca, N.Y.: Cornell University Press, 1968.

———. *Varieties of Nationalism: A Comparative Study*. Hinsdale, New York: The Dryden Press, 1976.

————. *Macro-Nationalism: A History of the Pan-Movements.* Westport, Conn.: n.p., 1984.

Subtelny, Orest. *Ukraine: A History.* Toronto, Buffalo, and London: University of Toronto Press, 1994.

Symmons-Symonolewicz, K. *Modern Nationalism: Toward a Consensus in Theory.* New York: n.p., 1968.

————. *Nationalist Movements: A Comparative View.* Meadville, Pa.: n.p., 1970.

Szporluk, Roman. *Communism and Nationalism: Karl Marx versus Friedrich List.* New York: Oxford University Press, 1991.

———— (ed.). *National Identity and Ethnicity in Russia and the New States of Eurasia.* New York: M. E. Sharpe, 1994.

Tismaneanu, Vladimir (ed.). *Political Culture and Civil Society in Russia and the New States of Eurasia.* New York: M. E. Sharpe, 1995.

Tivey, Leonard. *The Nation-State.* New York: n.p., 1981.

Walker, Christopher J. *Armenia: The Survival of a Nation.* New York and London: Croom Helm, 1990.

Ward, Barbara. *Nationalism and Ideology.* New York: W. W. Norton, 1966.

Index

About the Author

GEORGIY I. MIRSKY is a graduate of Moscow's Institute of Oriental Studies and has taught at the Institute of International Relations in Moscow, American University in Washington, D.C., and the London School of Economics and Political Science. At this writing, he is senior research fellow at the Institute of World Economy and International Relations in Moscow and a visiting scholar at the Center for International Studies at Princeton University.

ISBN 0-313-30044-5

HARDCOVER BAR CODE